Computer Telephony

Automating Home Offices and Small Businesses

Ed Tittel
Austin, TX

Dawn Rader
Netware Magazine
Austin, TX

AP PROFESSIONAL

Boston   San Diego   New York
London   Sydney   Tokyo   Toronto

Copyright © 1996 by Academic Press, Inc.

AP PROFESSIONAL
1300 Boylston St., Chestnut Hill, MA 02167
World Wide Web Site at http://www.apnet.com

An Imprint of ACADEMIC PRESS, INC.
A Division of HARCOURT BRACE & COMPANY

United Kingdom Edition published by
ACADEMIC PRESS LIMITED
24–28 Oval Road, London NW1 7DX

Tittel, Ed.
  Computer Telephony : automating home offices and small businesses /
Ed Tittel, Dawn Rader
      p. cm.
  Includes bibliographical references and index
  ISBN 0-12-691411-7
  1. Telephone systems--Data Processing. 2. Computer networks
3. Telematics   4. Business communications.   I. Rader, Dawn.
  II. Title.
  TK6392.T57   1996
  621.385'0285--dc20   95-53875
                                                               CIP

Printed in the United States of America
96 97 98 99   IP   9 8 7 6 5 4 3 2 1

Contents

About the Authors

Ed Tittel

Ed Tittel is the author of numerous books on computing and a columnist for *Maximize!* and *Windows NT* magazines. He's the coauthor (with Bob LeVitus) of four best-selling books — *Stupid DOS Tricks, Stupid Windows Tricks, Stupid Beyond Belief DOS Tricks,* and of the just-released *New & Improved Stupid Windows Tricks.* He's also a coauthor (with Deni Connor and Earl Follis) of the best-selling *NetWare for Dummies,* now in its second edition, and (with Steve James) of *HTML for Dummies,* now getting ready to go into its second edition.

Most recently, Ed has coauthored several titles for AP PROFESSIONAL, including *ISDN Networking Essentials* (with Steve James) and *The PC Networking Handbook* (with Dawn Rader, Mary Madden, and Dave Smith).

Ed's last "real" job was as the director of technical marketing for Novell, Inc. In this position he tried his best to control technical content for Novell's corporate trade shows, marketing communications, and presentations. He has been a frequent speaker on LAN-related topics at industry events and was a course developer for Novell in San Jose, where he designed and maintained several introductory LAN training classes. At present he serves on the program committee for the NetWorld+Interop trade show, where he helps to set tutorial, seminar, and conference session content and coverage.

Ed has been a regular contributor to the computer trade press since 1987, and has written more than 150 articles for a variety of publications, with a decided emphasis on networking technology. These publications include *Computerworld, InfoWorld, LAN Times, NetGuide,* and *IWAY.*

You can contact Ed at CompuServe ID: 76376,606/Internet e-mail: etittel@ zilker.net <URL: http://www.lanw.com>

Dawn Rader

Dawn Rader has been active as a networking researcher and editor since 1993. Her editing credits include *Network Design Essentials, E-mail Essentials, Internet Access Essentials, ISDN Networking Essentials,* and the *Guerrilla Guide to NetWare.* Previously Dawn was managing editor for *NetWare Solutions,* a magazine targeted at NetWare systems engineers and administrators, to which she was also a regular contributor. She also contributed to *The PC Networking Handbook,* another AP PROFESSIONAL book published in 1995.

Currently Dawn is employed as a full-time researcher and project manager at LANWrights, an Austin-based consultancy that specializes in network- and PC-related writing and research. She's also pursuing a degree in technical communications at Austin Community College. Dawn's areas of interest and expertise include client/server applications, groupware, high-speed networking, network management, computer telephony, and network storage management and backup.

When she has time, she also enjoys spending time with her husband, Bert, and their faithful flop-eared Labrador puppy, Benjamin Franklin Rader.

You can reach Dawn on the Internet at dawn@tab.com or on CompuServe at 73762,524.

Acknowledgments

Ed Tittel: We have lots of people to thank for making this book possible and for contributing so substantially to its contents and direction — first and foremost, the people who helped us research, write, and assemble this book. They include:

- Steve James, a long-time computer industry writer who has filled the research and documentation needs of organizations as diverse as The Psychological Corporation and the U.S. Fish and Wildlife Service. A former consulting environmental biologist, Steve has concentrated his efforts in the personal computer realm for the past 15 years. Along the way, he has authored and edited more than 50 magazine articles, users manuals, and technical papers, and has made some excellent friends. He's also the coauthor, with

Ed Tittel, of *HTML for Dummies and ISDN Networking Essentials.* Currently Steve divides his time among the keyboard, his family, and the great outdoors, where the thrill of competitive bicycling continues to lure him, despite his accelerating decrepitude. You can reach Steve on the Internet at snjames@wetlands.com. or at http://www.real-time.net80/~snjames/

- Michael Stewart, my chief researcher, right-hand man, WebMaster, and equipment guru for quite a while now. He's turning into quite a good writer as well. All I can say is that I've come to depend on him for many services, large and small. Thanks for being there when I needed you, Michael!

- Louise Leahy, one of the few "grizzled veterans" with whom I have the privilege of associating. The former executive editor for *MacUser,* she's now working in Austin as a freelance editor and compositor. She's shepherded this project through its final stages and polished our rough work. Thanks a million.

With this, the seventh book that we've done together for AP PROFESSIONAL, I'd also like to continue my ongoing thanks to Susan Price and Shelly Ryan for doing such a good job with our sometimes scattered materials. Finally, I'd like to thank technical editor John Collins for picking as many nits and issues as he could find and generally improving the value and accuracy of the book.

Next come the folks at AP PROFESSIONAL. First and foremost, we'd like to thank our project editor, Jenifer Niles, for sticking with us when things got wacky at the end of the project. Thanks also to Jacqui Young, for managing the many logistical details and minutae of pulling this book together. And then there's the production staff, managed by Karen Pratt.

Also, I'd also like to thank the many vendors and networking experts whose hard work and good advice made this book possible. If it weren't for the work all these people had done before Steve, Dawn, and I got started, we couldn't have marshalled the facts and figures you'll find in here. There's one standout individual who made this project possible in many ways: Harry Newton, publisher and editor of *Computer Telephony* magazine, and in many people's eyes the "godfather" of the CT industry. Harry, we couldn't have done this work without your help, inspiration, and your *Telecom Dictionary*. Thanks!

The other many individuals and companies that gave us information, evaluations, references, and resources are just too numerous to mention by name, but we'd like to wish them all a fervent and well-meant "blanket thank-you" just the same. Wherever possible and appropriate, you'll find their contact information in Appendix B. However, we reserve the right to thank Dan Kegel in person for putting together the best-ever online resource on ISDN!

Finally, I'd like to thank my family for putting up with me through the course of a time-consuming and all-absorbing project. So, Suzy, Austin, Chelsea, and Dusty, please accept my thanks for riding out yet another book with me, and my heart-felt apologies for missing out on part of the Christmas season while I was "busy"!

Ed Tittel, Austin, Texas, January 15, 1996.

Dawn Rader: A number of great people out there deserve my deepest thanks for their support during not only the process of writing this book but also in my life in general. I must begin with Ed Tittel. Let's just say that if everyone had a friend like Ed, there would be no hunger, poverty, war, and most of all, no excuses for not accomplishing the highest goals. Thanks, Ed: None of this would be possible without your never-ending friendship, guidance, patience, and wacky sense of humor!

Closer to home, I would like to thank my husband, Bert, for putting up with me during these last-minute crunches. Without his love and understanding, my portion of this book would never have been completed. Also, to Ben, Tiger, Boo, and Kittyhead: Thanks for keeping me company during those late nights.

In the family circle, there is no doubt in my mind that I have the greatest mother in the world. Mom, your encouragement and respect mean the world to me. If it weren't for you, I wouldn't have this wonderful life. Thank you for everything. I would also like to thank my wonderful grandmother, sister, and precious nieces, who never fail to put a smile on my face and warm my heart.

Thanks to Deni Connor and *NetWare Solutions* magazine for having given me a "real" job. I would also like to extend a very warm thank you to Mr. Art Hammer. Hammer, words cannot describe my undying appreciation for all that you taught me — thank you from the bottom of my heart. Last, but certainly not least, to the girls: Tina, Cheryl, Mimi, Roxanne, Mary Mary, Laura, Teresa, and Nan. They have all at one time or another lifted my spirits and shown me what real friend-ship is all about.

Dawn Rader, Austin, Texas, January 15, 1996

Introduction

Welcome to *Computer Telephony!* This book is aimed squarely at the following audiences:

- People who are curious about the kinds of hardware and software that are needed to let their PCs and telephones work together.

- People in a small or home office with PCs who want to install and use their computers and telephones together for things such as voice mail, call logging, autodialing, computer-based faxing, and more.

- People who want to leverage the information they've already collected in such programs as personal information managers (PIMs), scheduling or calendar programs, and electronic address books and phone directories, to improve their productivity and make better use of their time on the phone.

In short, we think that most people who now work without some kind of computerized telephone system at home or in the office will find this book quite interesting!

What Is Computer Telephony?

Only a few pieces of equipment are more prevalent in today's workplace than the personal computer; increasingly, the same is true in the homes of postindustrial workers and their families. This book explores the incredible synergy that can result when telephones and computers are used in concert, which is as good a general definition of computer telephony (CT) as its many incarnations will allow.

Ideally CT supplies the technology whereby the speed, power, convenience, and storage capacity of a computer augment and enhance the telephone's ability to bring people and machines together. As you'll see throughout this book, the sum of these two technologies adds up to much more than either of the parts.

Although the authors normally shrink from wild speculation, we're convinced that the marriage of the computer and the telephone promises to change the way we conduct our businesses and our lives. We also believe that this combination will forever alter the kinds of business and activities that we will undertake in the future, because the computer adds logic and memory to the communications abilities inherent in our modern global telephone system.

It's no accident that until recently CT has been a complex and expensive proposition. The lack of widespread standards, the proliferation of powerful proprietary telephone systems, and the failure to artfully blend personal computing with personal telephone use have blocked the marriage between these two technologies.

Until recently, access to advanced computer-based telephone services, such as voice mail, call forwarding, automated attendants, networked fax services, and the like, has been the exclusive province of companies large enough to spend the hundreds of thousands of dollars that were necessary to obtain such functionality.

The PC Made Them Do It!

In the past 10 years, however, the explosion of personal computers and the consequent economies of scale that result from very large installed bases and the industries that serve them have created a critical mass of technology and knowledge that permits a far more affordable kind of CT. (More than 120 million IBM-compatible PCs were in use by the end of 1995, according to a November 1995 Gartner Group study). The foundation of this phenomenon is the reality of a $99, 14.4 Kbps fax/modem, bundled with software that's sophisticated enough to drive it (and your telephone) from any reasonably equipped PC.

Likewise, the advent of PC-based multimedia has made formerly exotic equipment, such as sound cards, commonplace. And graphical user interfaces (such as Microsoft Windows) have permitted not only easy access to phone information while running other programs, but also permitted sound systems included with computers to play incoming telephone sounds while capturing speech from the computers' operators. All these things taken together can turn an average personal computer into a feature-laden telephone!

The Beef Is Here!

Based on 1995 figures from the U.S. Bureau of Labor Statistics, there were more than 6.2 million businesses in the United States with 10 or fewer employees and another 3.4 million home offices. This just happens to be the largest audience of its kind for computer technology anywhere in the world, and it also happens to be critically dependent on the telephone for its existence. Not coincidentally, it's also the primary audience for this book. As a form of shorthand, we refer to this audience as SOHO (an acronym for small office, home office).

We'll do our best to describe CT in general as we go, but our real goal is to inform small-scale users of this technology about the kinds of systems and options that are available and how they work. Therefore this book concentrates on the kinds of synergy that can be created between a small number of telephone lines (from one to six) and an equal number of personal computers. Many more complicated varieties of CT are available, but they're usually aimed at larger-scale users, with significantly higher levels of cost and complexity. As a rule of thumb, $400-600 per seat for complex telephony scales pretty well: This doesn't amount to huge sums for SOHO, but when hundreds or thousands of users (and phone lines) are involved, the numbers can get big in a hurry!

This high-end marketplace has been the breeding ground for many of the services and capabilities that are now becoming available in small-scale packages suitable for SOHO use. That's why you'll see us refer to such products from time to time throughout this book: We're not necessarily recommending such solutions, but they do provide useful examples of functionality that we expect to see on a desktop near you very soon, if it isn't already available in a SOHO-sized package.

What Can You Do with CT?

Surely the telephone deserves recognition as one of the most important (and omnipresent) pieces of equipment any place where modern humanity is housed. But under the right circumstances, the addition of a computer to a telephone makes all kinds of interesting activities possible, including:

- Construction of an electronic contact list or phone directory, from which calls may originate simply by selecting an entry and issuing some kind of "dial" command.

- Automatic recognition of incoming calls, where caller ID services are available and activated, with the ability to retrieve any records about the caller that may already exist on the PC.

- Automatic call logging, with time and date stamps, to provide detailed records of telephone calls and activity; many CT programs allow users to enter notes about calls into a log file while they're under way (which may then be retrieved the next time that number is accessed, either inbound or outbound).

- Comprehensive fax management capabilities, including easy access to outbound faxing from within any application (often as an extension of built-in "print" facilities) and automatic receipt, queuing, and notification of inbound fax messages.

- Automatic recognition of incoming call types, so that the same line may be used to handle voice and fax calls, with appropriate hand-offs to users or fax software, as required.

- Comprehensive voice mail services, including access to multiple voice mail boxes, screening of incoming calls, digital call recording on demand, and a variety of remote operation capabilities (record and manage multiple greetings, playback of messages in any order, forward or exchange messages, etc.).

- Construction and maintenance of "calling lists": prioritized collections of names and numbers to call that can be placed by the computer, so you'll be notified when the next callee on your list is reached.

- With text-to-voice translation services, easy to arrange telephone access to system files, faxes, and other information.

Believe it or not, this incredible range of features gives just a hint of the kinds of services and information that CT can deliver. But this diversity may also suggest more than is really practical: although all of the features and functions we've mentioned are available in some CT implementations, no single package offers all of these together.

Some packages may be strong on voice mail and message handling, whereas others may be stronger on faxing capabilities. Alas, CT's recent renaissance has created a certain amount of confusion in the marketplace. From the vendors' side, this is reflected in packages that contain interesting mixes of features that indicate their particular technical strengths or abilities as much as they match marketplace needs. From the consumers' side, this is reflected in a certain amount of confusion about what kinds of telephony services they want versus those they're willing to pay for. We expect that more standard collections of capabilities will include most or all of what we've mentioned here by the end of 1996, but the overall collection of CT's features and functions will continue to explode for some time to come!

What Do You Need to Use CT?

Beyond the obvious — namely, a PC and a telephone line — computer telephony requires some rather specialized combinations of hardware and software to accommodate a PC-telephone linkup and to perform its many and varied tasks. These include:

- Some kind of PC-telephone interface. Most frequently this will be a modem, but sometimes it could be an external device that attaches to your phone line and a communications port on your PC. It might be a special multifunction board that merges a sound card, a fax/modem, and a CD-ROM controller. Or it might even be a special-purpose multiline telephone interface that can allow a single PC to handle up to eight telephone lines.

- For those systems that permit you to use your computer as a telephone, you'll need to obtain either a sound card (the most common standard here is Creative Labs' Sound Blaster 16; "Sound Blaster compatible" is a common phrase you'll hear in the requirements for such things) or buy hardware that delivers fax/modem and sound card capabilities in a single package.

- No matter what kind of hardware your CT system uses, some kind of software is definitely needed to let the linkup between the PC and the phone line do something useful. This can range from a simple phone-dialing program to a complex and powerful fax-handling, voice mail, and call-logging system.

In general, the more bells and whistles you want or need, the more you should expect to spend to get them. You can purchase a simple minimal CT package for as little as $100, including the cost of a 14.4 Kbps modem and the necessary software. On the high end of the scale, you could spend as much as $1000 for a multiline phone card for one of your PCs that could handle up to six phone lines and another $300 to $400 for each PC on a local area network that can take advantage of the system's capabilities. In most cases the costs will fall somewhere between these two extremes.

Where multiple phone lines and computers are involved, there's another requirement that's implicit in CT: a network. The best way to bring computers together to share peripherals, data, and services happens to be a pretty peachy way to deliver telephone services among computers as well. We haven't yet seen too many instances in which a network has been purchased to distributed CT access, but we expect that a network's ability to deliver such services will only add to its value in most small and home office environments.

But Wait, There's More!

Until now our discussion of CT has assumed the use of conventional telephone technology. In CT circles this is called POTS, which stands for "plain old telephone service." This is an analog method of communication that we'll discuss in more detail in Chapter 1, but now suffice it to say that the bulk of CT revolves around POTS and ordinary telephone lines. The word "modem" is a contraction of "modulator/demodulator," which refers to the conversion process between the digital forms of data native to a computer and the analog forms native to POTS.

For two computers to communicate with each other, the sending computer must convert its signals from digital to analog form to send them over POTS and the computer on the receiving end must convert it back from analog to digital before it can interpret and understand the data. This adds to the overhead inherent in such communication and limits the capabilities of the computer according to the carrying capacity of the telephone system. That's why even a fast modem is limited to speeds of 33.4 Kbps or less (not including compression).

But there is a completely digital form of telephony that's becoming increasingly available throughout the world, especially in North America and Europe. It's called the Integrated Services Digital Network, usually known by its acronym as ISDN, and it provides a completely digital communications service over the existing telephone network. This eliminates conversion overhead and increases the speed and reliability of the communications involved. Today ISDN delivers 144 Kbps of bandwidth to its subscribers, of which 128 Kbps is usable for computer-to-computer communications.

ISDN also supports a variety of data-handling options, including sophisticated, fully digital telephones for voice traffic, which means that CT must also embrace ISDN in order to cover the full spectrum of telephony options. Normally when you buy a CT system, you'll have to decide in advance whether ISDN support is needed. Because it is significantly more expensive as well as a great deal more sophisticated, ISDN telephony remains relatively rare. Nevertheless it is gaining in use and popularity, so we'll alert you to related options, equipment, and software where appropriate throughout this book.

Whereas the price range for analog CT ranges from a low of $100 per computer to a high of $600 per computer, ISDN operates on a different plane. It's not unusual to spend $1000 per computer for hardware and installation of basic ISDN connectivity and another $600 to $1000 per computer for ISDN-based CT capabilities. Until these combined prices drop below $1000 per computer, we don't expect to see the same kind of explosive growth for fully digital CT that we now see for POTS-based CT on the desktop. For our price-sensitive target audience, its costs are still too outrageous to be considered seriously, even if ISDN can (and does) provide significant gains in performance and capability.

Then, too, only about 30 percent of U.S. locations (primarily in major metropolitan areas) can currently obtain ISDN services, and recurring service costs tend to be significantly higher than POTS equivalents. When all of these factors are combined, we see a continued strong interest in ISDN, with growth somewhat hampered by the higher costs of entry and use. In practice those small office and home office operations that already need higher bandwidths for Internet or other online service access will find that the incremental costs of adding ISDN-based CT are still relatively affordable, whereas those who don't have justification for such bandwidth probably won't want to incur the extra costs involved.

Can You Do It Yourself?

By this point you've probably gotten the idea that CT is powerful and useful but can also be expensive, and that it's not the simplest connection technology in the world to install and get working. Both of these points are true and should lead you to another question: "Can I do this myself?" If you're smart, you might even phrase the question as "Do I *want* to do this myself?"

Although your budget will have a strong bearing on your answer, we're inclined to suggest that you consider hiring a consultant to help with installation, no matter what your financial circumstances might be. Of course, you can still decide to go it alone, but it's worth considering that you may have to devote significant amounts of time and effort to get CT up and running. This is obviously more true for more expensive and complex systems, especially those you want to handle more than two phone lines. If you can install a modem and a communications software package, you can probably handle all the complexity in a low-end CT package with aplomb and panache!

We must warn you that doing it yourself might mean spending a "mere" 20-30 hours on the task, including researching the hardware selection, arranging for installations, and going through the installation on your PC. It could also mean spending an additional 40-80 hours or more on the phone with your modem vendor, your Internet service provider, the CT package's vendor, and your communications software vendor as you try to puzzle out why your chosen combination of components isn't working the way you know it should.

Therefore, if your time has value, you need to consider the potential "opportunity costs" of being a CT do-it-yourselfer. Our advice is that if 30 hours of your time is worth more to you than the costs of hiring a consultant for your installation, you should locate and hire a consultant without giving the matter much further thought. If you can't afford the costs or don't want to spend the money, be prepared to spend some significant time and effort in getting your CT installation up and running!. But remember that if you take the latter route, you may not get as much value as you should from your CT installation, either.

About This Book

Computer Telephony has been formulated with four primary goals in mind:

1. To help you understand enough of the workings, costs, and capabilities of CT to decide whether you want to use it.

2. To provide you with sufficient information about available CT hardware and software offerings to equip you to make informed purchase decisions.

3. To supply you with sufficient background and terminology to be able to survive the rigors of the installation process or of working intelligently with a consultant to handle that process on your behalf.

4. To acquaint you with the best sources of up-to-the-minute CT information so you can temper what's included in this book with the latest and greatest technical and product information.

To that end this book has been structured into three parts, with three appendixes, to provide the information you'll need:

1. Part I of the book introduces the fundamentals of CT technology and terminology, and explains what it is and how it works.

2. Part II introduces current CT hardware and software options, with rating and pricing information to help you select the items appropriate for your needs and budget

3. Part III covers installing and troubleshooting several typical PC CT setups to acquaint you with the process and to equip you to deal with the kinds of problems or questions you might encounter along the way.

4. Appendix A lists CT service providers and vendors to help you in your search for products, information, and assistance. Appendix B provides bibliographic and online resources to help you stay current on CT technology and products, including pointers to the very best print and electronic resources on CT. Appendix C is a glossary.

We suggest that you read this book from start to finish if you're relatively inexperienced with CT. If you're already somewhat knowledgeable, you can probably skip Part I and delve into those areas of Parts II and III that interest you. We also suggest that all of our readers sample the various appendixes, if only to determine what kind of information they contain and to see whether their contents might provide useful pointers to vendors, consultants, or other sources of CT enlightenment.

What makes our book different from some of the others in this area is that we assume little or no knowledge of computer telephony. Any technical terms we use anywhere in the book you'll be able to look up in our glossary (Appendix C). Whenever we introduce a new topic, we try to lead you into it as gently and completely as possible, so you'll be able to appreciate its significance directly and immediately.

Another thing that makes our book different from other CT tomes is that we don't attempt to provide an encyclopedia of all telephony-related protocols, services, terminology, and capabilities. Our book is designed as much to provide a set of techniques for you to do your own investigation and installation as it is to provide a road map of what's involved in working with CT.

Finally, this book is designed to provide useful tools and techniques to help you learn for yourself, and to supply you with the essential information for navigating among and coping with the many viewpoints, implementations, and discussions you're likely to find surrounding computer telephony. This is as much a matter of necessity for you as it is a matter of containing our subject matter, because CT is such a vibrant and dynamic area of technology. By the time you read this book, some of its contents are bound to be outdated; by providing you with tools and techniques to refresh and renew the information we provide here, we also enable you to work with current, usable facts, figures, and theories.

Whatever your approach to this book might be, we hope you find it useful. Please feel free to correspond via e-mail with any of us. We welcome your feedback — critical, complimentary, or otherwise. We hope a better second edition can result from your input, as well as from the continued stream of development in this rapidly growing technology area.

Part 1: Computer Telephony Technical Overview

Computer telephony is an exploding technical area in the computer field right now, promising to revolutionize the way the businesses and individuals work and play. But until recently, CT has always promised a lot more than it's been capable of delivering.

In the past five years, technologists have built new and powerful computing architectures around specialized, highly integrated and complex chips called digital signal processors. In keeping with the industry's tendency to turn anything worth talking about into an acronym, these chips are usually called DSPs.

The capabilities of these circuits are broad and flexible. Widely programmable, DSPs supply the kinds of signal-handling capabilities that can serve equally well for analyzing and recognizing audible signals — like the human voice — and for bit patterns — like the images that encode fax transmissions. Furthermore, any kind of signal transformation or modulation also falls within the purview of these silicon wonders. With a change of programming and the right kinds of connections, the same basic circuits can therefore handle voice, images, and signal transmissions.

Those looking for a single-factor explanation for the sudden takeoff of CT would be well advised to ponder the DSP. It makes it possible on a single computer interface board to cram all the logic necessary for a single device to support fax transmission and reception, to act like a modem, to perform voice and image recognition, and to provide all the capabilities of a sound card. Given the possible reductions in cost with a major boost in system function, it's no wonder that these chips have helped to spawn an industry!

In Part I of the book, we introduce the underlying terms and technologies that comprise and explain CT. Starting in Chapter 1, we begin with a discussion of the basics of digital and analog communications and explain what makes CT so interesting and special for computer-to-computer and human-to-human communication. In Chapter 2 we look inside CT systems a bit to examine the capabilities, transmission structures, interfaces, and protocols that make personal CT possible. Then in Chapter 3 we discuss those high-end CT systems that have been around the longest and have consequently shaped so much of the prevailing vision of what CT is and what it can (or should be able to) do. Finally, in Chapter 4 we take an in-depth look at the specifications for CT, including the application programming interfaces that have let software developers take advantage of the power and capability of CT equipment on desktop PCs.

Our goal in Part I is to equip you to understand the terms and concepts behind CT so that you can better understand the technology that's involved and its capabilities. Along the way, you'll find yourself learning more about the operation of the telephone system and how it can be used more creatively and effectively than you ever dreamed possible. We hope you enjoy the trip!

Analog and Digital Communications

The essence of computer telephony lies in the combination of the two most powerful pieces of office equipment in use today: the telephone, which can rightfully be called "the great communicator," and the PC, which provides the ability to handle so many tasks, both routine and extraordinary. In this chapter we'll investigate the fundamentals that support the marriage of these two technologies: the basic elements of the technology, hardware, and software that let these systems work together. This means taking a close look at how telephones and computers work, both separately and together. It also means understanding the differences between the analog and digital worlds that must be bridged in order for computers and ordinary telephones work together.

Note: if you haven't read the introduction (which precedes Part I), please go back and do so now. There we introduce some critical concepts and terminology, without which this chapter may not make sense. If you can't bring yourself to do this, please consult the glossary (Appendix C) to familiarize yourself with terms and acronyms such as POTS, CT, and modem.

The Basics of Communication

Before we talk about how computers and telephones talk to each other, it's essential to understand the very basics of the process of communication. At its most fundamental level, successful communications requires three things:

1. A physical link: Without some way for information to pass between the parties to a communication, no information can be exchanged. Computers usually rely on some kind of physical interface to a communications medium (such as a telephone or network wire, or even a satellite or other wireless link) to transfer data.

2. A shared set of rules: Without a shared language or a common notation, parties can't agree on how to represent information; without a shared representation, information cannot be exchanged. Computers most commonly use sets of rules, called protocols, to communicate with one another.

3. Content: The parties may be linked and share a common set of rules, but without something to say, communication is still impossible. For computers, this usually means sharing a common application, protocol, or data type.

These generalities cover all kinds of computer communications, ranging from a serial or parallel cable in a program like LapLink, to modems, networks, and other kinds of possible linkups. In the sections that follow, we'll talk specifically about how things work with conventional and digital computer-to-telephone connections.

Analog Communications

From the human perspective, analog communications are pretty simple: A microphone in the mouthpiece of the telephone translates the sound pressure waves of a human voice (and other sounds in the speaker's environment) into voltage pulses. These pulses are shipped across the phone wires from sender to receiver. In the handset of the receiver's phone is a loudspeaker that translates the voltage pulses into sound pressure waves, recreating the sound of the speaker's voice. The net result is that the receiver more or less hears what the speaker says. Because each handset has a microphone and a speaker, the roles can change: One party can speak while the other listens, and vice versa. If the parties get really excited, both (or all, for multiparty calls) can speak at once!

From a computer's perspective, things are a little bit more complicated. Communications software is necessary on both ends of the connection to allow the computers to exchange digital information, in the form of specific bit patterns (ones and zeros), one after another in an ongoing sequence, or series. (That's why this kind of information exchange is also called "serial communications.")

The earliest methods for enabling computers to communicate typically depended on stringing wires between pairs of machines and working out the programming details to allow each machine to understand what the other one was saying. The same approach works pretty well for hooking other devices to computers, such as printers, disk drives, terminals, and other kinds of peripherals. However, the limits of these wires could easily make themselves felt, simply because the strength of a signal is inversely proportional to the length of the wire it has to traverse. (Think of shouting down a long hallway: The farther down the hall your voice must carry, the louder you have to yell.)

From the beginning, the telephone system helped to provide the wires that could tie computers together, even those far apart, without having to worry about the lengths of the wires or the distances between the two machines. This required the development of technology that would let computers, which communicate by means of binary digits, or bits, use the phone lines, which were originally designed to conduct sound rather than binary data.

Devices that modulated the computer signals into audible tones to send across phone lines and then demodulated them back into computer signals on the other end were developed to let computers use the phone system to communicate. Today we call these devices modems (modulator/demodulator), and they are still the primary devices used in computer communication via telephone lines.

The voice heritage of the telephone system poses some interesting problems for computer communication, even after solving the binary-to-analog conversion issues handled by the modem. For one thing, the human ear can understand a conversation reasonably well when only a small portion of the audible sound spectrum (say 15 percent or so of the total range of human hearing) is provided by a phone link. This makes a tolerable vehicle for moving voice but a vary narrow pipe for transporting computer data.

Thus one of the ongoing issues in using telephone links between computers always has been the bandwidth, or the "size" of the data pipe that a telephone line provides. This remains true even today, when megabit-sized pipes are commercially available, and gigabyte-sized pipes are in use among long-distance telephone companies and other communications giants.

For continuous connections between one computer and another, such as those needed for a network connection between two machines, the telephone line that links them has to be up and running all the time. Because this means that the line is completely taken over by this use, it's called a dedicated circuit in phone lingo, and such connections cost a fair amount of money even today. When they first came into use in the 1960s, they cost a great deal more.

For the purposes of computer telephony, the computer is as likely to be assisting voice traffic as it is to be passing data traffic. Most of the connections used in CT are temporary rather than dedicated; that is, they last only as long as the call that's being handled lasts, and not a moment longer. In CT the computer's role is to help determine, establish, and regulate calls, both incoming and outgoing, and relieve the human operator of as much as possible of the mechanical tedium of dialing, receiving, and routing calls.

As long as analog telephones (a.k.a. POTS, or plain old telephone service) remain a viable means for human communication, there'll be an important role for analog CT. That's why we don't see a terrible urgency in the move from a mixture of analog and digital to all-digital telephony. As the infrastructure is upgraded over time, this move will happen on its own, slowly but surely. In fact, even in the United States, which remains a world leader in the area of digital communications, most industry forecasts put a complete switchover to purely digital communications as far out as the year 2040.

Communicating Digitally

Computers have always used digital signaling methods to control local devices and for communications over local buses. The development of the local area network (LAN) led to a slightly more complex form of digital communication — namely, communication between and among computers. LANs permitted powerful new applications for computer technology. In fact many industry pundits argue that the development of LAN technology was an important first step toward a new widespread use of computers, the linking of LANs into wide area networks (WANs).

Widespread adoption of WANs has led to large-scale use of the telephone network to complete the links among widely separated computers. Computer network nodes on a WAN may be connected not only by local cables but also by telephone links.

Normally this requires that digital computer signals be converted to analog signals for transmission over the phone systems and then reconverted on the receiving by modulating and demodulating equipment (modems). Even though this conversion causes considerable time delays and increases network overhead, the benefits of wide area networking make it both practical and necessary. Widespread use of telephone lines for data transfer has created a new use for phone switching and transmission equipment and has been a key factor in the push for a fully digital telephone system.

Evolution of the Integrated Digital Network System

The development of digital computer technology fomented a revolution in the way organizations created, stored, and transferred information. Many key innovations originally developed for computer technology were quickly adapted for use on the telephone network.

Analog to Digital (and Back Again)

Telephone networks depend on the coordination of many separate and distinct parts for their operation. Development of these parts has traditionally been concentrated in two major divisions: transmission and switching. Developments in computer technology have traditionally been adapted for use on the telephone network in order to lower cost and to improve the quality and reliability of service.

The first major use of computer, or digital, technology in the phone network was in transmission. Although most local subscriber loops in the United States are still analog, the more sophisticated transmission functions of telephony have been converted to digital. The first digital lines used in the United States were *digital first carrier systems* (T1), made up of two wire pairs — one for transmission and one for reception. T1 lines were introduced into the phone network to provide a high-volume link between central offices and between COs and tandem offices. Analog signals are converted to a digital bitstream and transmitted over the T1 line, where they are reconverted to analog on the other end.

Analog Signal Transmission. Analog signals are continuous signals consisting of waves traveling in cycles. Human voice, video, and music are all examples of analog signals. The frequency of an analog signal is measured in hertz (Hz), or cycles per second. The passband of an analog channel is defined as the range of frequencies that can be carried simultaneously. The bandwidth is the width of the passband required for transmission. Different channels may use different passbands within the frequency range of transmission.

The passband of an analog telephone link is defined as approximately 300 to 3400 Hz. The human voice produces sounds between 50 and 1500 Hz. Obviously, the passband of the physical phone link isn't adequate to carry the full range of human voice, but research has shown that the majority of human voice frequencies fall between 300 and 3400 Hz. Telephone links are optimized to carry these frequencies, which contain enough of the range of human sound to recreate clearly recognizable speech. The bandwidth of voice communications is limited on a telephone network, so multiple phone conversations can take place over the same physical channel, or link.

Digital Signal Transmission. For digital transmission over T1 lines and to take advantage of digital switching, analog voice must be converted into a digital bitstream. The continuously varying values of an analog signal are sampled 8000 times per second and are converted to digital values, using a coding algorithm called μ-law encoding. A continuous set of eight bits carries this digital value. After the value is obtained, it is mapped to one of 254 numerical volume, or amplitude, numbers.

Commonly an analog signal is generated, converted to a digital stream, transmitted, and then deconverted at the receiving end into analog signals. Ironically, the use of computer modems adds another set of conversions to each end of the stream, where digital data is converted to analog for initial transmission over the local loop and, on reception from the local loop, converted back from analog into digital.

Multiplexing. Using a common link for many simultaneous connections is called *multiplexing*. Multiplexing in the telephone network allows for multiple conversations or connections to occur over the same physical connection.

Analog and digital signals are multiplexed in different ways. The analog telephone network uses *frequency division multiplexing* (FDM) to carry multiple conversations. FDM apportions the total available bandwidth into channels, or bands, that belong to an assigned user for the duration of the connection. For voice transmission, each conversation is assigned a different passband, with a bandwidth of 3100 Hz.

Digital signals are multiplexed over a link through the use of *time division multiplexing* (TDM). TDM gives each separate channel the entire frequency range for a very tiny increment of time before switching to the next transmitter waiting in line. That's why TDM is sometimes called a "time-slicing" approach; nobody gets the whole bandwidth all of the time, but everybody gets a slice for a portion of each unit of time.

Switching. The first switching devices on the telephone network were electro-mechanical switches called *step-by-step* switches. As their name implies, step-by-step switches react to each digit dialed by the user and make physical connections in the switch to route the call. The next step in switch development was providing *common control* of the switching function within the switch. Common-control switching is based on a series of electromechanical relays, with instructions for handling the switching functions statically defined by the internal wiring inside the switch.

Stored-program switches were made possible by the development of the transistor. These switches allowed easier reprogramming of connections and call control within the phone network. The first stored-program switches were installed in the early 1970s. Essentially they were digital switches, so their inclusion into the telephone network, combined with the implementation of T1 lines, marks the beginning of digital telephony and the beginning of the evolution of ISDN.

The inclusion of digital switches and high-volume digital transmission lines required a high volume of analog-to-digital and digital-to-analog conversions within the network. Although these conversions were practical and necessary, given the evolution of the phone network, they also added considerable overhead and cost to transmission of phone calls without adding any value to the connections. Engineers in the phone network immediately began to convert more of their transmissions and switching functions from analog to digital in order to reduce the number of conversions required, and to eliminate as much as possible of the overhead and its associated costs.

LANs and WANs

Meanwhile, the development and implementation of computer technology continued at an incredible pace. New ways of constructing and using computers were envisioned, developed, deployed, improved, and replaced with more efficient methods in a ongoing quest for the best and fastest technologies.

One of the most significant changes in computing followed the move from batch-oriented mainframe processing to distributed computing. Following this change in physical organization, innovations pushed computing toward decentralized processing and storage. Most of this push resulted from the deployment of local area networks composed of powerful desktop computers spread willy-nilly around many enterprises.

At the same time, these newly deployed LANs were linked by telephone circuits to form WANs that vastly increased the desktop computer user's access to application processing, storage capacity, and sources of information.

The widespread implementation of LANs and WANs placed a new burden on telephone transmissions. Primarily designed and built to provide analog voice transmission, the telephone network was increasingly called on to transmit digital data.

As we mentioned earlier, digital computer signals are converted to analog signals (modulated) on the sending end of a transmission and are deconverted back to digital signal at the other end (demodulated). Modems are designed to handle this task to enable computer communications over the telephone networks. But because the infrastructure of the telephone network was increasingly shifting from analog to digital, it was invariably the case that computers had to go through an extra layer of modulation and demodulation simply to use what was primarily a digital medium in the first place.

The Move to an Integrated Digital Network

As more and more phone circuits are used for digital computer data transmission, new developments and evolution in digital hardware and software continue to bring down the transmission and switching costs and the overhead necessary for the operation of the telephone network. From the beginning, it has been obvious that conversion and deconversion of analog and digital signals over the telephone network should be eliminated for reasons of economy, expedience, and accuracy. As early as 1959, when the first experimental digital telephone technology was being tested and debugged, it was proposed that the global telephone network move from its analog beginnings and be converted into an integrated digital network (IDN), where switching and transmission facilities in the network could be combined for efficiency.

Users and implementers of wide area networks have always recognized the value and sought the implementation of end-to-end digital connections for transfer of computer information. Telephone network technicians sought out the cost savings, increased load capacity, and tighter control that can be provided by eliminating analog-to-digital conversions inside the system.

Bringing Digital Technology to Your Telephone

There's not much magic involved in getting computers to exchange information digitally. As the preceding discussion illustrated, the real trick is to convert the existing analog infrastructure dating back to telephony's earliest days from its analog roots to all-digital equipment and technology. The closer you get to your handset (which is what telephony professionals call your telephone), the more difficult this is to achieve.

Although the infrastructure that's shared between central offices and for long-distance communications is pretty much entirely digital in the United States (and in most of the developed world), the cables that stretch from there to your home or office aren't always up to handling the higher bandwidth and communications demands that digital communications can impose. One of the reasons that installing the most common form of digital telephony, the Integrated Services Digital Network (ISDN), costs more than installing a regular phone line is that the phone company's technicians have to diagnose and check every segment of cable between the central office and your house or office to make sure it's up to the task of handling this more demanding form of communication.

This exercise is called *line conditioning* and can require the phone company to move equipment, run new cables, or even add equipment in order to deliver digital telephony services. The installation costs may be as high as $500 in metropolitan areas, with correspondingly higher charges out in the boonies: Even so, these charges sometimes fail to cover the phone company's costs in bringing the service where it's needed. This helps to explain why service charges are often higher for digital services than for analog, and why you'll sometimes perceive a profound sense of reluctance to deliver those services to your door (because the phone company knows it will be a money-losing proposition).

The strange and wonderful legalities of a regulated communications industry are much too tortuous and complicated to explain in depth in a book like this, but take our word for it that there's an awful lot going on behind the scenes when it comes time to deliver any kind of digital telephone-based service to your home or place of business. Rest assured, however, that if the company is obligated to deliver digital telephony services it will ultimately do so, but if technical difficulties arise during the delivery, it may take quite a while before you have access to a working connection.

For data communications, taking advantage of a digital telephone link ultimately boils down to obtaining the right equipment to allow the computer to attach and exchange information over that link. This is usually a matter of research, purchase, and installation. For voice communications, additional equipment is required: to use a digital telephone line for voice or fax, you'll have to pay through the nose to buy either a truly digital telephone or a device that lets an analog phone attach to a digital connection. Because ISDN phones can cost anywhere from $400 to $1200 (and sometimes higher), many SOHO (Small Office Home Office) users elect to plug in their analog phones and fax machines without going digital all the way.

This is entirely viable, but it eliminates access to the advanced features that digital telephones can bring. Such features include:

- three or more party conference calling

- up to 15 levels of call waiting

- easily programmable call forwarding and call management services

- built-in phone directories with up to 250 numbers

- built-in CT integration with Windows-based software

All roads, including the digital one, lead to computer telephony applications — especially in this book. Given already available sophisticated software that lets voice and data share the same channel, ISDN's greater bandwidth permits those users who can afford it to take better advantage of such capability than their analog counterparts. Even for voice-only connections, ISDN's richer features and cleaner signals can improve overall telephone sound quality, while its built-in CT capabilities help to improve productivity.

Visualizing Computer Telephony

Whether digital or analog, adding the computer to the telephone brings powerful new capabilities into play. The computer adds the ability to see and select from on-screen lists of names and numbers, to interact with call logs and notes from previous calls, and to record and play back both incoming and outgoing digital messages, and lets the body of knowledge about the work under way with your telephone persist and be available whenever it's needed.

The overall result is to create an environment in which the telephone is an extension of your desktop. In this environment placing a call is just as simple as highlighting a field in a window and issuing a dial instruction. Likewise, fielding a call (and dealing with callers) can be handled easily and naturally via a pop-up on-screen window that notifies you of the call's arrival and awaits further instructions (pick up, send to voice mail, monitor, forward, etc.). By bringing sophisticated telephone functions to your computer's display, CT lets you use advanced telephone features and functions without having to master another keyboard (your telephone's) or another strange command set (your telephone system's).

CT Approaches

CT comes in two primary flavors in today's marketplace. Those organizations large enough (usually with 24 or more telephone lines) to operate their own internal telephone systems typically seek a way to interface PCs with such systems. This brings the power and capability of powerful (and expensive) private digital phone systems to users' desktops, but is usually beyond the scope and the means of SOHO operations. This kind of CT implementation usually depends on a link between a network server of some kind and a telephone system, where a LAN routes information exchanged between the network server and the telephone system's main controller, to an individual's workstation or his or her handset, as shown in Figure 1.1.

In smaller organizations or when no telephone system (or network server) is in use, CT is applied to one or more phone lines and one or more PCs. Here, a network may be present, but it need not play a pivotal role in supporting CT applications. This is an arena in which individual computers are interlinked with individual phone lines. This is the primary method for implementing CT for individuals and is a workable approach for most SOHO needs, especially if a network is

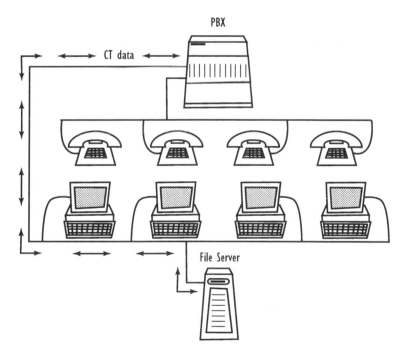

Figure 1.1: In larger organizations CT data is exchanged between a private phone system and a properly equipped network server.

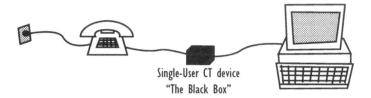

Single-User CT device
"The Black Box"

Figure 1.2: For SOHO users, the link between the telephone and the computer occurs directly at the PC.

present to facilitate local communication and information exchange among colleagues in the same office. This approach is depicted in Figure 1.2.

Although we will mention CT as practiced in the world of private telephone systems from time to time, please remember that our primary focus will be on those CT systems that make direct links between the user's phone lines and his or her desktop PC.

Summary

In this chapter we've reviewed the basics of analog and digital signaling, as applied to both human and computer communication over the telephone. Along the way we've explored how the phone company's own communications infrastructure is laid out and have identified the local loop between the central office and your own telephone as the final but formidable analog holdout. We've also discussed the basics of computerized telephone communications and the fundamental configurations for CT systems. All of this information will stand you in good stead as we move forward to the next chapter, where you'll learn more about the details of CT services and functions. In the meantime, is that the phone we hear ringing?

CT Services & Functions

By now you should be pretty excited about computer telephony, even if in a vague and general kind of way. You already have a pretty good idea of the kinds of things that CT can do in combining the power of the PC and your telephone to create its strange and wonderful features and functions.

In this chapter we'll take a closer look at the services and functions you'll be most likely to find in CT systems and products. This will mean introducing and explaining some specialized terminology and explaining what such features and functions can do.

The three primary types of external information that CT systems must handle include:

- voice, or normal human conversation on the telephone

- data, or normal computer-to-computer communication via telephone lines

- fax, or normal facsimile transmissions between one fax machine (or fax/modem) and another, which involves transmission of specially encoded graphical images, or facsimiles, of the pages being shipped from sender or receiver

In addition, CT supplies another set of functions that are critical to using this technology effectively — the ability to coordinate and control the telephone's behavior for both incoming and outgoing calls. This involves a fourth type of data for CT systems to handle, related to call setup, control, and management. Some would argue that this is the most important type of data that CT manipulates, since it inevitably controls how the other three types of data will be handled. Whatever your viewpoint on this may be, it's clear that the function of call control and management is what makes CT so useful and attractive to its users.

In the sections that follow, we'll examine these four kinds of data and explain how they're represented and handled within CT systems and applications. This will be a general theoretical discussion, not an in-depth look at particular products' features and functions. (For that information, please consult Part II of this book, which will cover such things directly).

Call Setup, Control, and Management

In the simplest of terms, CT lets the computer tell the telephone what to do and when to do it. In practice this boils down to a handful of activities:

- Dealing with CID (caller ID) or ANI (automatic number identification) information from incoming calls, possibly including database lookups or call log retrievals. Most CT systems integrate some form of computer storage of names, numbers, and dialing codes with telephone control to make it easy to place, receive, and process both incoming and outgoing calls. Mundane though it may seem, most users report that the biggest advantage of CT is its relief from "dial-it-yourself" button-punching.

- Routing calls based on caller identification to either voice mail or to the phone itself. Many CT systems provide a "do not disturb" feature that routes all calls to voice mail, except those that originate from a predefined list; likewise, a "reject calls" feature can direct any call whose information is contained on another list straight to voice mail.

- Call monitoring and screening, which is possible on some voice-mail-capable CT systems, since they can simultaneously record incoming messages while playing them back to the PC's operator. Such systems usually include a "pick up" feature so that such calls can be answered immediately or not, at the operator's discretion.

- Call forwarding, automatic ringover to a backup operator, conferencing, and other advanced call control features. these functions are supported in many CT systems, and typically operate much as they would on a feature-laden handset, except that the "buttons" that control their behavior are on screen rather than on your phone.

- Computer as telephone. Properly equipped PCs (with sound cards, microphones, and speakers) can take over the role of the telephone completely, since they can control the phone line, pick up the operator's voice, and play back incoming sounds.

This is not an exhaustive list of all control and management features, but it is a reasonable "wish list" of what careful buyers should look for in a midrange CT system for their desktop.

Voice-Based Services

Computers can handle audible information as a source of data in two ways. Both are based on the sophisticated signal-processing capabilities inherent in the modern generation of Digital Signal Processor (DSP) circuitry. One method is called "speech recognition," which refers to a broad-based capability to recognize a set of verbal commands to navigate or control a system. For example, If you call Delta Airlines to make a reservation, you can now say the word "one" to make a menu selection instead of pressing the "1" key on your phone's keypad. Speech recognition systems can recognize sounds from a broad range of speakers, so their set of commands and options has to be kept somewhat narrow, as is the case when navigating most Interactive Voice Response (IVR) systems such as the Delta reservation system.

The second method is called "voice recognition": Unlike speech recognition systems, these kinds of systems have deep but narrow capabilities, usually tailored for one particular speaker's voice (hence their name). Voice recognition systems may be used for more complex system controls (like the kind of vocal replacement for the keyboard a motion-impaired computer user might want) or for data entry (taking speech and turning it into text for use in a word processing or an e-mail application, for example). Properly equipped PCs can even be operated remotely with such tools, enabling a user to "tell" his or her computer to handle complex tasks over any normal telephone connection.

Another kind of audible aspect of CT systems is also gaining considerable popularity. Used for output rather than input, it's called "text to speech" and refers to a computer's ability to phonetically sound out text, based on a set of rules for "reading out loud." When coupled with IVR, remote telephone access, fax management, and technologies such as Optical Character Recognition (another task that the incredibly versatile DSP can handle), this means that a user can call his or her computer from any telephone and have it read any waiting faxes, e-mail messages, or text files on demand.

As the preceding examples demonstrate, CT is really a two-way street. Not only does it bring the organizational power and intelligence of the computer to the telephone, but it also opens the telephone as a remote conduit to a computer's contents and capabilities.

User-Phone System Interfaces

At the desktop, the predominant interface to the telephone is a graphical, windowed user interface (such as Microsoft Windows, the Macintosh OS, the OS/2 Workplace Shell, or UNIX Motif or X Windows). In this environment all kinds of telephone information is flashed onto the screen in response to incoming calls or is available at the push of a button or click of a mouse from the CT system's own interface when placing or responding to calls. The emergence of multitasking operating systems makes it possible for an incoming phone call to "interrupt" an application in progress, using a pop-up window to indicate an incoming call, and displaying whatever information can be gleaned about the caller from CID or ANI data. Because of their sudden, random appearances, these windows are called "screen pops" in CT-speak, and they help define much of the interaction style for CT applications.

From the screen pop, users can generally access other capabilities of a CT system in reactive mode — call logs, annotations, call-tracking information, and so on. By iconizing their CT software or running it in background mode, users can also launch the CT application any time they like by double-clicking the icon or using a shortcut key sequence. With this kind of setup, computerized telephone access is never more than a click or a few keystrokes away. This ease of access, combined with the flexibility of gathering and manipulating names, phone numbers, and call data, is what gives CT so much of its power and utility.

IVR (discussed in the preceding section) is another example of a CT interface. Although IVR is most commonly used for remote operation over the telephone, several CT systems also support voice-based operation at the desktop. (We're tempted to add that this makes it more important than ever before to be careful what you say around your computer!)

Simple, intuitive graphical and audio interfaces to CT make it a useful addition to your desktop, creating the possibility of a better telephone than its old-fashioned stand-alone counterpart.

Handling Voice and Data

A new technology called Simultaneous Voice and Data (SVD, another outgrowth of the ever-versatile DSP chip, also known as Digital SVD, or DSVD) lets the same telephone link be used for multiple purposes, most commonly to support the transfer of computer data at the same time that a conversation is under way. This is a direct consequence of the minimal demands that human voice encoding places on today's modern telephony equipment and circuitry: Even with a spirited conversation, there's still room left over to move data from one computer to another.

Using SVD requires that both parties to the conversation be equipped with the right kind of gear, so your modem or other communications hardware can share a channel with your telephone handset (or its fully-computerized equivalent). This typically requires a standard, so that users can place such calls without having to worry about compatibility with the equipment on the receiving end. An emerging ITU (International Telecommunications Union) standard for DSVD is called TrueSpeech and is incorporated in products from companies such as AT&T, Multi-Tech, Sierra, and U.S. Robotics. This new speech-compression technology (to be designated as G.723 by the ITU when it is formally endorsed in 1996) will enable visual telephony applications over the public telephone network, as well as a variety of other teleconferencing applications.

Today the majority of modems and CT hardware still lack DSVD capability, but it's clearly becoming more prevalent, and we expect this capability to be standard in modems and CT equipment across the board by mid-1997.

Fax Handling

One of CT's biggest benefits is that it bundles all the various types of information that might arrive by telephone under a single umbrella, accessed from a single interface. This means that users can check a single message box to retrieve voice mail, faxes, file uploads, and in some implementations, even electronic mail.

By itself, facsimile remains one of the most heavily used methods for exchanging documents among individuals and businesses. This is especially true outside the United States, where fax alone seems to have overcome the many electronic incompatibilities that seem to rear their ugly heads when electronic information must cross over actual physical borders.

CT's ability to integrate fax handling with other forms of telephone communication also adds another useful characteristic: Properly equipped CT systems can recognize whether an incoming call is voice, data, or fax and can route it accordingly to the proper device. In situations typical of smaller SOHO operations or remote offices, this can let you get by with only one or two phone lines, where you might otherwise be tempted to bring in separate lines for voice, data, and fax. As usage of one type or another increases, however, it will eventually become necessary to dedicate a line for exclusive voice, data, or fax use.

CT's ability to integrate fax handling with other applications also lets the synergy provided by the combination of OCR, text-to-speech, and remote access come into play, as we mentioned earlier. This same integration also extends fax capability to the entire desktop for outgoing transmission: In most cases, sending a fax is delivered as a special-purpose print driver. This lets applications handle faxing as another kind of print operation; the driver solicits the destination number(s) as it prepares to send the fax. When supplying information for outgoing faxes, it's just as easy to supply the name of a defined distribution list for broadcast fax capability or to provide a list of destination numbers for a one-time delivery.

Sophisticated fax services also commonly include delayed, scheduled fax transmission. This allows faxes that aren't time-sensitive to be sent during off-peak hours, when long-distance charges are lower and sending and receiving equipment is generally more accessible. CT technology also makes it easy to establish a faxback service. Since this consists of a telephone-based document selection system in which users select the documents they want faxed to them, it's an ideal application for IVR (for document selection), keypad entry (for the destination fax number), and fax services (to send the selected documents to the target number).

In fact, fax integration with other services in CT makes it possible to construct all kinds of crossover capabilities. Since Internet e-mail is basically free, a fax response to e-mail lets users request information without incurring the costs of a long-distance call and lets the receiver handle a request without paying for toll-free call-ins. The combination of e-mail and faxback is a natural, and several CT systems are beginning to include such features.

In the long run it's the combination of fax, voice, and data capabilities under a single CT interface and control structure that makes the difference. Although lots of interesting applications that leverage this synergy are available today, we expect to see all kinds of new, innovative uses popping up in the near future.

Handling Data: Modem Protocols

For most computer users, moving data (as opposed to voice) means using a modem, separate from voice communications. Until SVD becomes ubiquitous, the separation of voice and data will probably remain the norm. When it comes to using a modem, there's a plethora of potential protocols that you may encounter.

Most modem standards (in fact, all the ones that we cover here) start with the notation "V." (pronounced "vee dot"). That's because they're all part of the same ITU family of standards, sometimes called the V Series Recommendations, that deal with data communications over the telephone. The beauty of standards, especially international ones like these, is that when everyone conforms to them, interoperation of equipment becomes far less problematic.

The V Series modem standards involve several technical areas, each with its own requirements for compliance. Today these include:

- Speed, or the bits per second (bps) or kilobits per second (Kbps) rating associated with the standard

- Error control, which refers to the specific encoding schemes and error detection/correction algorithms in use

- Data compression, which refers to the mathematical techniques used to squeeze data into a shortened form for transmission (compression), reversed on reception (expansion, decompression) to return it to its original form

You'll also see some interesting notation following some V Series standards. ITU uses the suffix "bis" to designate the second item in a series of related standards and "ter" to designate the third item (that's as high as they go these days). That's why you'll see designations such as V.42bis and V.27ter in Table 2.1.

Table 2.1 lists all the V Series standards we could find. Here's how to interpret the various columns when you read this table:

- Name: the V. designation for the standard

- Year: the year the standard was finalized (This is a great clue as to what's current and what's hopelessly outdated.)

- Speed: the bit rate for the standard

- Error: the names of the error-handling algorithms supported (none, if empty)

- Compression: the names of the compression algorithms supported (none, if empty)

- Comm: "Simplex" indicates that only one-way communications is supported and that sender and receiver cannot change roles; "half-duplex" indicates that only one party may send at any time but that parties can switch roles; "full-duplex" indicates that both parties can send and receive simultaneously.

- Misc: miscellaneous information, possibly noteworthy (you decide)

Armed with this information, Table 2.1 should make sense to you. After the table, we'll also provide definitions for the most current V Series standards, which in the table are indicated by boldface.

Table 2.1: V-Series Standards

NAME	YEAR	SPEED	ERROR	COMPRESSION	COMM	MISC.
V.13	Simulated carrier control (lets full-duplex modem emulate half-duplex)					
V.14	Lets synchronous modem carry async characters, default mode for V.42 modem talking to a non-V.42 modem					
V.17	1991	14,4000	Fax standard for Group 3 encoding, including simplex V.32bis			
V.21	1964	300	Asynchronous operation		Full-duplex	Like Bell 103
V.21ch2	1964	Standard for fax operation at 300 bps				
V.22	1980	1200	Asynchronous, synchronous operation		Full-duplex	
V.22bis	1984	2400	Asynchronous, synchronous operation		Full-duplex	Fallback to V.22
V.23	1964	1200	Asynchronous, synchronous operation		Half-duplex	
V.24	1964	Defines interchange circuits between DTE and DCE, similar to RS-232-C				
V.25	1968	Specifies automatic calling and/or answering equipment, similar to RS-366				
V.25bis	1968	Popular for AS/400 and other mid-range systems' auto-call/answer equipment				
V.26	1968	2400	Synchronous		Full-duplex	4-wire leaseline
V.26bis	1968	2400			Half-duplex	
V.26ter	1970	2400			Full-duplex	Seldom used
V.27	1972	4800	Synchronous		Full-duplex	4-wire leaseline
V.27bis	1976	4800	Synchronous		Full-duplex	Uses equalizer
V.27ter	1976	4800	Synchronous		Half-duplex	Used in GP3 fax
V.28	1972	Defines functions of all circuits for RS-232 interface				Equiv: EIA-232
V.29		9,600 also used for fax transmission at 9,600; still widely used today			Full or half	4wires=full 2 wires=half
V.32	1984	9,600			Full duplex	Use w/V.42
V.32bis	1991	14,400			Full-duplex	Use w/V.42

Table 2.1: V-Series Standards, continued

NAME	YEAR	SPEED	ERROR	COMPRESSION	COMM	MISC.
V.32terbo	1994	19,200			Full-duplex	AT&T std
V.33	1992	14,400 & 12,000			Full-duplex	4-wire leaseline
V.34	1994	28,800			Full-duplex	
V.35	1968	varies				Group band use
V.42	1989		LAP-M, MNP 2-4			
V.42bis	1989			LZ (4:1)		Implies V.42
V.54	1976	Modem loopback test circuit, includes local/remote digital/analog capabilities				
V.Fast	1994	28,800			Full-duplex	Pseudo-standard
V.110	1984	ISDN DTE to serial interface				Rate adaption
V.120	1988	Protocol encapsulation on ISDN, statistical multiplexing of B channel				

A close examination of Table 2.1 shows that there are an awful lot more V Series standards than are worth attending to. Only the four items in boldface — V.32bis, V.34, V.42, and V.42bis — are worth detailed discussion. Each of these is covered generally in the following sections.

V.32bis

V.32bis is an ITU standard for full-duplex transmission on two-wire leased and dial-up lines at 4800, 7200, 9600, 12,000, and 14,400 bps. As a superset of V.32, V.32bis provides full backward compatibility with V.32. Modems operating at a rated speed are transmitting data at that speed; with compression schemes such as V.42 and V.42bis, they can achieve data transfers at rates up to 57,600 bps. V.32bis also includes a rapid rate renegotiation feature to support quick, smooth rate changes when line conditions change. Even though V.34 offers faster speeds, many modems in use today conform to V.32bis.

V.34

This is the newest, fastest current modem standard and handles speeds up to 28,800 bps. (An extension that may ultimately be called V.34bis is under development right now; it supports speeds up to 33,400 bps.) These modems use a feature known as line probing to identify the capacity and quality of their current phone line, helping to ensure maximum throughput. This standard includes a half-duplex mode of operation for fax applications. V.34 modems also use a new handshaking technique that identifies them to local telephone equipment, which helps to explain their strange, faxlike warbling negotiation/handshake tones. Prior to this standard's adoption, some manufacturers developed "best guess" implementations, some of which were labeled V.FC (for "Fast Class") or V.Fast. Unfortunately not all these modems can interoperate at their highest speeds, so use them with care!

V.42

V.42 is an ITU standard for modem error checking that uses LAP-M as the primary protocol but also provides MNP Classes 2 through 4 as alternatives for compatible operation with other modems. V.42 may be used with V.22, V.22bis, V.26ter, V.32, and V.32bis modems. LAP-M is based on HDLC, is used as the primary error-checking protocol, and is the basis for all future error-checking extensions. MNP is supported as an alternative protocol, primarily for backward compatibility with older, less capable modems.

V.42bis

V.42bis is an ITU modem data compression standard using a Lempel-Ziv compression algorithm developed by British Telecom to deliver up to 4:1 compression ratios. V.42bis automatically implies the V.42 error-checking protocol. Please note that compression provides benefits only on data that hasn't already been compressed; if you're already using file-compression software prior to file transfer, compression will not add much to performance.

V.29 (Fax)

Even though it has a higher number than the next standard, V.29 is older than V.17. V.29 defines Group 3 fax behavior for machines that communicate at 9600 and 4800 baud (still the most common speeds for fax communications). However, V.29 was initially developed for full-duplex communications over four-wire leased lines. It has since been adapted for two-wire leased and dial-up lines, with the half-duplex communications required for fax transmission and reception.

V.17 (Fax)

V.17 is a new ITU standard for simplex modulation used in Extended Group 3 Fax applications. The standard provides 7200, 9600, 12,000, and 14,400 bps trellis-coded modulation, Modified Modified Read (MMR) compression, and error-correction mode (ECM). It also defines special sequences for half-duplex operation during negotiation and data transfer.

Stand-alone Computer Telephony

Stand-alone CT describes the relationship among the telephone interface hardware, the underlying telephone system, and the user's PC. It is meant to indicate that a single PC and telephone line could provide CT functionality without requiring access to a network on the PC side or to a private or "virtual" telephone system on the phone side. (In many RBOCs, it's possible to lease Centrex services, which let any handset behave as if it were part of a digital PBX system, including voice mail, call forwarding, call transfer, multiparty conference calls, and other features not normally available on "dumb" telephone handsets.)

Since this is precisely the set of circumstances that defines the kind of telephone and computer configurations most common in the SOHO environment, stand-alone CT is a major focus of this book. The configurations needed for such systems typically take one of three forms:

1. The CT system assumes that a fax/modem and sound card are already present in the PC and relies on the presence of certain hardware features to support its software capabilities.

2. The CT system requires that an external device be attached between the telephone line wall jack and a modem or a serial port on the computer.

3. The CT system requires a specialized CT adapter card that is configured for and installed into a PC. (This applies especially to situations where two or more phone lines need to be routed through such a system).

Since the complexity of the hardware required for each form increases as you read down the list, it should come as no surprise that the expense goes up correspondingly. But since the functionality and capability also increase, it remains as true for CT as for other technical areas that "you get what you pay for." As you'll see in Chapters 5-9, the range of capabilities is even more staggering than the potential costs involved!

The stand-alone CT system remains the mainstay of SOHO operations. That's why they'll be an important focus for the rest of this book. We'll cover numerous other options along the way, as much to provide potential coming attractions for stand-alone systems as to explain the capabilities of networked systems that either emulate or require private telephone systems.

Summary

In this chapter we've covered the basic services that CT can provide and the functions that CT systems can deliver to their users. We've also discussed what CT systems can do for voice, data and fax communications, and have explored the synergy resulting from uniting these communications under a single common interface. We've also examined the modem standards you're likely to encounter in the marketplace, with a clear indication of the ones that are most important. Finally, we've described the kind of CT system that is most likely to appeal to SOHO users, as a way of defining the real focus to this book. In the chapter that follows you'll have a chance to see how the other half lives, as we investigate the larger and more complex CT systems used in networked organizations that use private telephone systems.

Networking the Telephone

At this point you should already realize that most of the features and functions that are important in computer telephony have emerged from larger business telephone environments. Bigger organizations have long been able to afford the kinds of expensive, specialized systems that were necessary to provide CT functions before the advent of the DSP made this kind of technology more compact and affordable.

It's important to realize, too, that even though private telephone systems may be large, complex, and expensive beasts, they're often essential elements of any sizable organization's physical plant. In fact, any time the number of phone extensions exceeds 30 or so, there are often savings to be had by changing the normal 1:1 ratio of phones to telephone lines that prevails in most homes and SOHO operations.

Whatever the size, CT systems must handle the same primary types of information: the triumvirate of voice, data, and fax that we introduced at the beginning of Chapter 2. Likewise, the need for call management and control persists and is usually greater in private telephone systems, where a significant amount of the voice traffic may be within the confines of the system rather than requiring a local or long distance outside connection.

In the sections that follow, we'll examine these four kinds of data again, but this time in the context of private telephone systems and the kinds of equipment that they use. To that end, we'll begin with a discussion of the basic elements involved in such systems and move on to an examination the roles that private branch exchanges and network servers play in such environments. We'll then talk about how incoming calls are handled and outgoing calls placed in such environments. We'll conclude with a discussion of CT's role in this kind of environment and the features and functions it can bring into play. As in Chapter 2, this will be a general theoretical discussion. (We will cover some elements in greater detail than in Chapter 2, because we won't be covering these particular systems in much detail anywhere else in this book.)

The Pieces of the Puzzle

Any time the scale of telephony gets sizable — more than 30 lines or more than 40 or 50 extensions — the level of complexity starts to grow quickly. For one thing, paying for 30 telephone lines, even at a low rate of $20 or $30 a month, adds up to $600-$900 a month. (Even when purchased in bulk, $50 per line per month is a good average cost for business lines.) There is also the additional expense of long-distance charges, which can easily run double or triple the preceding totals.

For another thing, installing and maintaining the infrastructure needed to handle that many lines and phones is also costly and labor intensive. Even a relatively modest telephone system can involve several miles of cable, one or two wiring closets, and one or two major pieces of equipment (such as operator consoles, and the computers that make and manage internal and external telephone connections, generically called a "telephone switch," or more simply "the switch"). It's easy to spend around $250 per connection for wiring, while the major pieces of equipment can cost anywhere from $10,000 to $50,000 for a system of this size and scale, depending on how much growth is anticipated over the life of the system and what level of sophistication and function the system is expected to deliver.

There's also the cost of "personal" equipment involved: Everybody needs a handset, and some people will want speakerphones or headsets as well. Let's figure on around 100 pieces of such equipment for our hypothetical telephone system. At an average cost of $120 per item (multiline, multifunction handsets and speakerphones will often cost more, in fact, and headsets somewhat less), this collection of gear adds up to $12,000.

No properly equipped office will be without some tools, some spare pieces of equipment (to replace defective or broken items while they're in the shop or replacements on order), and someone to maintain the system after it's been installed. Figure on yearly costs of around $2500 for spares, repairs, and tools. A system of this size won't need the allocation of a full-time person, so figure on absorbing one quarter of the salary of an IS person with telephony skills, for a cost of about $15,000 a year, or on spending the same amount on an outside consultant to handle new installations, repairs, and system changes on an as-needed basis.

Some of these numbers are large enough to compete with the impact of buying a car on an ordinary household budget, and they add up to some pretty scary totals. What we've described here amounts to the following:

- $22,500 to $102,500 for up-front equipment costs

- $15,000 for wiring and installation

- $1500 per month for business service, $3000 per month for long distance

- $1250 per month for a part-time system administrator

- $210 a month for spares, parts, and repairs

From the perspective of a yearly budget, we're talking about a start-up cost of $37,500 to $117,500 for equipment, wiring, and installation and a yearly recurring cost of $71,520 (or $5960 per month). For a 50-person organization, the average per-head monthly phone bill comes to $119.20, not counting equipment capitalization costs.

As organizations get bigger, per-head costs will come down somewhat, but the overall outlays get bigger and bigger. And yet the pieces remain the same: wiring and premises equipment (the infrastructure and the phone system), end-user equipment (handsets, headsets, speakerphones), and recurring costs (staff or consultant, line service, long distance). Because the money involved can be pretty significant, it's no wonder that vendors have spent significant amounts of time and effort building products to capture part of this market. It's also no surprise that organizations have expended serious time and effort to manage and control related costs (especially recurring monthly costs, which over the five- to ten-year life of the average phone system dwarf start-up outlays).

Because the investment in telephony is large, the payback has to be demonstrable. And although the costs in CT systems are considerable, companies continue to plow big chunks of cash into this technology — obviously the paybacks are considered worthwhile. This helps explain why most of the significant advancements in CT have come out of this marketplace and why the model for CT continues to be ruled by this group's approach to using the telephone as an instrument of commerce and profit, as well as communication.

Key Systems and Private Branch Exchanges (PBXs)

To really understand how the telephone network operates, you need to understand what goes on behind the scenes when your telephone rings to announce an incoming call or when you pick up the receiver and start to dial an outgoing call. In learning about this, you'll also learn about the various types of telephone switching equipment, the roles and capabilities of switch elements, and how telephones really work. After reading this section, you'll have a pretty good idea about how telephone connections are made and broken and the pieces and parts that make this happen.

Handling Telephone Lines

Before you can appreciate the beauty and majesty of a private telephone system, you need to be familiar with how telephone lines are treated as groups (called line consolidation). It's also important to understand how telephone calls get connected from the caller to the callee (referred to as call routing, or more simply, routing).

The Power of Consolidation

Almost any private telephone system will attempt to consolidate lines in order to save on service and wiring charges. This process in telephony-speak means maintaining a less than 1 : 1 ratio between telephone extensions and the lines that service them. Since the odds are slim indeed that everyone who has a phone will want to use it at exactly the same time, organizations can get away with ratios that are sometimes as great as 10 : 1 (that is, only one line for every 10 telephone extensions).

In fact, this is how the phone company delivers lines for your use anyway. As the biggest phone service provider in your neck of the woods, the phone company can no more afford to supply a 1 : 1 lines : phones ratio than any other business. Nor could you afford this in your home; it's a safe bet that you have many more extensions than lines there, too.

When you pick up your phone, you'll usually be connected to the first available line. Occasionally you'll hear the message: "All circuits are busy now. Please try your call again later." This means that all lines that are connected to your nearby central office are in use and that there's no more capacity available to service your request (made in picking up your phone and waiting for a dial tone).

This is also why leaving your phone off the hook causes loud tones to be issued from the phone company's equipment. Until you hang up, you're taking up a circuit that somebody else could be using.

Routing Means Making Connections

Routing explains how the telephone network links caller to callee, whether the device in use is a telephone, a modem, or a fax machine. (In most cases the underlying phone system doesn't even care). In the telephony world your 10-digit phone number acts just like an address: The first three digits supply your area code, which identifies a geographical service region; the next three digits identify a telephone exchange, which is usually a collection of telephone equipment somewhere within a few miles of your home or office; and the final four digits identify the particular telephone line that services the devices attached to it.

When a call is placed, the equipment looks for an area code to determine whether an interarea transfer must be made. If so, the local phone company's requests from a long-distance carrier a line that connects the local area to the remote area identified by the area code. If not, the local phone company looks for a line that connects your local exchange (identified by the first three digits of a seven-digit local number) to the local exchange you're calling (identified the same way). If you're calling someone on your own home exchange, the central office merely needs to make a connection between the line associated with your final four digits with the line associated with the last four digits of the number you are calling.

Routing comes in the processes involved in identifying the source and destination for a call and in deciding how to establish the connection. It works very much like network routing, in that such selections are usually guided by a look-up table that identifies connections that can link up the source and destination or that have access mechanisms that can calculate or otherwise determine a valid circuit path (or route) between the two parties.

Now that you understand the relationship between telephones and the lines that service them and how calls get from sender to receiver, we can talk about the kinds of telephone systems that are often used to handle line consolidation and to provide the initial step in call routing. We'll begin with key systems, which represent the lower end of the telephone system spectrum (up to 100 extensions or so). Then we'll introduce the PBX (or Centrex, as the phone companies call it), which, although it can handle small installations as well as large ones, is usually installed in environments with 100 extensions or more.

Key Telephone Systems

The main difference between key telephone and PBX systems is in switching capability: Key systems can't transfer calls from one extension or number to another unless that function is supplied by the central office. (In the world of telephony, central office is usually abbreviated CO and is the phone company's local exchange, associated with the first three digits of a seven-digit phone number.) Otherwise, the two kinds of systems are similar in their basic capabilities.

All key systems support access to multiple lines and some can deliver access to as many as 20 distinct lines on a single handset. Because the key system provides no switching functions, dialing outbound requires no extra number ("9" for an outside line is fairly common on most PBX systems).

Key system telephones can be equipped with different sets of lines to reflect organizational needs or requirements. Thus accounting could have access to a small set of lines for its handful of employees but manufacturing to a larger set for the 100-plus employees on each shift. Because the accounting lines would be distinct from manufacturing, however, the accounting employees won't have to share their lines with the larger group of shift workers.

Most key systems use analog lines rather than the digital telephone lines used by PBX systems. Today many so-called hybrid key systems are available, which support a mix of analog and digital equipment and lines. Some can even manage connections with digital telephone services, such as ISDN, transparent to the system's users.

Key systems don't usually require special environments for their equipment, either, because their smaller size reduces power and climate control requirements. All you need to do is plug them into a wall outlet, and they're ready to go. (It is a good idea, however, to have an Uninterruptible Power Supply for this equipment.)

The three criteria you should use in selecting a key system would have to be:

1. Cost: Whether budget is a major concern or higher costs are difficult to justify

2. Size: Whether the number of lines and extensions is under 30 and 100, respectively

3. Performance: Whether blazing fast call handling and lots of sophisticated options are unnecessary and internal switching is something you can live without.

Key systems' feature sets are improving as well: In addition to hybrid capabilities, many of them can integrate voice-processing applications quite nicely, and some can handle SVD (Simultaneous Voice and Data) and network linkups. Advanced key systems (which you own and operate yourself) can even outperform Centrex (which you lease from the phone company, which maintains the system on its own premises) at a lower overall cost these days. Prices for small systems start at under $1000, and cost between $100 and $350 per handset; digital systems can cost as much as $40,000 fully configured but offer correspondingly better features, functions, and performance. Thus key systems appear to have a secure niche for the foreseeable future, as an appropriate intermediate step between personal CT systems and PBX-based systems.

The Private Branch Exchange (PBX)

PBXs supply the same technology that the CO uses to connect an inbound call to your telephone and to supply an open line when you place a call. The underlying technology that makes it all possible is called a telephone switch, or more simply, a switch. A switch is a device that makes and breaks connections (such as the light switch on your wall); it can be mechanical, electrical, or electronic and in the telephone world is used to request, set up, maintain, and tear down connections between pairs (or sets) of lines that are connected to the switch. All you care about is that one of those lines connects to your handset and is ready to ring or provide a dial tone, as circumstances dictate.

From a physical perspective, a switch is nothing more than a matrix of electrical circuits, where any incoming line can be physically connected to any outgoing line through a series of intermediate relays and connections (each of which is opened or closed by flipping a switch). A telephone switch is a special-purpose computer with a number of slots (as few as 10 or as many as several thousand), each of which can accommodate an adapter card to attach one or more phone lines. Within the switch, a control program provides the logic and knowledge necessary to make and break temporary connections as needed, while the connections between the adapter cards provide the electrical pathways that interconnect lines as the control program dictates.

In addition to making and breaking physical connections between lines, switches supply many more features and functions that have largely defined CT up to the present. Centrex and PBX define the two major types of switching systems in use today. In most cases the primary difference between the two varieties is that under a Centrex system, the phone company owns, operates, and manages a switch on its premises, and leases services to customers over analog phone lines, whereas the PBX systems are almost entirely digital, and are usually owned and operated by individual organizations on their own premises.

PBX systems usually have fairly stringent power and climate control requirements. Because some of them can be quite large, they'll often have their own separate power and A/C systems. The telephone company, in fact, routinely operates COs with switches that service thousands of lines and may consist of tens of thousands of interface cards, with floor after floor of cabling and interface racks, and a battery of special-purpose computers to handle the ceaseless making and breaking of connections among those lines and to provide a broad range of services for the users.

PBX service offerings are staggeringly broad, but here's a core set that you're likely to encounter on most of them:

- Call block: This lets users prevent calls from particular numbers from ringing a particular number or group of numbers; conversely, it can be set up so that extensions managed by the switch are prevented from dialing out to certain numbers.

- Call forward/transfer: This essential switch function is handled by the switch's ability to break a connection between one internal extension and an outside line and to establish a new one between that outside line and another extension. More sophisticated implementations allow rollovers to a defined operator (or hierarchy of operators), call forwarding from one extension to another, and the like.

- Call waiting: As long as an outside line can be held open by the switch, the caller may be kept on "hold" until the recipient picks up that line and completes the call. The switch provides this capability.

- Caller identification: Automatic Number Identification, also known as caller ID, allows the recipient to be informed of the caller's number prior to accepting the call (either while it's ringing or waiting on hold). Some systems can even look up numbers in a database and supply the caller's names instead of (or along with) the numbers. The availability of caller ID ultimately rests with your local phone company, because it must supply that information to your telephone system before it can be used.

- Conference calling: This takes advantage of the switch's ability to manage multiple lines simultaneously, allowing three or more callers to be bridged together in a single virtual telephone connection.

- CT interfaces: The switch is a powerful computer in its own right, often with sophisticated voice and data-handling capabilities. As the focus of telephone activity in those organizations where the interfaces are present, switches are a natural place to integrate CT capability and to provide an interface to other CT systems. Today, many switch vendors support a variety of CT Application Programming Interfaces to permit external CT applications to interact directly with the telephone system. (The standards and technology involved for this are discussed in Chapter 4.)

- Digital telephone support: Most business telephones are digital — that is, they convert analog voice signals into bit patterns for cleaner, more reliable transmission over telephone lines. Because most such phones are attached to PBXs, it should come as no surprise that the overwhelming majority of PBXs are digital, too. Hint: A six-wire RJ-45 phone jack usually indicates that the attached phone is digital.

- Intercom/Internal calls: PBX systems provide extra internal communications links that can activate the speakerphone on appropriate premises equipment (even while the phone lines are in use). These can also be used for internal voice calls from one extension to another. (The PBX may have a limited number of outside lines, as dictated by the mathematics of line consolidation, but it can permit any two extensions under its management to connect to each other.)

- ISDN support: Modern PBXs may support standard ISDN Basic Rate Interface (BRI) devices, but they can be capable of handling Primary Rate Interface (PRI) devices as well. This capability allows ISDN telephones and peripheral devices to use completely digital connections. PRI technology supports "bandwidth on demand," which can advance applications, such as video teleconferencing or LAN-to-WAN connections, through existing digital telephony connections and services.

- Speed dial: Certain telephones can be programmed with internal telephone lists so that a one- or two-digit key sequence can issue a complete external dial string to the switch. In most Centrex and PBX systems the feature is supplied from the central computer at the switch; in key systems this information resides in individual telephones.

- SVD (Simultaneous Voice and Data): Newer PBX systems even support mixing voice and data information over the same (usually digital) telephone line so you can be transferring a file to somebody else's computer while you're talking about what it contains.

- Voice mail: Because switches are built around computers, it's no big deal to attach some extra disk drives and supply voice recording and playback facilities through the switch. Callers who can't reach the person at an extension can elect to record a message, which recipients can play back later on.

In short, the PBX is the communications hub in many organizations. It can provide a bewildering variety of other functions besides those we've mentioned here (including the infinite series of automated menus that seem to exist on so many phone systems in the world). In reality, the PBX is where computer telephony got started and where its biggest users and enthusiasts still hold sway.

Local Area Networks (LANs)

A local area network (LAN) is a communications network generally used to interconnect employees' computers in an office environment. Because LANs were originally designed to allow users to share peripherals and information, it makes sense to include telephony devices in the list of elements to be shared. Thus LANs allow users access to databases, services, and applications that they might not otherwise be able to afford on an individual basis.

Not only are devices and information more accessible in a LAN environment, but it is easier for multiple employees to collaborate on information and to push projects through the chain of command. LANs in these types of environments commonly provide interoffice e-mail for employees. When implementing telephony services, this "electronic in-box" can contain not only interoffice e-mail but also voice mail and fax messages. This kind of implementation is often referred to as "unified messaging."

The primary benefit of unified messaging is efficiency. Rather than having employees check in different locations for different types of messages, all messages are available under the same umbrella on the users' PCs. Voice mail capabilities in a telephony-enabled LAN environment are superior to those voice mail systems that support only a telephone dial pad interface. If voice mail messages are available at the desktop, they can be viewed and acted on in order of importance rather than in the order in which they were received.

The bottom line is this: LANs make it easier for people to communicate, and so does telephony. By integrating these two technologies, more information is available to the end-user. In fact, the combination of local area networking and telephony makes access to information simpler and easier and enables end users to act on information more efficiently.

Making CT Work in the Enterprise

The secret to a successful deployment of fully computerized CT in a company that's big enough to have its own private telephone system is to bring the computers on the network together with the computers that run the telephone system. Once this happens, everything that used to require an arcane sequence of keystrokes on your phone's dial pad becomes accessible through a graphical on-screen interface.

In this magical marriage of telephone and computer systems, real databases rather than strange two-digit push-button sequences can drive speed-dial activities. You can select voice mail from an on-screen list of incoming messages, each of which is identified by the caller's number (and possibly the caller's name), in any order you like. You can send a text message to a distribution list with some recipients receiving the message as a voice mail recording, others as an e-mail, and still others as a fax — all through the same telephone system.

Bringing individual computers together with the telephones that so often sit next to them is not a trivial undertaking. In the world of big-business telephone systems, it's typically not cheap, either. Most such enhancements cost at least $300-500 per user for software, in addition to the up-front hardware costs needed to "build a bridge" between the switch or key system and the PC network.

Yet companies all over the world have justified the additional cost and effort because the productivity gains and convenience are simply too valuable to ignore. That's why computer telephony is taking off all over the place and why companies with large, complex telephone systems are as delighted with the new possibilities that integration can supply as are SOHO users, who can put systems in place with much less effort and expense.

Summary

In this chapter we've looked at the world of big-time telephony and have examined the impact of CT in this environment. Suffice it to say that those who have mastered the complexities of managing their own private telephone networks are well equipped to handle the impact of adding CT to their bag of tricks, but all can appreciate the tangible benefits that it can incur. In the next chapter we'll take a peek inside the hardware and software interfaces that help to cement this union, as we investigate some of the most important (and fastest growing) of the burgeoning crop of CT standards and technical specifications in use today.

Telephony's Technical
Specifications

To provide telephony, or Computer Telephone Integration (CTI), it's vital to understand the underlying standards governing the technology. This chapter covers the types of telephones and connections incorporated into telephony. The components we examine range from single- and multi-line systems that use advanced telephone features such as caller ID, call forwarding, and voice mail, to the hardware that links all the other elements together.

From there, we cover the applications programming interface (API) developed by Microsoft and Intel, and the Telephony API (TAPI), a call control program interface used primarily on the desktop in the Windows environment. We then examine the other side of the fence and explore Novell's and AT&T's Telephony Services API (TSAPI), an API that focuses on the client/server environment.

We also explore another important element, Tmap which was developed by Northern Telecom. Tmap lets TAPI applications interoperate with TSAPI applications. Then, we take a look at Dialogic's Signal Computing System Architecture (SCSA), a scaleable architecture that consists of both a hardware and software model for providing telephony functions. We'll also investigate Integrated Services Digital Network (ISDN) technology and explore its relationship with telephony.

Telephone Types and Connections

When it comes to telephones, a bewildering array of options is available. There are single-line and multi-line phones, either of which can be analog or digital, and can use either tone or rotary dialing (although the latter is found less frequently now). This section explores the kinds of telephones and connections that can help lay a foundation for successful telephony implementation.

Phone Facts

Today's telephones vary in appearance and functionality. For the purposes of this book, we won't focus on rotary or pulse dialing, due to the growing standardization on tone dialing.

The components shared by all types of phones are:

- the handset, which contains the transmitter and receiver

- the switch hook, which signals the beginning and end of telephone transmissions

- a dial pad, which transmits signals to the telephone network

- two cords, one that connects the handset to the phone unit and one connecting the phone unit to the telephone network

Tone Transmissions

Modern telephones dial out and transmit information using tone dialing. Tone refers to dual tone multi-frequency (DTMF): These are the signals sent by dialing the digits zero through nine on the telephone's dial pad. These signals can be used as tools to transmit information. For example, it's not unusual to encounter an automated attendant that gives you a menu of options for which you enter numbers to make selections. In fact, such tones play an integral part in most telephony applications.

Inside the Handset

When you talk on a telephone, two components play a key role The first is the transmitter, the device into which you speak. Inside the transmitter is a diaphragm, a thin piece of material (usually duraluminum or thin phosphor bronze), and a support system that holds the transmitter in place. Voice transmissions are sensed by the diaphragm, which vibrates in response to sound waves and produces electrical signals. These electrical signals are then transmitted across the telephone network into the telephone receiver at the other end of the call. The receiver contains a magnet and a diaphragm which moves in response to the current generated by magnetized coils in the receiver and translates signals back into sound waves.

One or More Lines

Most home environments have a single-line telephone that has only one line to dial out on. Multi-line telephones, however, can have a number of lines and generally come with function keys. These functions vary from phone to phone, but most have Hold, Intercom, Last Number Redial and Do Not Disturb buttons. On a multi-line telephone, you can talk on one line while having calls holding on other lines. In an office environment, multi-line phones are generally hooked up to key or PBX systems, as described in Chapter 3, Networking the Telephone.

Bells and Whistles

There are many telephone features available that play a key roll in telephony applications. These features include display panels, speakers and call holding, call forwarding and conferencing. There are many different types of telephones to choose from, and some include more advanced features than others.

PC Phones

A number of telephones specifically designed for use with telephony are now available. Some of the features these phones provide include caller ID compatibility, character display screens, programmable function keys, serial ports for direct PC attachments, and even special telephone function keys that activate PC-based rolodexes or other telephony applications.

One example on the market today is the Computer Telephone 8130, developed by AT&T. This two-line telephone is caller ID-compatible, includes a speakerphone and telephony management software and costs around two hundred dollars. The software is a Windows application that includes a telephone emulation screen and a built-in telephone directory, among other features.

Fujitsu has also developed telephones specifically to transmit voice and data over ISDN lines. Their SRS-2000 sends up to 19.2 Kbps over analog lines, and up to 64 Kbps per ISDN B-channel. The SRS-1050 can transmit data at speeds up to 38,400 bps over analog, also with 64 Kbps per B-channel. These phones offer all kinds of advanced features that come with digital telephony, including call waiting up to 12 levels deep, comprehensive call forwarding and conferencing capabilities, and voice-and-data transmission over a single line.

TAPI Architecture and Specifications

As noted earlier, TAPI is an acronym for the Microsoft/Intel Telephony Applications Programming Interface. Before we get into what TAPI does, it's important to understand the underlying API architecture.

What is an API?

An API is a collection of interfaces and procedure calls, usually embedded in a software developer's toolkit. With a particular API, application developers can write programs once that will interface with various kinds of equipment and applications that adhere to that API. There are many kinds of APIs, and the API you use depend on what services you wish to provide, as well as which types of devices the application is designed for.

TAPI Basics

TAPI (also referred to as Windows telephony) was developed by Microsoft and Intel as a graphical environment to control calls on the telephone network. It defines how telephone calls are redirected, forwarded or transferred, among many other telephony-focused features and services. TAPI was created to provide computer-based telephone network access, a visual interface for telephone features and functions, and a platform for personal communications management.

TAPI and WOSA

TAPI is part of the Windows Open Standards Architecture (WOSA), a system that provides a set of open-ended interfaces to enterprise computing services. WOSA incorporates multiple APIs, providing an open set of interfaces to which applications are written.

TAPI, like other WOSA services, is comprised of two interfaces:

- the API developers write to, in constructing telephony applications and services, which provides a link between end-user applications and telephony capabilities

- the service provider interface (SPI), which establishes a connection to a specific telephone network, letting general applications deal with individual systems without having to customize for each system

A service provider interface for telephony can be likened to the printing environment, where printer vendors provide print drivers for Windows-based applications, and application vendors don't have to concern themselves with such details. The SPI end provides specific information for supported hardware, without requiring tedious tweaking and tuning for each application. Thus, in the purest sense, TAPI is a powerful form of middleware. TAPI is designed to bring together telephone systems and telephony applications for both telephone system vendors and telephony application developers—without requiring complete knowledge of what's on the other side.

In addition to the API and SPI, TAPI includes a Windows Dynamic Link Library (DLL) to supply basic telephony objects and methods. This DLL code enables Windows to manage applications in conjunction with telephone devices and network services.

What Does TAPI Do?

TAPI controls network and phone devices, not the actual information—the media stream—exchanged between such devices. Some useful examples of media stream information include voice, fax, and electronic data. TAPI is used in conjunction with other WOSA APIs in managing a media stream, providing audio, fax, and data transmission functionality along with telephony services. All the APIs work together to provide interoperability with existing audio hardware and applications, so telephony becomes an extension of the potentiality of what's already installed on a desktop machine.

Telephone Troubles

The primary obstacle in linking a telephone to a PC is the complex underlying telephone network. A wide variety of incompatible services, equipment and protocols makes it difficult to tie all these elements together. TAPI was created to provide a standard application programming interface that permits application developers and end-users to use the benefits of the telephone, while insulating them from the underlying technologies. TAPI allows PC applications to govern telephony functions, such as establishing, answering, and ending calls, as well as holding, conferencing, and transferring such calls.

TAPI operates independently of the telephone network and equipment while mediating between a telephony application and the telephone network. TAPI is also independent of the specific physical connection between the telephone and the computer, which allows a wide variety of configuration options. TAPI uses advanced call managers to maintain control of the phone system via the desktop PC.

TAPI Topics

Because TAPI is hardware and network independent, it offers a variety of features. TAPI services come in three levels:

1. basic telephony

2. supplemental telephone service

3. extended telephony

Basic telephony provides a set of functions that communicate with POTS (plain old telephone services): it makes and receives calls only. Supplemental telephone services furnish more advanced features, including call hold and transfer. Extended telephony provides specific APIs that enable developers to access additional hardware- and service provider-specific functions.

Applications that incorporate TAPI include the following:

- Advanced call managers that create a graphical and intuitive series of menus on a desktop PC, providing easier access to telephone features, such as conference calls and voice mailbox messages.

- GUI transmissions that provide the now familiar "drag-and-drop" method for performing telephony functions. This opens the door to a series of easy to use and understand features such as simultaneous voice and data transmissions.

- Information services provided by TAPI, such as an online news retrieval system that delivers important news gathered from a news service straight to your e-mail box.

- Integrated messaging, which is probably one of the more important TAPI functions. With TAPI, you need maintain only a single system for receiving, storing and acting upon voice, text, graphical, and (in the near future) video messages, sometimes referred to as a "universal in-box." This puts an end to checking an e-mail box for interoffice messages, and then checking separate boxes for fax and phone messages—with integrated messaging, all messages can be picked up from the same place.

- Personal information managers that provide automated dialing through GUI-based rolodexes, and collaborative application sharing over phone lines.

- Remote control functions that incorporate the ability to control a PC from another location. TAPI provides both host and caller modules that do away with detailed programming otherwise needed to control modems and other communications devices.

These features are just the beginning of the features that are available with computer telephony. Integrated messaging alone has the potential to change the way we do business. With the advent of simultaneous data and voice collaboration, the need for travel diminishes. With some of the other features, a more logical and organized method for doing business should soon be coming of age.

TSAPI Architecture and Specifications

TSAPI, or NetWare Telephony Services, was developed jointly by Novell and AT&T Global Business Communication Systems. It's based on a set of protocols defined by the European Computer Manufacturer's Association (ECMA), and focuses on implementing call control via a NetWare LAN. The basis of the TSAPI approach is linking the services provided by a LAN with those provided by a telephone network. Telephony services are provided by three items:

1. the client/server API, to which telephony applications are written

2. the Telephony Server NetWare Loadable Module (NLM), which passes information between the PBX and the NetWare server

3. the PBX driver, which provides an interface for a particular PBX model

Together, these elements can combine to create powerful call handling capabilities.

TSAPI Pieces

The pieces that make up TSAPI are similar to those fitted together to build TAPI. The API principle is the same, as is that of the PBX driver at the Service Provider Interface level. The main difference between TSAPI and TAPI is the Telephony Server NLM. In addition to providing network authentication services, this NLM provides a Computer Supported Telecommunications Applications (CSTA)-compliant interface for routing information (called TSAPI service requests) between the server and the PBX.

TSAPI, like other NetWare services, uses NetWare's Service Advertising Protocol (SAP) to broadcast across the LAN that its services are available. TSAPI also manages the flow of messages from different applications running on the network, while also delivering requests to the telephone switch.

Three additional TSAPI ingredients are:

1.   Call control

2.   Voice processing

3.   Speech synthesis

Call control provides the core services for PBX-to-NetWare communication, as well as the API for developing client/server applications. It offers features such as call conferencing and transferring, and auto-dialing. Voice processing encompasses interactive voice response (IVR) systems and voice mail. Speech synthesis provides speech recognition and speech-to-text conversion. Speech synthesis features make it possible to access voice mail, e-mail, and fax documents through either a telephone or a PC.

TSAPI Software

NetWare Telephony Services comes with two diskettes: the server component diskette, TSRVDSK1, and the workstation/client component, TSRVDSK2. The following list explains the contents of the TSRVDSK1 diskette and their functions:

- PINSTALL.NLM: installation file

- TSRV.NLM: NetWare Telephony Server software

- TSLIB.NLM: windows library for server-based applications

- OSSASN1.NLM: enables CSTA mapping between the client application requests and the PBX

- PATCHMAN.NLM: applies the SPXFSFIX.NLM

- SPXFSFIX.NLM: for NetWare v3.11

- CLIB.NLM: required minimum version 3.12

- MATHLIB.NLM: required minimum version 3.12

TSRVDSK2 contains the following:

- IPX.OBJ: generates a dedicated IPX driver

- IPXODI.COM: Internet Packet Exchange Open Data Link Interface communications protocol file

- CSTA.DLL: Telephony Services Library For Windows, requires Windows 3.1 and VIPX.386

- TSCALL.EXE: CSTA Windows application

- TSRVOAM.EXE: Operations, Administrations, and Maintenance server configuration utility. Must be run from the SYS:SYSTEM/TSRV/SDB directory.

- NWCALLS.DLL: Windows Dynamic Link Library

- NWIPXSPX.DLL: Windows Dynamic Link Library

- NWNET.DLL: Windows Dynamic Link Library

- WBTRCALL.DLL: Windows Dynamic Link Library

All of these software parts work together with the NetWare server and the telephone network to offer telephony features. A brief description of a TSAPI installation follows. By examining the installation process, each component's function can be more clearly identified.

Putting the Pieces Together

The following information is an excerpt from Novell's July 1994 AppNote (Applications Note), Implementing and Configuring NetWare Telephony Services. This discussion of the telephony services installation process is not intended to supplant the documentation that comes with the product. Rather, it is an overview serving to identify the steps and the server processes associated with installing telephony services.

Step 1

- Prepare the server hardware components that connect to the PBX and to the network.

Step 2

- Run PINSTALL from the server (or from the TSRVDSK1 diskette).

- During the installation, the installer will be asked to enter the path where the client software should be copied. The response to this question determines where the MS Windows components will be copied. If a directory is specified that does not exist, NetWare creates the directory.

- Note: NetWare will create only one new directory. For example, suppose the path specified is: server/ SYS:TSCLIENT/CSTA where TSCLIENT exists as a subdirectory under SYS, but CSTA does not exist. NetWare will create the CSTA subdirectory and install the client components in that directory.

Step 3

- Verify that the proper versions of CLIB, MATHLIB, and Btrieve are loaded (version 3.12 or higher). For NetWare 3.11, the SPXFSFIX patch must also be loaded.

- If these NLMs are not loaded, they should be copied from the TSRVDSK1 diskette into the SYS:SYSTEM directory. After copying these files, you must reboot the server before continuing.

Step 4

- Load the PBX driver provided by the vendor and bind the necessary protocols.

- Note: Until the protocols are bound to the PBX interface card, the Telephony Server will not advertise its presence.

Step 5

- Start the Telephony Server by typing the following commands at the server console:

LOAD TSRV

LOAD OSSASN1

Step 6

- Check to see if the Telephony Server is properly installed by typing DISPLAY SERVERS at the server console. The Telephony Server should appear in the list of servers. It will have a name that contains a "#" character. (For example, the name of the telephony server used at Novell for this Application Note was ATT#G3_SWITCH#CSTA#PRV-NMS.) If the Telephony Server does not appear, check to make sure the PBX driver interface card is properly bound.

Step 7

- Log into the server as Supervisor, launch MS Windows, and run the TSRVOAM application found in the telephony directory created during installation. This is the OA&M utility used to configure the server and users. No users will be able to access telephony services until this step has been completed.

- Note: A sample script file is included with the software that illustrates options for configuring the server. Refer to the NetWare Telephony Services documentation for more information.

Step 8

- After configuring the server, run the TSCALL application and test for a PBX connection. The application will first ask you to select a NetWare Telephony Server and then authenticate you with that server.

Example: Novell's Corporate Installation

The telephony server installed at Novell's corporate headquarters is a COMPAQ DESKPRO 386/33 computer with 16 MB of memory, one NE2000 network adapter, and one AT&T PC/ISDN interface card. Its cache buffers are at 67 percent with 20 active connections. The PC/ISDN card has an on-board MC68000/10 Mhz microprocessor and is connected via an RJ41S connection to a single port on a BRI (Basic Rate Interface) card in the G3 PBX switch (see Figure 4.1).

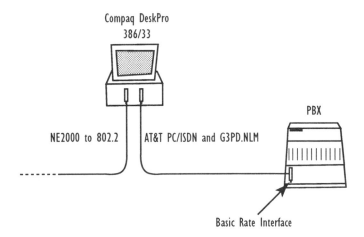

Figure 4.1: Telephony server configuration at Novell's corporate headquarters.

This telephony server is available to all users on Novell's Corporate internetwork; however, users located off-site do not have a direct connection to the AT&T Definity G3 PBX located in Provo. So even though users in Salt Lake City or Germany may attach to the server and load the TSCALL application, the PBX cannot ring the handset at the remote site because there is no direct connection.

However, if a remote site has a data connection and a direct connection to the PBX, the user can use the telephony server. Both a network line and an OPX (Off Premise eXtension) must be in place for this to work. This scenario exists in small branch offices where one or two lines connect the office to a larger site (see Figure 4.2).

This is just one example of how telephony services can be implemented. Obviously, many different types of networks and PBXs are supported. For a listing of TSAPI-compatible devices, contact Novell at (800) NETWARE or visit their World Wide Web site at http://www.novell.com.

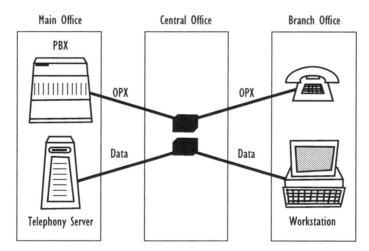

Figure 4.2: Example of telephony services solution using an off-premises extension.

Tmap Architecture and Specifications

Originally, developers were forced to chose between developing TAPI- or TSAPI-based applications when creating telephony applications software. Otherwise, they would have to write to multiple APIs. Northern Telecom developed Tmap to provide interoperability between TSAPI and TAPI. Using Tmap, TAPI applications can run without changes on LAN-based TSAPI. On the other hand, TSAPI switch integrations can run with any TAPI application. This often called "running a TAPI front-end with TSAPI back-end telephony services." In many cases this makes good sense, especially if you're already using NetWare and have a PBX.

The Tmap Treatment

Tmap is a regular service provider to TAPI, and a regular client application to TSAPI. It translates from the TAPI SPI to the TSAPI Telephony Services Library for Windows. Tmap must be installed on every client that requires this functionality. The Tmap environment is more easily understood in a graphical format, as shown in Figure 4.3.

As Figure 4.3 indicates, each PC creates a logical pairing between a PC and a telephone. These PCs make telephony service requests over the LAN using TAPI. TAPI then transfers the request to Tmap, which translates the request into a TSAPI client library request. The TSAPI client library then sends the request over the network to the NetWare server running the Telephony Services NLM. The NetWare server that contains the PBX-specific driver then translates the requests into commands that can be interpreted by the switch.

Using Tmap to develop telephony applications means that developers no longer have to write their applications to multiple APIs. They no longer have to consider whether the underlying technology is NetWare- or PC-based. For users, this opens up any TAPI- or TSAPI-based solution over the network without compatibility concerns.

Tmap is available from Northern Telecom, which provides technical support through their CTI developers' support organization. Better yet, there's no charge

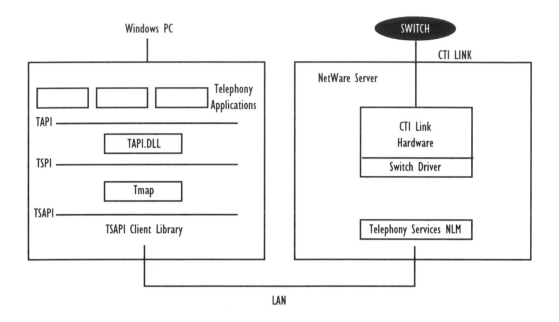

Figure 4.3. The Tmap environment.

for the Tmap software. For more information, try their Web search engine at http://www.nortel.com/english/search.html, using "tmap" as your search term. It will turn up all kinds of interesting resources from Northern Telecom's numerous Web sites!

SCSA Architecture and Specifications

The Signal Computing System Architecture (SCSA) was developed by Dialogic—with the participation of over 70 other companies—as an open architecture for providing telephony services in a client/server environment. It offers call control, processing for multiple media types (fax, voice, e-mail, and text), and even converts between different types of media.

The SCSA framework is made up of a software model and a hardware model. Each model can be used in a standalone environment or in conjunction with each other. The following sections take a closer look at each of these components.

The SCSA Hardware Model

The SCSA Hardware Model outlines open, software-independent, distributed switching fabric interfaces and protocols for real-time telephony communications. In the hardware model, an open platform is described to enable components from multiple vendors to work together via a Multinode Network Architecture (MNA). MNA provides communications regardless of the size or scale of the environment. It provides a standard time-division multiplexed (TDM) bus architecture and switching model permitting bus access for all devices.

This model was developed to connect numerous technologies, such as fax and voice processing, to each other and to telephony applications. The model utilizes a real-time communication bus (SCbus). The SCbus is separate from the host system bus and can be installed on a number of hardware platforms.

The hardware model was designed using open standards in order to simplify development of telephony systems. The model lets developers use a single architecture that encompasses both large and small telephony systems, and which is interoperable with other telephony standards. Because Dialogic is a driving force in the computer telephony industry, its major objective has been to provide a development system that is scaleable, open, and most important, that focuses on future as well as current applications.

The SCSA TAO Framework

On the software side, the SCSA Telephony Application Objects (TAO) Framework consists of standard, open, hardware-independent software protocols, interfaces, and services. The SCSA TAO Framework is composed of APIs that allow various client applications to reside on a server, along with call control and media processing resources. The SCSA TAO also provides a service provider framework and a standard communications protocol. SCSA was designed to specify the relationship between hardware and software components.

SCSA TAO can be broken down into several parts. First, there are the SPIs. These provide a standard protocol for communication between telephony applications and a specific hardware device. Second, there are the SCSA APIs. These are the interfaces that SCSA uses to communicate with an application. Third there is the SCSA Message Protocol (SMP), which is a message transport that facilitates API/SPI communications.

SCSA Services

Some of the services provided by the SCSA framework are listed below:

- The Session Manager places and maintains the client/server connection. This service uses a login security measure to verify that users are authorized to use the requested services.

- The Group Manager configures resource groups dynamically depending on the type of application that's running, providing those services necessary to support call processing applications.

- The Conferencing/Connection Manager interconnects groups controlling call processing resources. This Manager is completely independent of the operating system.

- The Container Manager provides operating system-independent data storage. It supplies a file system that delivers location-independent access to files, as well as a standard name-space convention.

- To provide fax services, the T.611 Fax System Service allows fax service requests based upon the ITU T.611 standard.

- System Administration encompasses application installation and removal, monitoring system statistics, control of SCSA system services, and creating and sustaining the server file system.

- The SCSA Call Router performs application call routing, and establishes protocols for call setup, teardown, placement and routing.

- The Switch Fabric Controller provides the interface that controls the hardware switching fabric.

The SCSA architecture was developed by multiple vendors to ensure product compatibility, and to provide a full range of services and capabilities. With that kind of backing, it's easy to see why this technology has a noticeable impact on the Telephony market.

The ISDN Relationship

The Integrated Services Digital Network (ISDN) is just now beginning to become widely available. It's a digital telecommunications technology that provides more reliable and versatile transmission than regular analog telephone lines. ISDN defines a set of internationally standardized protocols to ensure interoperability among ISDN devices. It was designed to replace existing analog telephone lines to integrate voice, video, data, and other services. ISDN provides these services at higher transmission rates than traditional analog telephone lines.

Changing Channels

There are two interfaces to ISDN.

1. The Basic Rate Interface (BRI) provides two B-channels and one D-channel (2B+D), the two bearer B-channels at 64

Kbps and a data D-channel at 16 Kbps. The B-channels are for voice, video conferencing, fax, Internet access, and more. The two channels can be converged, called bonding, to provide 128 Kbps throughput. With some advanced devices, you can bond up to eight ISDN lines for a maximum transmission rate of 512 Kbps. The D-channel identifies information about incoming and outgoing calls; it also can be used to access slower-speed data networks.

2. The Primary Rate Interface (PRI) is a 23B+D interface, and is the ISDN equivalent of a T-1 circuit, providing transmission rates of 1.544 Mbps. See Figure 4.4 for a look at BRI and PRI internals.

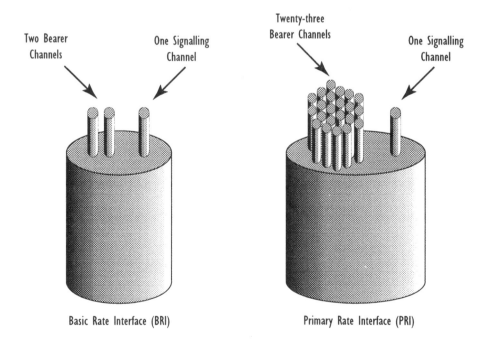

Figure 4.4: A look at BRI and PRI.

ISDN Components

ISDN connections can be made in various ways; the following section examines ISDN components, and how they are used to provide ISDN connections.

To begin with, there is terminal equipment (TE). This equipment can be categorized into two types: TE1 and TE2. TE1 devices are devices with built-in ISDN support; TE2 devices do not have native ISDN support. Terminal equipment consists of computers, telephones, modems, fax machines, and just about any other device that can be attached to an ISDN line. Terminal adapters translate signaling from TE2 devices into an ISDN-compatible format.

The S interface connects TE devices to a PBX. NT2 devices encompass PBXs, or any other device that provides on-site switching. The T interface connects NT2 switching equipment to the local loop. An NT1 device is one that connects the site to the telephone network. These components work together to link a site to the ISDN provider.

ISDN Telephony

ISDN is related to computer telephony in that it provides reliable data transmission rates, which can be extremely important when transmitting voice and video. In most cases, ISDN is also less expensive than private or leased data networking lines. It is interesting, however, that pricing varies depending on your location. At the time of this writing, the cost of installing an ISDN line for business varied greatly. For example, in Texas, ISDN installation runs around $485, while in Virginia it costs only $64. Over time and with growing availability, these prices should drop and converge.

Currently, there are numerous telephony-enabled ISDN devices available from vendors, such as 3Com and Motorola. These products include integrated voice/data/fax boards. While these products are roughly twice the price of a 28.8 modem, they offer up to four times the throughput.

As ISDN technology becomes more pervasive, expect the telephony market to grow still further to take advantage of the higher throughput speeds of ISDN.

Especially as the video conferencing market takes off, reliable and adaptable lines such as those provided by ISDN will be required.

Summary

This chapter covered the technical specifications of telephony. We examined the types of telephone features and capabilities that are available for integration with telephony systems. We discussed Microsoft's and Intel's TAPI, and its approach to computer telephone integration. We explored the components of Novell's and AT&T's TSAPI, and how it implements telephony services in a client/server environment. We explained how Northern Telecom's Tmap software developers toolkit creates compatibility between TAPI and TSAPI. We also examined Dialogic's SCSA, an open standard that is sure to gain momentum in the telephony industry. Finally, we explored the relationship between ISDN and the telephony industry and how that relationship is sure to flourish.

While the scope of this book is to explain how to implement computer telephony, it's important to understand the specifications that build the framework for a successful telephony system. A greater understanding of telephony hardware and software options is possible through learning about the underlying technology.

Part II: Current CT
Hardware and Software

The hardware and software CT offerings available for the PC are surprisingly varied and numerous. In Part II we'll examine how to determine your CT hardware needs. Then we'll proceed to examine a number of hardware and software offerings that you might use to equip your PC, or a small network of PCs, with a reasonably functional CT system.

The number of options for internal and external interfaces and other aspects of CT hardware can sometimes be confusing. That's why we concentrate on explaining what items of hardware and software are necessary to establish and use a working CT system. That's also why we try to contrast and compare the various options and to explain the pros and cons of particular implementations and approaches.

We start you off in Chapter 5 by presenting a laundry list of features and functions that can help you to determine your ISDN hardware and software needs. In Chapter 6 we provide an overview and a questionnaire that can help you to determine your CT needs and help you decide whether you need to involve a consultant or can handle system installation for yourself.

In Chapter 7 we examine the various options available for internal and external CT PC adapters, with discussions of the leading vendors and their interface products. In Chapter 8 we shift our emphasis to examine CT software and whole systems and network termination equipment. Then, in Chapter 9, we discuss the various options for telephones and other business-use equipment that can (or should) be integrated into a state-of-the-art CT system.

Our goal in Part II is to arm you with information about what kinds of CT products are available for your PC, to expose you to the various vendors that participate in this marketplace, and to try to share with you our own experiences (and the experiences reported by others) in using this equipment and software. We feel that you'll be much better equipped to purchase and configure what you really need if you understand what's available and what kinds of tradeoffs you must make to pick one product over another.

Advanced Telephony Services

Telephony environments can deliver a rich collection of services and features. Some of these were originally introduced by the telephone companies, often as a way of enhancing their plain vanilla POTS services. Many are provided by telephony applications themselves, and still others result from adopting standard telephony Application Programming Interfaces (such as Microsoft's TAPI and Novell's TSAPI) within such applications or systems.

We examine an impressive list of telephony services in this chapter: caller ID, call logging, phone books, notes databases, electronic voice mail, voice recognition and speech synthesis, selective message retrieval, inbound call screening, voice-controlled outbound dialing, message monitoring, message filtering, message handling, intelligence, smart agents, and programmability. The following sections go into more detail on each of these services.

Caller ID

Caller ID was developed by AT&T and Bell Laboratories in the late 1970s. A member of the custom local-area signaling services (CLASS) group of telephone services, caller ID is available from the local telephone company for a monthly fee. The data-link layer of caller ID is based on the Bellcore TRTSY-000030 specification. (You can call 800-521-2673 to purchase the latest copy of the caller ID specification.)

Caller ID includes both single and multiple message formats. The single message format sends only the number of the person calling; the multiple message format sends the calling number and the business or customer name to which that number is registered. The caller ID service transmits the number of the person calling to a device that reads and translates the information.

Although caller ID's original use was to allow residential telephone customers to ward off harassing phone calls, its business implications were immediately evident to many in the telephony industry. By integrating caller ID with certain business applications, efficiency, productivity, and customer service can all be improved. There's no reason why recognizing a number can't precipitate a database search for all information relevant to that number, including call logs from previous calls, customer information, preferences, and more. In fact, these capabilities drive much of the truly sophisticated capabilities found in some call-handling systems, especially those used in high-tech customer support situations.

Is ANI-Body Home?

Automatic Number Identification (ANI), the technology behind caller ID, transmits the number of the person calling between the first and second rings of the call. What happens from there can vary tremendously, depending on the equipment in use at the receiving end of the call.

Database Queries

In an office or call center environment, a database of all customers can be created and once the number of the person calling is transmitted via ANI, a database query can be made. That person's information can then be delivered to the desktop of the person receiving the call, via an on-screen pop-up box (usually called a "screen pop"). Using this type of application, a customer service representative can often know the customer's problem before picking up the telephone, especially if it's a follow-up on an already logged help or information request. This not only cuts down on the calling time, but also lets organizations deliver more personalized services to their customers.

Taking the Call

ANI and caller ID are also useful for people who get a lot of phone calls and end up taking every call to avoid missing important ones, which often leads to inefficiency and frustration. With the database query approach and a good telephony application, an employee can now see who's calling before he or she ever picks up the phone. In addition, such systems usually provide options that let users take a call, forward a call, or send the call to their voice mail system, among other choices. With such a system, employees needn't lose time taking unnecessary phone calls and are assured that they won't miss any important calls, when they arrive.

Available Caller ID Hardware

Unlike the caller ID boxes sold for residential use, caller ID boxes for office use offer various features and prices. One such box is the Whozz Calling 4 caller ID box from Zeus PhoneStuff in Norcross, GA. Whozz Calling 4 is a four-port box that connects to a PBX and accepts caller ID information for each line. The box costs $445.

In Huntsville, AL, Tel Control builds the MLX-41 and the MLX-82. These caller ID boxes handle four and eight ports, respectively, and include two RJ-14 jacks, two 9-pin serial ports, and carry two lines per connector. The MLX-41 costs $300; the MLX-82, $500.

The last device we'll examine is not a box but a voice card. Pika, from Ontario, Canada, now supports caller ID on all of its voice cards. A standard feature on Pika's Inline series of cards, caller ID costs $60 per line for its V-12 series. Other major industry players in the caller ID hardware market include Brooktrout Technology in Needham, MA; Dialogic in Parsippany, NJ; Multi-Tech Systems in Mounds View, MN; and Rhetorix in Campbell, CA, to only name a few.

Although it is not important how you receive caller ID information, it is important what you do with it once you've received it. The following sections take a look at some of the uses to which telephony applications can put this information.

Call Logging

Call logging, which means keeping careful track of incoming and outgoing calls, is a common telephony feature. With this type of service, a detailed summary of all calls is always available with a push of a button providing valuable business information.

Call logging means no more flipping through Rolodexes or rummaging through stacks of paper to find names and numbers; instead, a record of all calls is kept electronically and the information is always instantly available. Log information includes both parties to a call, as well as its duration and cost. Such information can prove useful to accounting departments in billing telephone costs to departments, groups, and other organizational units. It also provides a variety of ways to categorize and analyze call traffic, expenses, and other useful information.

Odds and Ends

Call summaries are pretty much plain vanilla when it comes to call logging. Some applications allow you to choose the method by which a summary is drawn up: by extension, department, or company division. Another important call-logging feature is traffic monitoring, which entails monitoring line usage in your organization. For example, if you have 10 outside lines, the application monitors the traffic on those lines and lets you know whether you need more phone lines or whether you have too many and can get rid of a few.

Other applications allow you to track interoffice calls to monitor how departments interoperate and to help you figure out whether you need, say, a foreign exchange line. A line brought in from another exchange, which turns repeated long-distance calls into local ones, is cost-justified if the line charges are lower than the current aggregated long-distance charges.

Many call logging applications are available, so it's important to know what logging features and functions you need before making a purchase. For instance, one application may provide detailed call summaries but not traffic reports. If you want to monitor usage of outside lines, this would not be the right package for your environment.

Phone Books, Notes Databases, and Outbound Dialing

The main impetus behind computer-telephone integration is efficiency. Telephony applications, such as an electronic phone books and database access, provide increase efficiency by cutting down on the time it takes to deliver quality customer service. By showing a customer's information on screen before an employee picks up the call, you've saved the time it would have taken for that person query a database directly. This not only saves time, but it also gives you the chance to update any or all fields in that customer's database entry. Every customer contacts, therefore, offers the chance to improve the quality of the information in the records.

The Electronic Phone Book

One of telephony's truly outstanding features is the electronic phone book. No more trying to find the office phone book or trying to remember where you put that business card: with an electronic phone book, everything is right there on your desktop. And once it's been retrieved, the number can be dialed for you with a simple point-and-click operation.

Electronic phone books have been around for a while now, but they gain added flexibility when integrated into telephony solutions. Rather than simply supplying some person's name, company, address, and phone number, the right application allows you to call that person by clicking on a dial icon or, with a speech recognition program, to simply say "dial." This makes placing calls far more efficient by eliminating most physical interaction with the telephone itself.

Another phone book application is called electronic yellow pages. Just about everyone has used the paper-based version of the Yellow Pages at one time or another only to find no entry for a particular company simply because it's a new operation that started up after the most recent version of the Yellow Pages was published.

By providing electronic yellow pages—which really means a phone number search application that can locate companies by named categories—the information can be updated more frequently, resulting in more successful searches. This in turn speeds access to your calling parties and lowers the need for external information calls (to 411 or similar search databases operated by your local phone company).

Notes Databases

Entirely new functionality can be added to telephony by tying in database applications. For sales representatives, for example, automatic calling and customer updates can take place while the sales rep makes sales calls. The customer record is kept up to date, and reps can more efficiently manage customer calls.

Contact management software also falls into this category. A number of applications are currently available that provide telephony-enabled contact management. ACT! from Symantec in Cupertino, CA, is caller ID-compatible; it provides call options, such as transfer, forward and conference calling, and automatic call logging, among many other features.

Other contact management software includes Maximizer from Modatech Systems in Vancouver, Canada; Goldmine from Elan Software in Pacific Palisades, CA; and TeleMagic from TeleMagic in Dallas, TX. A number of other database and call management applications are available; careful shopping around should uncover the products that best fit your needs.

Outbound Dialing

In order to dial out using your PC, a box that provides dialing functions must be connected between the PC and the telephone. These boxes provide an interface the telephony application uses to control dialing via ports that connect the box to the phone line and PC or PBX. Some boxes, such as Teltone's T-311 Telephone Access Unit, interface with communication management software, making contact management more efficient by providing a way to use an electronic contact form to dial a contact. Whatever the details of the application, it is hard to overstate the convenience of pointing to a database record and initiating an outbound call, while simultaneously logging and monitoring the call!

Electronic Voice Mail

Also called voice messaging, voice mail is one of the major application areas in computer telephony. Many voice mail systems in use today force employees to listen to messages in their order of arrival. This can be a real time waster (not to mention an expensive activity if the user is calling long distance to retrieve his or her messages). Electronic voice mail puts an end to this type of manual message retrieval.

By implementing electronic voice mail, you allow users to retrieve only those messages that they want to hear. Some electronic voice mail applications provide a graphical user interface (GUI) for message retrieval, and this "mailbox" can be integrated with fax messages and other forms of interoffice communications. With this kind of interface, caller information can be recorded by speech-to-text recognition or by capturing the call's ANI information. Some applications show, among other things, the caller's name, number, time of call, and length of message. This not only saves time, but also provides a mechanism to store and delete messages at will.

Electronic voice mail applications are widely available. Some examples are ViewCall from Active Voice in Seattle, WA, and CallWare from CallWare Technologies in Salt Lake City, UT. This is just the tip of the iceberg when it comes to electronic voice mail, but both systems provide on-screen menus of pending messages and let users retrieve the ones they want in any order they like.

Bits and Pieces

Voice mail systems are made up of several components. These components and their related functions are detailed in the definitions that follow:

- I/O cards: These cards provide the physical connection to the telephone lines and equipment, and also accept the touch-tone signals typically used by callers to communicate with the voice mail system.

- Central Processing Unit (CPU): This unit contains the processing power of the voice mail system. With PC-based voice mail, a PC processor is used.

- Codec (abbreviation for coder-decoder): These circuit boards convert spoken words into digital format (encoding) for storage and back to analog format (decoding) on retrieval of a message.

- Software: This is the application that integrates PCs and a PBX (in large systems) or PCs and individual telephones (in smaller systems), providing control over the voice mail system's features and functions.

- Voice mailbox: This is an electronic location where messages are held for each voice mail user. It is generally accessed via the desktop or via phone lines, using a password entered from a touch-tone telephone.

- Disk drives: Disk drives are the repositories for recorded messages, both incoming and outgoing.

With all the components in place, a voice mail system can successfully perform basic voice mail operations. No two voice mail systems are the same, and their requirements may differ, depending on the system you choose. All of them, however, will supply some version of the functions and capabilities we've just described.

PBX Mail

Some voice mail applications communicate directly with a PBX but are also capable of directly connecting to outside lines. Voice mail is generally provided by a series of cards placed into a PBX, for large systems, and directly into a PC for smaller ones. These cards contain ports (usually two, four, or eight) that connect to voice mail users. The number of ports available determines the number of users who can use the voice mail system simultaneously. Messages are stored on a network file server, an ordinary PC, or on a PBX for later retrieval. Some PBX vendors sell voice mail systems that work in harmony with their particular PBX models. Although these applications integrate well with their particular PBXs, many do not offer advanced telephony features. In general, PC- and network server-based systems are both cheaper and more advanced than many of their PBX-based equivalents.

Speech and Voice Recognition

Speech recognition (speaker independent) indicates a computer's ability to understand human speech in general. Voice recognition (speaker dependent) indicates a computer's ability to understand your voice (or some other particular voice). Speaker-dependent systems are trained to recognize a particular voice and are able to master large vocabularies. Speaker-independent systems can recognize any caller, regardless of background noise and the accent of the person speaking, but typically they can handle only limited sets of words and phrases. As you'll see in the sections that follow, there are several different aspects to consider when examining a speech- or voice-recognition system.

Discrete versus Continuous

With discrete recognition, users can speak single words, such as yes and no, when prompted. This allows callers to vocally choose menu items as opposed to entering numbers, and is especially useful for areas where DTMF tones are not widespread. Continuous recognition, or word spotting, allows users to speak a series of words among which the computer can pick out key words and perform the functions requested.

Although these systems continue to improve by leaps and bounds, no system can achieve 100 percent accuracy. As an example, with a continuous-recognition program, you could speak the words "Connect me to the accounting department." The recognition application would be able to detect "accounting" and connect you with that department. With discrete recognition, you could speak the word "accounting" when prompted, but the system wouldn't necessarily be able to pick it out of a stream of spoken words.

Recognition Hardware and Software

This section reviews some of the available recognition hardware and its individual features.

- Advanced Recognition Technologies (ART), from Cupertino, CA, offers SmartSpeak, a speaker-dependent, discrete software engine.

- BBN Hark, from Cambridge, MA, has the Hark Telephony Recognizer, a speech recognition system for client/server environments.

- Corona, of Menlo Park, CA, offers speaker independent continuous speech-recognition software.

- Dialogic, from Parsippany, NJ, offers the Antares 2000, a continuous-recognition card.

- PureSpeech, of Cambridge, MA, offers a speaker-independent, continuous- recognition engine.

- Telaccount, from Narberth, PA, has SpeechEasy, discrete voice-recognition software.

These are just a few of the available recognition products. Numerous buyers' guides are available detailing other systems.

Selective Message Retrieval

The beauty of telephony derives from enabling users to act on information more efficiently. Selective message retrieval is one important piece of the efficiency puzzle. When people arrive at the office in the morning, they're often faced with a message triathlon:

1. They go to the community fax box and pick out their faxes. This is a pain, and there's no security; everyone's faxes are at least potentially subjected to public scrutiny.

2. They check their voice mail messages. This can be a real hassle if an employee has returned from vacation or a trade show and has dozens of messages. The employee must listen to each message serially, often rewinding to jot down important information. All of this is done via a less than intuitive touch-tone pad.

3. They log on to the network to read their electronic mail.

Only then is the triathlon over and the day's real work can begin!

All of this can be avoided with the right telephony application. All messages voice, electronic, and fax (not to mention the imminent arrival of video clips in a mailbox near you) — will be waiting in a single in-basket for each user. By scanning the contents of their in-boxes, users will immediately be informed about pertinent information. They can act on it quickly, without having to wade through other, less important items, which can be handled as time and activities permit.

Inbound Call Screening

This is where caller ID information really shines. When a call comes in, the ANI information is queried in the database. The information associated with that number appears on the screen of the person receiving the call. That person then has the option of taking the call, forwarding it to someone else in the company, or sending the call to voice mail. The options available vary from application to application, but connect, forward, and voice mail are generally included. The usefulness of inbound call screening is evident: An employee who is busy or working under a tight deadline, can send calls to voice mail unless a call is pertinent to the task at hand. When the task is complete or ready to be put aside, he or she can review and respond to incoming messages in optimal order.

Voice-Controlled Outbound Dialing

Some dialers can be controlled by voice command, performed by using one of the speech/voice recognition technologies discussed earlier. Even with a small vocabulary, systems can "hear" key words in a phrase and act on them accordingly.

A market example of voice-controlled outbound dialing can be found in Voice Control's 2060 Voice Dialer. Retailing for $299, it allows an employee to program and store up to 50 telephone numbers to be automatically dialed by the box on voice command. A software method for voice control, Wildfire, is available from Wildfire Communications. A real dazzler, this system can dial out to a variety of numbers from voice commands, and has other helpful features.

Message Monitoring, Filtering, and Handling

The ability to monitor a message directed to voice mail is another option that is becoming more widespread. This option allows a user who isn't sure whether to take a call to forward it to the voice mail system, while still monitoring the message being recorded (much like using an answering machine to screen calls at home). If a call is important, the caller can then be picked up out of voice mail, but if the call is routine or unimportant, the message can be left in the system for a later response.

We once read a humorous example of this feature in Computer Telephony magazine: "If you receive a pop-up box that lets you know your mother is calling, you have the ability to monitor the call. That way, if she's just telling you what a rotten kid you are, leave her in voice mail; if she's screaming that she won the lottery, pick up the phone and start groveling!"

Intelligence, Smart Agents, and Programmability

When people refer to intelligence in a computer environment, they're usually talking about the ability to program agents to perform specific tasks. Agents are software resources that automatically execute a variety of tasks and can interface intelligently with a wide range of devices, including telephones, fax machines, e-mail, computer applications, databases, and telecommunication systems.

Agents can be programmed to perform operations according to specific criteria. An agent in a telephony application could be programmed to retrieve information based on a complex set of information, conditions, and call data: For example, you could set up your system to look for calls from particular numbers on certain days of the month and have them forward a message to your pager. Let's say you set up a particular number as a system-failure hotline; you could tell the agent to screen for that number any weekday and to page you immediately with a particular message when that number is called.

By programming smart agents to perform such functions, you come out ahead in two areas: You save valuable time by not requiring a human to perform that task, and the task can be performed after business hours, so you get the most out of the system's automated capabilities.

Summary

In this chapter we covered a number of advanced telephony services. We took a look at caller ID and ANI technology and explained how their use can provide a more efficient way of handling calls. We examined call logging and explained how its use can not only help telephone cost allocation but also determine how numbers and information are available to you on your desktop. We then showed the advantages of tying into electronic phone books and databases. From there we examined electronic voice mail and how it enables employees to act more effectively on information, and discussed the use of voice- and speech-recognition technologies.

We also investigated selective message retrieval in place of the "message triathlon." We looked at inbound call screening and how it, too, helps employees do their jobs more efficiently. Voice-controlled outbound dialing and message monitoring, which allow employees to interact more intelligently with their calls and messages, were also covered. Finally, we examined how smart agents can perform complicated tasks.

When implemented correctly, these advanced telephony services can make life a lot easier. If there are any two words that come close to fully describing such services, they would be convenience and efficiency. That's what telephony is all about: efficiently dealing with and acting on information with a minimum of fuss and effort.

Determining Your CT Needs

Are You Ready for Computer Telephony?

If you've skipped Part I of this book and started here, that's OK. The idea here is to explain only what you need to know in deciding if computer telephony is for you. If you don't understand an acronym or buzzword, check the glossary or return to Part I for the details. It would probably be a good idea to at least skim through Chapters 3, 4, and 5. This chapter assumes you're at least somewhat familiar with the terms and concepts explained in those chapters.

Today computer telephony is one of the "Top 3" buzzwords sweeping the computer industry. You may be thinking seriously about getting Integrated Services Digital Network (ISDN) for personal or business use, or you may be wondering if you should get some kind of telephony program for your computer that will eliminate playing "phone tag" with your clients all day long.

Even now, you may not be sure what CT really is, how it really works, or if it will be really cost effective. Not to worry: You're way ahead of the pack. Just by being curious enough to buy this book and learn more about computer telephony, you're in the forefront of industry knowledge and experience!

Deciding whether to jump into the world of computer telephony using digital or analog technology isn't as complicated as it looks. To be sure, there are a multitude of different products available and more keep popping up every day. All we can say is "Welcome to the bleeding edge of technology!" You can be thankful that competition among a variety of good products insures that your needs will be answered with reasonably-priced and well-supported products. As recently as the spring of 1995, this was not the case.

Our advice is: Don't let the plethora of CT products overwhelm you. You need only one or two of them to get your connections up and running, and we'll help you choose them.

The telephone companies (RBOCs—Regional Bell Operating Companies) are knowledgeable about phone services, whether analog (POTS), Switched 56, or T-1 service. They're also fairly well-educated in the intricacies of the new kid on the block, ISDN — or at least some of their employees are. As someone (who must remain nameless) so cogently stated: "All of the ISDN workers went to the same classes, but not all of them stayed awake and walked out with the same knowledge." At least you'll be able to call your local telephone service provider, ask for ISDN assistance, and eventually find a person who knows what ISDN means. This is generally true if you live in an urban area in the many parts of the United States. Rural areas will have to wait for ISDN service just a bit longer.

A Brief Review of Phone Service Options

This is just a quick comparison of the phone service options available today. Think of it as the "menu" that you can order from when obtaining CT services for your small office or home operation.

Switched 56 versus ISDN BRI

A Switched 56K telephone service provides 56 Kbps of digital bandwidth via a standard pair of phone wires. This service is what businesses used to purchase when they wanted digital instead of analog service, but didn't need the bandwidth or expense of T-1 service. The CSU/DSU required by the Switched 56 service is generally expensive since these devices are primarily aimed at larger markets, rather than individuals or small offices. Even so, it's possible to obtain the necessary hardware for between $1,000 and 2,000 in most locations.

An ISDN BRI (basic rate interface) provides two B (bearer) channels and one D (data) channel via a standard pair of phone wires. Each of the B channels can carry 64 Kbps of voice or data, while the D channel is used to control the B channels or possibly for X-25 data (credit card verification, and the like). Many people are changing from the Switched 56 service to BRI service because the price differential favors ISDN.

Although ISDN has been around since the early 1980s, until recently there hasn't been sufficient standardization to spark widespread usage or proliferation of its less expensive equipment. The rapid rise in popularity of the WWW on the Internet has caused an explosion in the number of available ISDN packages and an approximately 50% drop in prices during 1995. Combined TA/NT1 cards are now priced under $500 — significantly cheaper than the Switched 56 equivalents.

T-1 versus ISDN PRI

A T-1 telephone service provides 1.544 Mbps of bandwidth or 24 lines at 64 Kbps each. This service requires either a fiber optic cable or two pairs of standard phone wires. Depending on the RBOC's tariffs, fractional T-1 service (a part of the 1.544 Mbps) may be offered at a lower rate than the full 1.544 Mbps. Otherwise, you will pay for the bandwidth whether you are using it or not.

To use a T-1 you will need a CSU/DSU and the appropriate software, all of which is somewhat costly since historically only larger companies have purchased this type of equipment. In general it will cost over $5,000 in equipment just to get started, exclusive of your computer.

An ISDN PRI telephone service provides 23 64 Kbps B channels and one D channel via a standard telephone wire pair. The cost of installation varies depending on the RBOC that provides your service. More and more manufacturers are introducing PC-based CT equipment for ISDN PRI lines, especially for UNIX and Windows NT systems. ISDN bridges, routers, NT1s and TAs are generally less costly per PC than the CSU/DSU equipment needed for T-1 applications.

This is especially true if you have a small Novell network and will be using TSAPI-compliant equipment for only a few people. Either two or three BRI lines or a PRI (if you need the 23 lines) will support more people for less total cost than several analog phone lines or a fractional or full T-1. Unless your business requires a large amount of data to be transferred rapidly via the phone lines (in video conferencing for instance), or you're planning on reselling unused capacity, a PRI or T-1 is generally overkill at 23-24 lines.

A Word or Two about PBXs

Here's another thing to keep in mind: Today's PBX systems don't integrate easily with computers, primarily because there's no real standard in the PBX field. Therefore, building your own telephony system around one or more ISDN BRI lines using a couple of standalone PCs or a small network of PCs may be just the solution for your situation. This equipment is perfectly able to handle PBX-style call routing via TAPI or TSAPI-compliant software and Windows-based applications, without requiring any PBX at all.

How do you decide?

Before you can determine which approach will work best for your needs, the very first step is to answer truthfully the questions below. There's a lot riding on the answers, so take your time and research your options thoroughly. You'll have to live with (and pay for) the consequences for a long, long time, so some time and effort spent here is clearly justified by the results.

Do I really need high-speed, computer-controlled, digital phone service to my home office or small business office?

For business use at home or in a one-person office, the main reason to install digital phone service (ISDN or T-1) is to gain faster access to information sources such as the WWW (World Wide Web) and other Internet or on-line business services. Secondarily, you'll also get more phone numbers at a lower cost per line when compared to adding analog lines. As an added benefit, you will be able to use computerized fax services and digital telephony (answering via computer and digital telephones) just like the big companies do. In general, if you already have two analog lines, the cost of digital service may be less than or equal to your current costs, with the improved speed and control as no-cost extras.

If you have a small business office with two to eight people, each of whom needs fast access to the WWW and other Internet or on-line services, ISDN BRI service may be an appropriate way to go for voice, data, and multiple ISDN phones. If your computers are already networked, installing ISDN gets more complicated, but will allow you to share your ISDN lines and services via the network. You can use one of several TSAPI-compliant hardware and software systems to effectively simulate your own PBX right on your network using your computer screen as the control panel, often for a significantly lower cost than buying the "real thing."

If your business is telephone intensive (for example, a real estate office or mail-order company) but not necessarily a telemarketing business, you probably won't need an expensive PRI or T-1 service. If you need more than 4 phone numbers, it would be smart to check with your local telephone company about rates for multiple BRI services vs. a fractional T-1 or PRI service. Because "the numbers don't lie," you can let costs guide your selection process pretty effectively.

Small business owners or operators may find that the cost of equipment and CT software, digital line installation and monthly fees are offset by increased employee productivity. If you aren't confident about running a network integrated with digital telephony, add the costs of hiring a consultant who is familiar with your type of network to suggest the appropriate equipment for your particular needs, and who will install and maintain the equipment. Consultants can seem expensive at first, but they can save you money by keeping you and your employees working, rather than wasting time fooling around with your network and telephony problems. Take our word for it — we learned this first-hand!

What can computer telephony do for you?

Individual Business Use

For outgoing calls, expect a good personal Windows CT application to have a phone/address book integrated with an auto-dialer that supports a speed dial list. It should include call logging by date and time with extra space for notes. You should be able to send a fax while on a voice call, simultaneously.

Some of the more expensive packages include Automatic Call Distribution (ACD) to send a voice message to a list of people. For incoming calls, the application should have a screen pop up with information about the caller when the phone rings (using Caller ID). You should have the option of answering the call or sending it to voice mail. The application should automatically receive an incoming fax without requiring your intervention. If you are talking on the phone when a call arrives, the application should automatically send the call to voice mail. The application should work with serial devices on analog phone lines, and with digital devices and lines (ISDN, switched 56 through T1). Finally, it should be both TAPI- and TSAPI-compliant.

On the low end of the price scale, you can use a voice/fax/modem, your analog phone line and a CT application to perform adequately if not expeditiously most of the functions mentioned above. The next step up involves using a serial ISDN "modem," a BRI line, and TAPI-compliant CT application; this should accomplish basic tasks more quickly and easily. Exchanging the ISDN "modem" for an ISDN bridge/router type LAN card increases data transfer speed further, but it's difficult to find one that does voice and fax right now.

Small Office Use

For small office use, each employee may use one of the types of CT system we just described on individual PCs, or you can use a network-based solution. If you're using a Novell network, you can get a TSAPI-compliant CT application and multi-line card for your NetWare server that provides CT functions to everyone on the network.

Novell says its NetWare Telephony Services can cost as little as $108 to $259 per workstation, if you're already using NetWare. Generally speaking, networking solutions are aimed at more than eight or more persons on a LAN, and tend to be somewhat labor-intensive (especially from a maintenance standpoint). However, this software and hardware is available today, and appears to work quite well.

Can you afford the costs of phone company installation?

As of late 1995, the cost of installing a single BRI (2B+D) ISDN service in the U.S varied from $40 to $485. The average installation fee was in the $150 to $250 range. PRI and T-1 installation services also vary widely in price, depending on the RBOC. Call your local RBOC and ask for their current installation charges. Ask around and find out if there's any competition in your area, too — you may find a better deal just by shopping around! One case in point was recently advertised on the Internet.

Cherry Communications has been promoting the following service via the Internet:

Until recently, it was said that you only needed a T-1 if you spent over $5,000/month on long distance, and that T-1s cost $1,500 to install and at least $400 a month. A free T-1 install, $200 a month, and traffic at 6¢. We lease T-1 equipment for $200 monthly. It costs you nothing to install a T-1 line. The carrier pays the local telephone company to install a 1,544,000 bps private digital link at your site. Under the new T-1 math, the carrier absorbs the $1500 install cost of the T-1 circuit. The long distance rates are $.0599/minute and lower to anywhere in the U.S. You pay $200 per month for this private line. How else can you get two dozen digital phone lines with Caller ID, ANI, and DNIS — at that price? http://www2.connectnet.com/users/cherry/ Send email to cherry@connect-net.com Fax (619) 551 - 8944 Tel (800) 879-0505 — ask for the Internet Rate Desk.

Can you afford the monthly phone company service fees?

The RBOCs and other phone service providers seem to be constantly changing their tariffs and therefore their rate structures. Maybe they're not as bad about it as the airlines are about ticket prices, but it's sometimes hard to tell the difference.

Rates for ISDN BRI Business service in the United States currently run from a monthly fee of $15 to $112.50, with per call usage charges of $0.00 to $0.10 per B channel per minute. Rates for PRI and T-1 may be determined by calling your RBOC. It's also a good idea to ask around your community to find out how these costs translate into average monthly charges (the more similar the operation from which you get information is to your own, the more closely their experiences and costs will apply to you).

Can you afford your ISP's installation or setup costs?

ISDN is the maximum bandwidth that most ISPs provide via dial-in connection. Most provide a single B channel but some are offering BONDed B channels to 128

Kbps (at twice the price, of course). The going rates for ISPs (Internet Service Providers) to set up an individual, non-business ISDN account using SLIP or PPP varies from $25 to $200 across the U.S.

Most ISPs charge more for a business account setup with multiple user numbers. In their defense, it takes a knowledgeable network person upwards of thirty minutes per user in setup time; the process is far from automated at most ISPs. Some of this cost theoretically goes toward the labor involved in the setup process. The remainder is usually intended to help defray the provider's up-front hardware costs.

If you want more bandwidth than an ISDN BONDed connection, you will need to talk with your ISP about dedicated lines. You will probably need this only if you are going to run your own WWW site and anticipate a large volume of traffic.

Can you afford your ISP's monthly service fees?

ISPs like to stay competitive in their ISDN rates, and therefore frequently change their rate structures. Without going too far out on a limb, we've observed that most ISPs offer two different ISDN services: dedicated and dial-up. Most such connections use either SLIP or PPP protocols, depending on the provider's own server software and its ability to measure and bill for connect time.

Dial-up SLIP/PPP rates generally range from $30 per month with 45 hours for a single B channel connection (with additional hours charged at $1 per) to $29 per month with 30 hours for a single B channel connection (with additional hours at $2 per).

Flat rate monthly charges for unlimited time — and since nobody can use the connection you're using if you use it all the time, these connections are often "dedicated lines" — range from $150 for an uncompressed single B channel to $400 for two compressed, BONDed B channels. The rates for dedicated lines appear to vary — at least in our immediate vicinity — more than dial-up lines, so you'll want to shop around as much as you can when looking for such service.

It's also important to remember that ISDN equipment takes less than one second to "connect" to your ISP. Therefore, if you are being billed for "connect" time, you may be able to keep your charges quite low by setting your equipment to time-out after only a few idle seconds (this is discussed in Part III). In general, when buying ISDN connections, you should expect to pay at least $30 per month and possibly as much as $60 to $100, even if you spend as little as 3 hours per day on line.

Can you afford digital phone equipment for your PC?

For an individual PC, the cost of an ISDN NT1 and TA — whether it is an adapter card, bridge, router, or ISDN "modem" — ranges between $300 and $1,000. Some manufacturers have developed marketing agreements with local telephone service providers or ISPs whereby you can purchase their hardware in a package deal with the service. It's possible to get a combined TA/NT1 for as little as $200 in a package deal. Here again, shopping around can result in significant savings.

ISDN "modems" with both analog modem and ISDN T/A capabilities have become available during 1995. The Motorola Bitsurfer and IBM WaveRunner are a couple of the more outstanding examples. These are external devices that plug into your computer's serial port. Some of them include a built-in NT1, making them more expensive but also more convenient. They're popular primarily because they're relatively easy to install and set up, and they provide combined modem and ISDN capabilities in a single, external box with an external power supply. These kinds of devices range in price from $300 to about $600.

Generally, expect to pay around $500 for an ISDN adapter card with built-in NT1 and a POTS port. A separate NT1 costs between $200 and $400 with power supply (and sometimes a built-in battery backup). External ISDN bridges or routers generally range between $800 and $1500 depending upon their features and their routing capabilities.

The bottom line is as follows: an adapter card costs about half as much as a separate NT1 and bridge or router combination, and about two thirds the cost of a separate NT1 and ISDN "modem." Most adapter cards are new to the scene as of early 1995, so it's reasonable to look for more functionality and ease of use in the future, along with lower prices as economies of scale begin to kick in.

In the ISDN PRI or T-1 hardware arena, the equipment is built for multiple phone lines (usually 4 or more) with prices starting at around $700 and quickly going into the thousands. See Chapters 7 and 8 for additional information on this equipment.

Can you afford the time required to deal with the local phone company?

Most RBOCs and other telephone service providers have business order lines staffed by reasonably knowledgeable personnel that can help you with your needs. However, this doesn't mean that everything will progress smoothly, rapidly, or without requiring your close supervision.

If you're interested in ISDN service, here's some of what you'll encounter on the way to ISDN nirvana. If your location is near an ISDN switching station, there may be unused phone wire pairs available to you; if not, you may have a long wait for the necessary hookup. If your location and wiring is less than 10 to 15 years old, and the local phone company isn't swamped with installations when you call, you may get lucky and have to wait only a couple of weeks for installation. Otherwise, it can take up to six weeks or longer, even if your location meets most of the other conditions we've mentioned. During this period, you will be spending your valuable time on your POTS phone to more than one TPC (The Phone Company) employee trying to get things going or figuring out what, if anything, is happening.

Since ISDN to residential locations is relatively new, there will be more problems than you have with your current analog system. When an ISDN service goes "down," you don't get a weak or buzzy line, you get a big, fat nothing. Zip, zero, nada! Generally, an ISDN service is either up and working or it's stone-cold dead. Sometimes it will alternate live and dead sporadically, a few seconds at a time. This really makes the phone company happy. It usually means one of the cards in a remote computer location is going bad, and, of course, these are difficult to find.

Remember too that if you lose power to your NT1 device, your ISDN service is dead (that's why battery backup is nice during the occasional power outage). This "dead or alive" characteristic is quite different from POTS, which draws its power from its own sources, not from your house or office wall plug. However, that same plug is exactly where your NT1 or computer gets its power. Remember this when determining whether or not to hire a consultant, or whether or not to go completely ISDN with no POTS phones for backup. Like the mighty mainframe, we think POTS will still be around for a long, long time!

Can you afford the time necessary to do it yourself?

Assuming you are a knowledgeable computer user who feels comfortable installing cards inside your computer, but not an electrical engineer or hot-shot programmer, it can take you from one day to three weeks to get ISDN equipment installed and running properly in a single computer. Installing a multi-line card in a server with its software, whether ISDN BRI, PRI, or a T-1 with a CSU/DSU, will take considerably more time and knowledge. You should seriously consider hiring a consultant for this type of installation unless you are a network guru with an electical engineering background.

For most SOHO users, installing an external NT1 with a serial ISDN "modem" device can take only an hour or two. If you try to install an ISDN adapter card that is actually a network card in a computer that already has another network card installed, try to get it all running under Windows for Workgroups or NetWare, and the provisioning (setup) on your ISDN line isn't exactly what you ordered, it may take you three weeks or more.

This time estimate includes several hours on the phone to the customer support personnel of your chosen ISDN adapter card, to Microsoft or Novell for networking advice, to your telephone service provider for switch and provisioning information, and to your Internet service provider for connection testing and debugging. It also involves seemingly endless changes to your PC's configuration files (that is, to CONFIG.SYS, AUTOEXEC.BAT, WIN.INI, and SYSTEM.INI), and to its CMOS setup maps.

Warning! This estimate is by no means a worst-case ISDN horror story. Unfortunately, a certain amount of thrashing around happens all too frequently, given the variety of new cards and other hardware in PCs today. This sort of thing happens much less frequently in the Macintosh world, because of the standardization of the operating system and its interface managers. In any case, be aware that it's going to take you longer than you anticipate to get everything up and running smoothly. If you plan for this, and arrange for expert help to be on tap if and when it's needed, you'll lose a lot less sleep during this sometimes excruciating process.

Can you afford to hire a consultant?

If you're getting ISDN or a T-1 for a profitable business that needs your time and attention to keep it profitable, consider hiring a qualified consultant. Do a quick cost/benefit analysis that compares your lost time and lessened efficiency against the consultant's fees. Keep in mind that a good consultant can assist you in choosing the proper equipment for your business, both now and when you need to expand.

If you're getting ISDN for personal business use only, and like most of us have more time than money, keep on reading and do it yourself. As the working wife once said to the out-of-work husband, "Honey, your time is valuable but not costly." Choosing the right ISDN equipment and ISP, and knowing how to deal with the phone company, should make your initial ISDN experience less trying than you might expect.

And your options are ...

Are you still with us? Good! That means you're either committed to getting your own computer telephony system up and running or you should be committed — or both. To aid you in your next set of tasks, please find the section below that best describes your situation and read it completely and thoroughly.

In each of these sections we've condensed the answers to the previous questions and customized them for the specific group the section addresses. For these situations, it is assumed that the service will use eight or fewer lines, and that either existing analog lines or an ISDN BRI is the optimum choice.

Home Office Use
(Voice and Data + POTS phone with CT software)

You are a work-at-home consultant or have a one-person office. You already use a modem with your Internet account and CompuServe, AOL, and so on. You have three POTS lines: for voice, for your computer, and for your fax machine. You want to consolidate your phone lines at the lowest possible price. You want to make use of a PIM and contact manager with CT application software to track your incoming and outgoing calls.

One possibility is to purchase a Compaq Multimedia computer with its built-in voice/fax/modem and Compaq Phone Center software, or if your modem is a voice/fax ready model, get Phoenix Technologies to sell you their Telephone Center package (which it looks like they OEM to Compaq). Otherwise, purchase one of the following packages or one like it:

Diamond Multimedia (San Jose, CA, 408-325-7000) TeleCommander 2500XL uses a 14.4 Kbps modem and the 3500XL integrates a 28.8 Kbps modem and their TAPI-compliant software. The card includes 16-bit sound, fax send/receive/forward, fax-on-demand, voice mail, data transfer, pager notification, and call screening and forwarding. In addition, it includes NetCruiser and VocalTec's Internet Phone capability (phone calls via the Internet). All of this for $209 and $299, depending on modem speed.

Bottom Line

The total hardware and software cost is between $200 and $300. You can drop one of your phone lines since the software will handle the switch to fax or internal voice mail automatically. Eliminating one business line saves you about $30 per month in phone charges. You will have gained some efficiency via the CT application and lowered your recurring monthly costs, all for a minimum initial outlay.

Home Office Use
(ISDN Voice and Data + POTS phone with CT software)

You are a work-at-home consultant or have a one-person office. You already use a modem with your Internet account and CompuServe, AOL, etc. You have three POTS lines: for voice, for your computer, and for your fax machine. You want to install an ISDN service to replace the data and fax phone lines and to increase your on-line speed and bandwidth. You want to make use of a PIM and contact manager with CT application software to track your incoming and outgoing calls.

You feel comfortable installing cards in your PC and are enough of a hacker to alter your CMOS setup without calling AMI. You will either leave your computer on all of the time for your fax machine or you'll not worry about it after hours. You have enough time to spend doing it yourself and want to keep the initial cash outlay to a minimum.

For this scenario you will need the following:

1. ISDN service from your local telephone company. Installation $150. Monthly fee $60.

2. Combined ISDN "modem/TA" with external NT1 and POTS port $600

3. PP software and TCP/IP stack and network drivers. Freeware or Shareware.

4. Your current modem software.

5. CT application software that is TAPI-compliant with drivers $200.

6. Windows TAPI Server service from your Internet Service Provider $50 setup plus $30–$60 per month

Bottom Line

The total installation and hardware cost will total around $1,000. Monthly fees will run approximately $120. Eliminating two business lines saves about $60 per month in phone charges, so you breakeven on phone service. Your ISP charges will jump from $20 to $60 for a net increase of $40 with ISDN over POTS usage for all lines.

Small Business Office
(ISDN Voice and Data, multiple ISDN phones)

Your office is relatively high-tech with you and your partner using PCs on a Windows for Workgroups (WFW) or Win95 Ethernet network. You have separate POTS lines for voice for each of you with no receptionist or intercom functions. You both want faster access to Internet and other on-line information services which will undoubtedly be offering ISDN connections in the near future.

You also want to be able to e-mail more easily to your clients and send/receive large files more quickly. You want to use your networked PCs to efficiently handle your telephone calls and contacts. You will soon need a receptionist and want to use the network with fax and voice mail. You are adept at working with your hardware and feel comfortable with the amount of your time it will take to set all this up.

You are at the point where you need to carefully determine if you need an ISDN and/or network consultant or really want to do it yourself. Assuming you want to do it yourself, here is the simplest and least expensive scenario.

For this application you will need the following:

1. Two ISDN BRI service lines from your local telephone company. Installation $450. Monthly fee $120

2. ISDN NT1 with UPS $250

3. ISDN TA internal adapter card with S/T port 2 @ $400

4. ISDN service from your Internet Service Provider 2 @ $50 setup plus $60 - $120 per month

5. CT Software with TAPI drivers for Windows and Win95 $400

6. PPP software and TCP/IP stack and network drivers for WFW. Freeware

Bottom Line

You have replaced all of your POTS lines with the two ISDN services (4 numbers total), installed a separate NT1 and used ISDN TAs without built-in NT1s in your computers. You plug your POTS phones as well as your fax into the NT1. You need the UPS for your NT1 to keep your phone lines up and going if the power goes out.

The total installation and hardware cost is about $1,550. The monthly telephone fees will run approximately $124 per month, which is what you were paying for analog. Your ISP charges probably increased from about $40 to $120 per month. This results in a net increase due to ISDN of $80. However, you are getting the benefit of the ISDN speed and bandwidth.

Summary

If you're still with us, you are really, really set on getting yourself deeply into this computer telephony thing. Don't worry overmuch about the myriads of acronyms, products, and unintelligible jargon. If you can understand what we've presented in this chapter, you can purchase, install, configure, and use your own individual or small office CT application with at least an ISDN BRI line and appropriate equipment on your own computer.

If you want to replace your existing POTS phone system with ISDN, you'll want to get a separate NT1 with its own UPS or you'll be without phone service whenever the power goes out. Even with a UPS, keeping one POTS line in service is good insurance. In the next chapter, you'll move on to grappling with the specifics of ISDN hardware and software.

Generally speaking, when this book was published in early 1996, CT applications for analog modems were the most prevalent with TAPI and TSAPI-compliant applications for Win95 being introduced almost daily. The external ISDN "modem" with internal NT1 was the product of choice for those who wanted to keep the analog modem's ease of use while gaining the speed of ISDN. Internal ISDN adapter cards with built-in NT1 and POTS plug are the most cost-effective for personal and individual business use — provided that you have the time to hassle with installing and configuring them (and provided their manufacturers provide Windows or Win95 TAPI drivers for their use with the available CT software).

Computer Telephony Interfaces

To supply voice, fax, and data communications from a single interface, it makes sense to use an interface card that supports all of these technologies. In the past, voice boards were typically constructed as single-function boards. But now, aided by the use of more powerful integrated circuits called Digital Signal Processors (DSPs), manufacturers can deliver fax, data, and voice support on the same interface card. Today a number of interface cards are available that can handle all these services together and, in some cases, deliver even more. This chapter covers such multifunction interface cards, with an emphasis on products already on the market.

Combination Interface Cards

Voice, data, and fax are the three types of information most commonly exchanged in modern offices. The following section examines several so-called combination interface cards, including their features, functions and pricing information. You'll find vendor information after the product descriptions.

Features and Functions

This section explains some of the common features and functions that are found on combination interface cards. Keep in mind, however, that each combo card comes with different feature sets; this is just a standard list.

- Binary file transfer: This handles transfer of nontext files, typically for specific applications. (Note: Such files would lose information if sent as text.) This capability adds general file transfer to the multifunction card's arsenal.

- Caller ID detection: This is the ability to accept caller ID (CID for analog lines) or Automatic Number Identification (ANI, for digital lines) information for display on a user's PC. For a complete discussion of caller ID technology, see Chapter 5, "Advanced Telephony Services."

- Direct Inward Dial (DID): DID allows callers outside a private branch exchange or other private telephone system to connect with a particular internal extension instead of going through an operator or automated attendant.

- Error Correction Mode (ECM): This is a method for sending and receiving data that eliminates transmission errors by sending mathematically encoded bit streams so that the receiving computer can verify that all bits were properly transmitted.

- Modified read encoding: This is a two-dimensional coding scheme for transmitting fax information that handles data compression of vertical lines and concentrates on squeezing down space between the lines and within given characters.

- Transmission of text files as fax: By sending text files via fax, an interface card transmits only the characters in the file, not formatting information. The advantage here is that every word processor or text editor can access the file's contents. (This comes in handy when transferring data between dissimilar systems.)

Brooktrout Technology

Brooktrout offers many different boards, each having different communication capabilities. The Brooktrout TR114A offers two communications ports, runs at 14.4 Kbps, and supports DOS, Windows NT, OS/2, UNIX, and QNX. Its features include transmission of text files as fax, DID support, modified read encoding, and ECM. The TR114A costs $1995. The Brooktrout TR114C supports all of the above features, but has four ports and costs $3295. Many vendors that offer complete turnkey CT systems use Brooktrout hardware in their systems, and the company enjoys a strong reputation for speed, powerful feature sets, and quality engineering.

Commetrex

Commetrex manufactures the MultiFax card, which can handle up to 60 ports with the addition of the necessary multiport serial cards. The MultiFax supports 9.6 Kbps fax transmission and is designed to be used in the OS/2 environment. It can also transmit text files as faxes, supports DID capability, and can handle modified read capability. The MultiFax costs $250 per port, in blocks of 2, 4, and 8 ports, and works with the company's PowerFax software, as one of a handful of fax automation packages available for OS/2.

Dialogic

Dialogic offers a series of four-port boards that vary from 9.6 to 14.4 Kbps transmissions. All the boards support DOS, OS/2, and UNIX. Other features include caller ID detection, fax transmission of text files, and modified read capability. Their prices range from $2445 to $2950. Dialogic is also a big supplier to the OEM market for CT systems, and its products are both widely used and highly regarded.

Linkon

Linkon offers a variety of four- and eight-port combination boards, all at 9.6 Kbps. Each of the boards supports both Windows 3.x and UNIX, with support for Windows 95 and Windows NT under development. Available features include caller ID detection, modified read, fax transmission of text files, and binary file transfer (including voice/data on the same channel). Prices range from $2945 to $5490.

Pika Technologies

Pika offers combination boards that come in configurations containing from 1 to 12 ports at 9.6 Kbps. These cards all support DOS, Windows 3.x, Windows NT, OS/2, UNIX, and QNX. Features included are DID and modified read. Caller ID detection is an option that adds another $65 to the cost of each port. For the basic capabilities, the cost is $200 per port. Pika cards are also widely used in the OEM marketplace and enjoy a reputation for quality and good price/performance ratio.

Vendor Information

The following vendors offer telephone network interface cards. Although not all vendors offer combination cards, all are viable resources for product information and comparison. For further contact information, please see Appendix B in the back of the book.

A&A Connections

Alliance Systems

Amtelco

B&W Electronics

Bicom

Brooktrout Technology

BusLogic

Commetrex Corporation

Contact Network

Dialogic

Dinatel

Exacom

First Pacific Networks

GammaLink

Hark Systems

LANart

Linkon

Micom Communications

Mitel

Multi-Tech Systems

National Instruments

Natural MicroSystems

Newbridge Networks

NewVoice

Olicom USA

PCSI

Pika Technologies

Promptus Communications

Quiknet Technologies

Rhetorex

Source

Voice Technologies Group

Voiceboard

Multiline Adapters

Multiline adapters, sometimes called multiport boards, also contain multiple DSPs to digitize and process voice, data, and fax. Some of these boards can transmit data and voice simultaneously, a technology referred to as simultaneous voice and data (SVD). Different adapters use different technologies to perform these functions.

Features and Functions

The following is an explanation of some of the features and functions commonly delivered with multiline adapters. Again, this type of hardware comes in many shapes and sizes, with a number of features and functions.

- Bell 202: This AT&T specification for modems supports asynchronous data transmission speeds up to 1800 bits per second and requires a four-wire line for full-duplex transmission.

- Enhanced call processing: This is the ability to incorporate the use of Interactive Voice Response with other call-processing features.

- PEB interface: PEB is an acronym for PCM Expansion Bus, a digital bus for sending voice transmissions among a variety of voice-processing cards.

- SCbus: This is an SCSA definition and describes a serial time-division multiplexed bus that carries information among devices using a signal processing mode.

- Voice compression: This is a method for electronically modifying a 64-Kbps PCM voice channel to obtain a channel of 32 Kbps or less, providing more efficient voice transmission.

- Voice digitization: This is the process of converting analog voice signals into binary bits for voice storage and transmission.

Let's Get Digital

In order to process voice, an adapter converts sound waves into digital signals. The process of converting these sound waves into numbers is called digitization. The device that performs this function is called a codec (coder/decoder). The system stores the binary code in an order that is directly related to the elapsed time of the original voice message. The transformation of the code back into sound waves is performed by the decoder, which produces a new wave form by reconstructing frequencies derived from the binary code.

A multiline adapter, created by adding fax and data capabilities to this type of voice processing, brings enormous communication power to the desktop.

Although large corporations can benefit from this technology, it is even more beneficial in SOHO operations, because it brings the power and functionality of advanced communications technology to small organizations.

Available Multiline Products

Various companies approach multiline adapter technology differently. Some offer internal adapters for communications, whereas others supply external units that provide the same functions.

Dialogic offers the VFX/40 and VFX/40E. Both are four-port voice plus fax boards. They offer four ports of enhanced call processing and 9.6 and 14.5 Kbps fax services, respectively. These boards incorporate an SCbus or PEB interface for compatibility with a wide range of call-processing products.

Multi-Tech Systems offers the MultiModem PCS, a simultaneous voice and data modem that transmits at 28.8 Kbps. It can send voice and data over the same analog phone line. Multi-Tech offers three models for standard serial ports the MT1932PCS, the MT2834PCS, and the MT2834PCS-ISI. For the Macintosh Multi-Tech offers the MT1932PCS-Mac and the MT2834PCS-Mac.

PCSI offers the CS8000 Access Multiplexer for integrating voice, fax, and data communications. The CS8000 can support up to eight voice/fax channels while simultaneously maintaining data throughput. Analog voice traffic is digitized and compressed to rates ranging from 5.3 to 32 Kbps.

Rochelle Communications provides the Rochelle Multi-Line Adapter, a concentrator that decodes caller ID information for up to six incoming lines. Features include Bell 202 signal demodulation, an off-hook detector that signals a host computer when an incoming call has been answered, RS-232 serial port connections, and support for DOS, Windows, Macintosh, UNIX, and OS/2.

Vendor Information

In addition, these vendors offer DSP chips, boards, and related software. For complete contact information, see Appendix B in the back of the book.

Ariel

Atlanta Signal Processors

Bicom

Dialogic

DSP Communications

DSP Group

Graychip

Innovative Integration

Multi-Tech Systems

OnChip Systems

PCSI

Radish Communication Systems

Rhetorex

Rochelle Communications

Voiceboard

Voice Technologies Group

White Mountain DSP

Summary

As we mentioned earlier, one excellent resource for telephony product information and reviews is *Computer Telephony* magazine. It provides up-to-date product information, as well as covering up-and-coming telephony technologies. As always, it's imperative that you evaluate your telephony needs before purchasing any products. If you're unsure about your needs, a good way to get the right system is to hire a systems integrator or telephony consultant who can evaluate your company's needs and work with you to develop the system that is right for you.

Computer Telephony
Software and Systems

Before obtaining telephony services, it's important to investigate the many options available from computer telephony software. The software application you buy will depend on the types of telephony services you want or need. Consequently this chapter focuses on the most important telephony software, features, and services information; we'll also indicate pricing, where that information is available. Following all these product listings is the relevant vendor contact information. This is by no means a complete listing of all such telephony information but rather a survey of the more popular options, according to published and online sources.

Computer Telephony Applications

Here's an overview of some available software options; wherever possible, we've included user interface examples, screen shots, and other information to give you a sense of what these tools look like and what they can do.

TeLANphony by Active Voice

TeLANphony is a telephony suite that supplies voice mail, fax, and incoming call capabilities based on the Repartee voice-processing system. Repartee's ViewCall module provides control of incoming calls using a Windows interface (see Figure 8.1). ViewCall provides call-handling options such as hold, transfer, voice mail, and message monitoring.

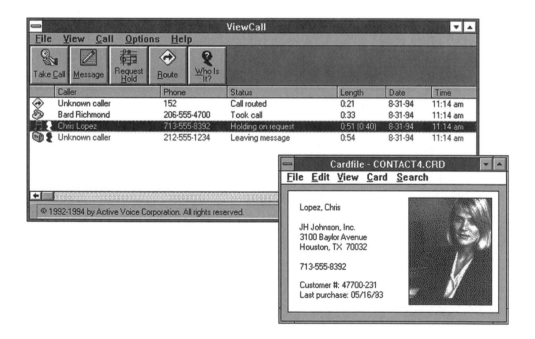

Figure 8.1: Active Voice's ViewCall module.

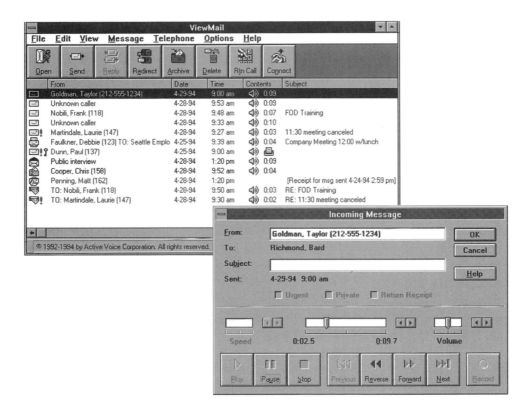

Figure 8.2: Active Voice's ViewMail module.

The Repartee ViewMail module provides universal messaging for voice and fax. Message information includes message status (new, old, archived for more than three days, return receipt, and so forth), the caller's name and number, date and time of the call, and the length of the message (see Figure 8.2).

AlgoRhythms' PhoneKits

PhoneKits, a Windows-based telephony package from AlgoRhythms, puts a full set of business phone functionality on screen. The four PhoneKits modules—PC

Phone, Call Log, Answering Machine, and Address Book—let users call anyone in their phone database by typing the first few letters of the last name of the person they want to call. Even better, users can highlight phone numbers in any Windows application and click on the PhoneKits icon, and the program will dial that number. Configuring an on-screen phone requires only a simple "drag and drop" operation from the dial pad (or using other controls) onto the phone screen. In addition, PhoneKits includes a range of useful fax, voice mail, call-tracking, and caller ID features.

AnswerSoft's AnswerSoft:Phone

AnswerSoft:Phone is a call management and control application that is caller ID-compatible and supports both NetWare Directory Services (NDS) and AT&T's Conversant interactive voice response. AnswerSoft:Phone can be customized by adding the following software modules to provide a universal in box for voice mail, fax, and e-mail messages.

- Sixth Sense is a PC- and server-based software agent environment that launches and controls distributed applications anywhere on the network. The toolkit supplies a scripting language that can create and manage process-related information flows for a high level of CT system automation.

- SoftPhone gives users access to advanced telephony services through a Windows-based, point-and-click style user interface.

- SoftPages provides access to business, residence, and government directory listings.

- On-The-Go! provides workgroup scheduling and notification software that integrates e-mail, paging, and other functions.

- MemPlus is a memory management and application launch program that allows Windows users to run a large number of applications simultaneously.

The AnswerSoft suite of products runs on Windows, Windows NT, OS/2, and UNIX platforms and supports TCP/IP, NetWare, NetBIOS, and Named Pipes networks. These products interoperate with most major databases and support many relevant computing and communications standards. Each product costs between $150 and $300 per user. AnswerSoft also provides system integration, custom development, and consulting services. Most of AnswerSoft's products are built to interface with PBX and other existing high-end telephony systems, but the company is making a strong push into the SOHO and PC server-based markets.

Applied Voice Technology's CallXpress3

CallXpress3 Desktop for Windows is a message management and call handling system built around a dedicated LAN-based telephony server. The system supports a universal in box for fax, e-mail, and voice messages and can deliver its data in text or speech form over the telephone or to your computer. CallXpress3 offers text-to-speech capabilities for faxes and e-mail for remote access. On the network, the system provides screen pops to alert users to incoming messages, as well as callback capabilities. Basic pricing starts at $7500; a usably configured system for 20 or fewer users would probably cost around $20,000, depending on the modules selected.

Aurora Systems' FastCall

FastCall provides caller ID detection and screen pops, can be programmed to launch an application when a particular call arrives, and supports outbound dialing, call transfer, conferencing, logging, and speed-dial capabilities. Aurora Systems has taken a unique approach to open telephony architecture. Instead of developing custom software to integrate CTI into an established call-processing environment, the company develops packages that emulate the actions usually executed by a user when he or she receives or generates a call and responds to the calling or called party. This makes it uniquely suited to SOHO environments, where established call-processing environments tend to be manual, if they exist at all.

Here's how it works: Suppose you're busy typing a letter into your word processor when a call comes through from an important customer. Typically your first move is to exit the word processing application and rev up the contact management program that contains a record of your last conversation with that customer. Aurora software lets your computer know that you want to exit word processing, enter the contact management package, and pull up that customer record. This approach works with most applications and dispenses with the need for custom software.

FastCall is based on a proprietary, patent-pending design that employs rules-based call handling in conjunction with a learning algorithm in furnishing CT functionality. FastCall for Windows links the telephone to the user's existing computer applications. The program works on PCs, mini- or mainframes, or across a LAN. It's fully compatible with the Microsoft TAPI.

For end users, FastCall automates handling of both inbound and outbound calls. The application pre-identifies inbound telephone calls, using ANI, DNIS, or touch-tone numbers, for simultaneous call and data file delivery. FastCall also supports screen-based telephony, transforming Windows into a smart phone. Answering, conferencing, transfer, and hold can be activated from the computer via FastCall control keys. Users can even extract a phone number from any Windows application and dial that number with a single keystroke, saving time and effort. Pricing for FastCall starts at $495.

CallWare Technology's CallWare

CallWare is a NetWare Loadable Module (NLM) that provides voice mail and call-processing capabilities written to Novell's TSAPI. CallWare is compatible with Novell's GroupWise and NDS, including application-integration capabilities and two-way data exchange at the click of a button. The ViewPoint user interface displays message details and recommends actions based on those messages.

For small offices using a NetWare network with a PBX (or equivalent Centrex services), CallWare is a powerful and useful call-handling system. CallWare pricing ranges from $50 to $125 per user, depending on the total number of licenses purchased.

ClearWave Communications' Intellect

ClearWave Communications' ClearWave Intellect is a useful combination of hardware and software for linking individual PCs and telephones. The product uses a battery-backed Intellect smart box along with Intellect software to provide advanced telephony services.

The smart box links to both the PC and telephones and, if caller ID information is available, supplies the software with information about incoming calls. If a number corresponds to an entry in the call log maintained by the program, the user will automatically see the record of the previous call as soon as the number is identified. The program lets users annotate the log in a pop-up window every time the phone rings, making it easy to integrate phone calls with other aspects of the daily routine.

ClearWave Intellect also supports Centrex service, visual message waiting and distinctive ring services. Other features include a message manager that tracks each call, a speed dialer that can handle up to 20 numbers, a universal phone book that supports voice, fax, and online service access calls, and selective call acceptance based on blocked or flagged numbers. A one-line version of the product retails for $289.

ConnectWare's PhoneWorks

PhoneWorks is a combination hardware/software computer telephony package designed for home office use. The software complies with the Microsoft TAPI Windows APIs, is caller ID-compatible, and provides voice, fax, and data message-handling capabilities. The associated hardware includes a 16-bit ISA adapter capable of 14.4 Kbps transmission. The package comes in single- and dual-line versions that retail for $399 and $699, respectively. Like other telephone/smart box combinations, this product is particularly useful for SOHO applications.

OCTus's Personal Telecommunications Assistant (PTA)

PTA is another TAPI-compliant desktop control center providing call control, DTMF dialing, caller ID detection, and more. Like many of the other stand-alone products, it uses a small external "black box" as the interface between your PC and the telephone. For stand-alone telephones PTA supplies the usual personal telephony package features: screen pops, call screening, point-and-click dialing, call logging, and more. By itself, this package provides plenty of useful SOHO-level telephony capabilities. When used in conjunction with a Centrex line or a PBX that supports Centrex features, the system makes all of the function buttons on a standard office phone (call forward, transfer, conference, and so on) available and easy to use on screen. The base-level PTA package retails for $179.

PTA also supports two very useful add-ons, each of which costs a paltry $59: one that provides electronic voice mail capabilities and another that enables fax messaging. The voice mail module writes incoming messages to your computer's hard disk and provides a menu-driven interface to all stored calls which can be accessed in any order. You can use the voice mail module to screen calls and pick up a call at any time or use it to put callers on hold until you can take their call. Incoming messages can be retrieved remotely, and you can change your greeting message the same way.

PTA's fax module is equally useful. It integrates with Windows as a printer driver, so you can send a fax from any program that supports the print command. Like voice mail, faxes are stored electronically and may be retrieved in any order. Because the fax services are integrated with the PTA phone book, you'll automatically be able to review call history and caller information for each fax you receive. The program also offers useful fax preview and customization capabilities.

SoftTalk's Phonetastic

From a Windows environment, Phonetastic displays caller ID information, provides screen pops, launches applications on specific inbound calls, and provides capabilities for call filtering, transferring, conferencing, and logging. As its price tag suggests, this is a LAN-based product that aims at interconnecting networked PCs with PBX systems. For most SOHO situations this is overkill, but the products integrate well with NetWare, and a Windows NT Server version is under development. For those with bigger needs (and budgets) pricing begins at $2495.

Tedas's Phoneware

Phoneware is a personal telephony application with both hardware and software components, but it also requires a Sound Blaster-compatible sound card in your PC to provide voice mail capabilities. Phoneware includes speech recognition for program navigation, outgoing call automation, digitized call recording, incoming voice mail message handling and services.

Normal voice mail features (set greeting, browse incoming messages, reply in any order) are augmented by the ability to create multiple mailboxes, use multiple greetings keyed by date and time, and password protection of up to 9995 individual mailbox IDs on a single system. The system also supports a call log, call monitoring, and caller ID screen pops. Phoneware will even let its users construct lists of outgoing calls and place them in sequence, at the user's behest. This product retails for $395 and is one of the most interesting examples of "personal telephony" that we encountered while researching this book.

Vendor Contact Information

Here are the addresses, phone numbers, and when possible, URLs for the telephony products described. In addition to these products, we have listed other telephony software provider information.

Active Voice
2901 Third Ave.
Seattle, WA 98121
206-441-4700

AlgoRhythms
12221 Merit Drive, Suite 1380
Dallas, TX 75251
Voice: 214-490-5487/Fax: 214-490-3050

AnswerSoft
3460 Lotus Dr., Ste. 123
Plano, TX 75075
214-612-5100

Apex Voice Communications
15250 Ventura Blvd., 3rd Floor
Sherman Oaks, CA 91403
818-379-8400

Applied Voice Technology
1141 NE 122nd Way
Kirkland, WA 9808
206-820-6000

AT&T
211 Mt. Airy Rd.
Basking Ridge, NJ 07920
800-247-7000

Aurora Systems
40 Nagog Park, Ste. 101
Acton, MA 01720
508-263-4141

Call Center Enterprises
1140 Kildare Farm Rd.
Cary, NC 27511
800-979-9699

CallWare Technologies
2323 Foothill Dr.
Salt Lake City, UT 84109
800-888-4226
World Wide Web: http://www.callware.com

CCOM
120 Wood Ave. S.
Iselin, NJ 08830
908-603-7750

ClearWave
P.O. Box 272278
Fort Collins, CO 80527-2278
970-221-1998
World Wide Web: http://www.clearwave.com

Comdial
1180 Seminole Trail
Charlottesville, VA 22906
804-978-2514

ConnectWare
1301 E. Arapaho Rd.
Richardson, TX 75081
214-997-4193
World Wide Web: http://www.connectware.com

Genesys
1111 Bayhill, Ste. 180
San Bruco, CA 94066
415-827-2711

Key Voice Technologies
1805 Glengary St.
Sarasota, FL 34231
800-419-3800

Microsoft
One Microsoft Way
Redmond, WA 98052
206-882-8080
World Wide Web: http://www.microsoft.com

Northern Telecom
P.O. Box 833858
Richardson, TX 75082
214-684-8589

Novell Telephony Division
2180 Fortune Dr.
San Jose, CA 95131
408-434-2300
World Wide Web: http://www.novell.com

Octel
1001 Murphy Ranch Rd.
Milpitas, CA 95035
408-324-3338

OCTus
8352 Claremont Mesa Blvd.
San Diego, CA 92111
6190-268-5140

SoftTalk
85 Wells Ave., Ste. 200
Newton, MA 02159
617-482-5333
World Wide Web: http://www.softtalk.com

Technically Speaking
333 Turnpike Rd.
Southborough, MA 01772
508-229-7777

Teknekron Infoswitch
4425 Cambridge Rd.
Ft Worth, TX 76155
817-267-3025

Summary

As the preceding list demonstrates, there is a wide variety of applications providing telephony services. Many more applications are currently available than those we mention here, and more keep arriving all the time. An excellent place to learn about applications as they are released is in *Computer Telephony* magazine, which offers comprehensive product reviews and listings monthly, as well as sponsoring an annual computer telephony trade show. You can get subscription information for *Computer Telephony* by calling 212-355-2886 or 800-677-3435.

Telephones and Business-Use CT Equipment

This chapter examines the technology behind a variety of communications methods. First, we take a look at teleconferencing and video conferencing technology, as well as at the equipment required for each. We also examine wireless connectivity and a variety of product information based on that technology. Then we list ISDN telephones and ISDN test equipment for those of you using ISDN services. After each section, we provide a list of companies that can supply the products. (You'll find contact information for all of them in Appendix B, "Vendor Information.")

Teleconferencing

There are a number of reasons for the recent popularity of teleconferencing. First and foremost, this technology can now support the applications needed for this type of collaboration. Second, companies are looking for more ways to reduce the overhead costs associated with business travel. By using teleconferencing, many of the duties that may have previously required an employee to travel to another location can now be performed without leaving the office. The types of functions that can be performed using teleconferencing technology include voice combined with on-screen presentations, document conferencing, remote control applications, and collaborative computing.

Voice combined with on-screen presentations allows one person to share an on-screen display, typically of slides or other training materials, with others on a conference call, while all parties can listen to an accompanying presentation and everyone can participate in Q&A at any time. Document conferencing requires the use of an application that lets multiple users edit, annotate, and rearrange the same document across the conference link, while simultaneously passing voice information among all the parties as these changes are discussed. Remote control applications let a user in one location "drive" a computer at another location, via a communications link. And finally, collaborative computing refers to a class of applications that lets users work together on a single piece of work or data — document conferencing is a subclass of this more general category.

The ITU's T.120 standard specification is what makes teleconferencing possible by providing the ability to successfully and securely transport information signals (data and voice) in a variety of formats. By complying with T.120, geographically dispersed and dissimilar systems with a variety of features are able to communicate and interoperate with one another.

Do You Get the Picture?

Video conferencing takes group communications one step further. The addition of such elements as eye contact and visual cues such as body language, drastically reduces the need for most business trips for routine, periodic functions (such as attending meetings). Because video teleconferencing equipment is still comparatively new to the market, prices are a little higher than many SOHO operations can afford. However, if business travel consumes a significant portion of your budget, an investment in video conferencing equipment quickly pays for itself.

The standard that provides interoperability for these types of systems is the ITU's H.320 standard, a multiplexing recommendation that specifies how each frame of information (audio, video, and data) is multiplexed onto a digital channel. This standard allows connectivity between dissimilar systems, supports standard compression algorithms, and, as an international standard, makes worldwide video conferencing available.

Because this technology is relatively new, a few wrinkles still need to be ironed out to improve the quality of video conferencing. One technology that should enhance video conferencing is ISDN. ISDN can transfer different data types simultaneously at higher speeds, so its use in video conferencing will likely replace conventional analog signaling. Because full-motion, real-time video is the ultimate goal, ISDN will no doubt be superseded by higher bandwidth media when they become more widely available.

The Benefits

Numerous benefits can accrue from incorporating teleconferencing or video conferencing into your organization. We've already discussed the potential travel savings from a reduction in time, airfares, and related expenses, but there is more than money to be gained from these technologies. When you decrease travel, you not only save time and money but also can conserve natural resources. In this age of conservation and concern for the environment, tele/video conferencing can be viewed as an environmental asset.

The Products

Access ISDN offers its PVS320 Video Conferencing for the Macintosh and the PC. It's a single card that combines audio and video compression and decompression and also supports an optional ISDN interface. The PVS320 provides multiport conferencing through support of H.320 standards.

Altec Lansing Multimedia offers the AVC 1000. This system transmits 30 frames per second, has four subsystems, video, voice, and a pen tablet. It is able to share graphics files, and has digital and still-video imaging capabilities. The system operates over regular telephone lines and costs around $800.

AT&T provides the Vistium Personal video system. It enables people to collaborate on Windows files, as well as providing audio and video capabilities. The price of the system (up to $400) will be refunded if you subscribe to either Accunet Global Switched Digital Service or a Software Defined Data Network plan.

Creative Labs provides voice, video, phone book with photo inclusions, interactive whiteboards, and real-time application sharing with its ShareVision PC3000 system. It comes with a voice card, fax/data modem, software, headset, video card, and a color video camera. The system is priced in the $1300 range.

Imagelink offers a system that includes a video-compression codec board, camera, speakers, microphone, and conferencing and shared whiteboard software. It is H.320-compliant and supports UNIX and PC technology. The cost is around $4700.

Incite offers an isoEthernet hub that delivers simultaneous voice, video and data. Pricing for this multimedia hub is $2450 and up.

PictureTel offers the PCS 50, an H.320-compliant ISDN-based desktop video conferencing and application-sharing system. The system includes LiveShare, a spreadsheet and document-sharing application that requires installation on only one of the video-conferenced PCs. The PCS 50 starts at $2495.

Polycom offers a unique teleconferencing tool called the ShowStation Document Conferencing Projector, based on its SoundStation audio conferencing system. It is similar to an overhead projector but is connected by telephone lines to remote locations. The ShowStation contains a 28.8 Kbps modem that sends and receives document images. Each component requires an analog line for transmission of sound and images. It is based on T.120 teleconferencing standards so it maintains compatibility with other teleconferencing systems. The system carries a suggested list price of $10,795.

SAT-SAGEM delivers the Meet-Me package, which is designed for the Macintosh and supports H.320 standards. It provides collaborative work and file transfer, support for multimedia services such as video conferencing, still-picture capture, and a collaborative whiteboard. It is capable of video-conferencing services with any standards-based system.

The Vendors

Several companies are listed here that weren't mentioned in the preceding sections. These companies also offer equipment for teleconferencing, video conferencing, and collaborative computing. For complete contact information for any of these organizations, please consult Appendix B.

> Access ISDN
> Adtran
> Altec Lansing Multimedia
> AT&T
> ConferTech
> Creative Labs
> Eagle Teleconferencing
> Hewlett-Packard
> Incite
> Imagelink
> Intel
> Inter-Tel
> LiveWorks
> MCI
> Northern Telecom
> Polycom

SAT-SAGEM
Siemens PNCO
Teleconferencing Technology
Video Server
VTEL

Wireless and Satellite Equipment

Wireless technology is also available for telephony use. This section outlines relevant wireless technology and related equipment. Later in this section we'll also briefly examine satellite technology and equipment and how they can play a CT role as well.

Goin' Mobile

Office computing has changed. It is no longer enough to communicate just from the desktop. Today's traveling professionals need require communication from various locations. With the incredible growth of cellular technology, such employees can access the information they need anywhere, any time, with help from cellular fax and telephone equipment.

Cellular Basics

Cellular phone transmissions are switched across transceivers in separate multiple broadcast areas called cells. A mobile user's connection is maintained while traveling through these cells, even though different transceivers may be used along the way.

The standard adopted by the cellular industry for cellular communications, is CDPD, or Cellular Digital Packet Data. This is a wireless data protocol standard that examines transmission of data packets.CDPD technology leverages existing cellular services by using spare packets on cellular networks for data transfer. The CDPD standard also incorporates the Transmission Control Protocol/Internet Protocol (TCP/IP). With TCP/IP support, mobile users can access Internet services and e-mail remotely.

Cellular Products

Megahertz makes a cellular-capable PCMCIA Ethernet modem capable of transmissions at 28.8 Kbps. It connects with Motorola and Nokia cellular telephones. The 28.8 Kbps PCMCIA Ethernet modem costs around $550.

PCSI offers Ubiquity Cellular Communications Systems, modems that provide a wireless CDPD modem, a cellular circuit-switched modem, a high-speed wireline modem, and a wireline phone. Other lines include the Ubiquity 2000 Cellular Communications System. Prices start at $1300.

Readycom combines voice mail with the mobility of cellular communication in its ReadyTalk two-way voice messaging service. ReadyTalk allows users to receive, store, and respond to messages with the ReadyTalk handset. The ReadyTalk Service costs between $20 and $30 per month the ReadyTalk handset is priced at $250.

Telular produces the Phonecell SX product line for providing a gateway to cellular communications. Included in the product line is MaxJack, which can incorporate the use of fax machines, computer modems, answering devices, and related hardware with cellular communications. A single-line unit is priced at $1000.

Cellular Vendors

The companies listed here also offer equipment for teleconferencing, video conferencing, and collaborative computing. For complete contact information for any of these organizations, please consult Appendix B.

> Megahertz
> PCSI
> Readycom
> Telular

Satellite Stuff

Satellite technology is another newcomer to the telephony market. The first U.S. licenses for mobile satellite service were awarded to Loral Qualcomm, Motorola, and TRW. Loral Qualcomm is in the process of launching its 56-satellite GlobalStar system. Loral is building the satellites and Qualcomm provides the ground station.

Motorola's Iridium is a low Earth-orbiting, 66-satellite system. Motorola has built an international partnership with manufacturers and telecommunications providers to provide Iridium services.

TRW is in the planning stages of providing Odyssey, its 12-satellite, intermediate orbit system. All of the systems mentioned in this section must get local approval to provide satellite communications.

This is still technology in the making, but keep your eye on this market. As the technology advances, prices will drop, allowing SOHO users access to worldwide communications.

ISDN Telephones

Because ISDN is a powerful tool for transferring data, it takes an ISDN telephone to take advantage of ISDN-specific call management features. They cost extra money, but such telephones put the power of advanced call management into the hands of SOHO users. Features commonly supported include caller ID detection, managing multiple calls on a single line, conference calling, call transfer, and more, depending on the make and model. The following section examines available ISDN telephones and their features.

ISDN Telephone Features

Access ISDN offers the A-1000 series of ISDN telephones. The phones have autosensing capabilities or can be programmed manually.

AT&T Network Systems provide the 8520T ISDN voice/data terminal. The set has a seven-line display screen and 20 buttons that provide such calling features as call transfer, redial, caller ID detection, priority-call notification, and call logging. It also contains a 144-entry personal telephone directory. The telephone transmits data at 64 Kbps and is able to provide simultaneous voice and data communications over a single ISDN line. The retail price for the 8520T is $1010.

Cortelco offers ISDN telephones that are software programmable with flash memory so upgrades are downloadable. The telephones offer speed-dial capabilities, speaker phone, caller ID detection, and 10-call logging. The telephones cost $385 for the 18-button model and $495 for the 30-button model.

Fujitsu carries a variety of ISDN telephones that are capable of simultaneous voice and data transmissions. The SRS-2100 transmits 38,400 bps synchronously and 64 Kbps synchronously. The SRS-1050 has a data transmission rate of 38,400 bps.

Tone Commander offers a line of telephones with ISDN capabilities. The products range from 5 to 480 lines. The Tone Commander 40d120 requires no terminal adapters, has a four-line display panel, a 1000 name database, and key-customization features. The 40d120 costs around $2300.

ISDN Telephone Vendors

Several companies are listed here that weren't mentioned in the preceding sections. These companies also offer equipment for teleconferencing, video conferencing, and collaborative computing. For complete contact information for any of these organizations, please consult Appendix B.

Access ISDN

AT&T Network Systems

Cortelco

Fujitsu

Lodestar Technology

Siemens Stromberg-Carlson

Tone Commander

ISDN Test Equipment

For most small or home office settings, ISDN testing equipment is probably not in your purchasing plan. In general, ISDN testing is a job best left to the ISDN service provider. However, we found one ISDN protocol analyzer from Frederick Engineering (call 410-290-9000). The ParaScope BRI is a hand-held ISDN protocol analyzer that monitors and simulates network and terminal equipment devices. It verifies ISDN link integrity, isolates network equipment problems, and decodes and analyzes the D and B channel protocols. The ParaScope communicates with a PC via a PCMCIA port and operates on rechargeable or alkaline batteries. The price is a whopping $4995.

Although you may want your very own BRI analyzer, the truth is you will probably never need one. If you suspect that your line isn't working properly, a quick call to your phone company's repair line will get it checked and fixed right away in most cases, at a much lower cost than the lowest-priced BRI analyzer. The only BRI analyzer that costs under $3000 that we've found is the PA 100 protocol analyzer at $2495, also from Frederick Engineering.

Without a protocol analyzer, however, it is almost impossible to resolve the finger pointing that commonly occurs between the service provider and the equipment vendor or the customer. If you are in a company that's plagued by ISDN problems, a knowledgeable technician with a protocol analyzer may be able to resolve these problems quickly and at a lower cost than the opportunity costs for the time and productivity lost due to an inoperative ISDN line.

The UPA 100 is a compact unit (9.5" x 7.5" x 1.5") that connects to the serial port of an IBM-PC compatible or Macintosh computer. It captures the messages passing between the subscriber's equipment and the network, decodes them into plain English, displays them on screen, and places them in a buffer for later analysis. Circuit-switched and packet-switched decodes for National ISDN, Northern Telecom DMS 100 Custom, and AT&T #5ESS ISDN are supported. When you need a piece of equipment like this, nothing else will do, so you might want to see whether any service companies in your area can provide one with a technician for an hourly rate, or check to see whether a short-term rental or lease might be available.

ISDN Test Equipment Vendors

For complete contact information for Frederick Engineering, please consult Appendix B.

Summary

This chapter examined a wide variety of communications and products. First, we examined teleconferencing and how it can help to save money in travel-intensive organizations. We then examined some cellular technology that provides access to information from anywhere. We then took a brief look at some available ISDN telephones and test equipment. As always, it is critical that you evaluate your needs before making any purchases, so that you end up with the telephony solution that is best suited to your business needs.

Part III: Getting Started with CT

Once you've made your selection of the appropriate CT hardware and software for your PC, the real fun begins. Now it's time to get serious! You may need to arrange to have additional telephone lines (or even ISDN service) installed, handle any associated wiring changes, and obtain all the necessary cables and equipment. Only then can you get down and dirty and begin the installation process.

We begin this long, arduous, and sometimes painful process with the most basic of all questions: Should you do it yourself or hire someone else to install CT for you? In Chapter 10 we debate the pros and cons of flying solo versus bringing in a real professional. The remainder of Part III is devoted to stepping through the ordering and installation processes involved in bringing CT to your PC or your network. Even if you don't do it yourself, you'll find these chapters useful and interesting, because they'll help you understand what your expensive hired gun is up to and can point you at some things to request, some things to demand flat-out, and others to avoid at all costs!

We continue the process toward a working CT system in Chapter 11, as we review the steps and requirements for a home or small-office CT installation. Here we talk you through researching your hardware needs, purchasing the necessary system elements, installing and configuring the wiring and other equipment, and more. In Chapter 12 we cover the same ground from a different perspective, as we lead you through the mechanics of a small office/home office CT system installation.

Chapter 13 proceeds to discuss common CT troubleshooting tactics, tips, techniques, and approaches that you might find helpful if and when your CT experience hits a snag. Chapter 14 concludes Part III (and the subject matter of the book) with an overview of the most common questions and answers on CT subjects, culled from Internet newsgroups, users' groups, and *Computer Telephony* magazine.

Our goal in Part III is to step you through the process of ordering and installing a simple CT setup and then cover the basics for troubleshooting your installation and answering the most common questions you're likely to have. We want you to feel comfortable with the process and to understand not just the steps involved but also the perils and pitfalls you're likely to encounter along the way. Let us close this introduction to Part III by wishing you a quick and painless installation or at least an all-knowing and infallible source for support when you need it!

Choosing the Right CT Stuff

Assessing Your Situation

In this chapter we'll discuss how to review your current environment, software, and equipment. Since every journey has a point of departure as well as a destination, you need to know where you're coming from before you try to get anywhere else. That's why we'll take a look at a couple of typical installations—one in a home office, the other in the offices of a small business—to establish the foundation of the introductions and enhancements in the succeeding chapters. After that we'll take a look at the pros and cons and the ins and outs of obtaining professional help from your friendly neighborhood CT consultant (as well as some other interesting alternatives).

Scenario 1: Home Office Use

To our way of thinking, this is the scenario most likely to be of interest to our readers, since those of you who don't have a home-based business—along with 3.6 million other at-home workers at the end of 1994, according to the U.S. Bureau of Labor Statistics—would probably like to understand what setting up a home office (to complement your "home away from home") might be like. For this scenario the most typical situation is one in which one or two phone lines already handle voice and data over conventional POTS telephones. In many cases some simple form of CT software is also in use (probably telecommunications and fax software and, less often but increasingly frequent, computer-based voice mail).

Current

Location:	Home
Business:	Consultant
Number of people:	1
Online via:	Modem
Online services:	AOL, CompuServe, Internet
Fax:	Yes
Voice:	Yes
Answering machine:	Yes
Number of POTS lines:	3
Computers:	1 PC
Software system:	Windows 3.1

Desired

Number of phone numbers:	2
Voice/Data/Fax:	Yes
Computer voice mail:	Want it
Internet usage:	Faster
Phone call tracking:	In and out

Caller ID on screen:	Want it
Computer dialing:	Want it
Expected growth:	None

Scenario 2: Small-Business Office

On the other hand, there were another 6.2 million businesses in the United States by the end of 1994 with 10 or fewer employees (Source: U.S. Bureau of Labor Statistics). This kind of situation usually involves something a bit more complicated, such as a small key-based telephone system or Centrex multiline services purchased from your local telephone company. It's also not atypical to find digital lines, where ISDN may be used for both voice and data and where a mixture of POTS phones and ISDN phones may already be in use. Based on recent market surveys, that's what we assume here:

Current

Location:	Office building
Business:	Sales representatives
Number of people:	3
Online via:	Modems
Online services:	AOL, CompuServe, Internet
Fax:	Yes
Voice:	Yes
Answering machine:	Yes
Number of POTS lines:	3
Computers:	2 PCs
Software system:	Windows for Workgroups 3.11
Networked:	Yes with WFW

Desired

Number of phone numbers:	4
Voice/Data/Fax:	Yes
Computer voice mail:	Want it for each person
Internet usage:	Faster
Phone call tracking:	In and out
Caller ID on screen:	Want it
Computer dialing:	Want it
Receptionist in network:	Want it
PBX simulation:	Want it
Intra-office dialing:	Want it
Expected growth:	1–2 employees < 12 months

Do It Yourself or Hiring a Consultant

You will need to answer only three questions to decide whether you want to do it yourself or hire a telephony consultant:

1. Can you afford spending a considerable amount of your time talking with your local telephone service provider, selecting and ordering your computer telephony hardware, fiddling with your telephone wiring, installing computer hardware (NT1, TA, network cards, etc.), finding an Internet Service Provider (ISP) that provides ISDN or other direct connection, installing or reconfiguring your computer's Internet software, and troubleshooting your digital system?

2. Are you comfortable installing hardware into your computer, setting it up, wiring telephone lines, and installing drivers and Internet software yourself?

3. Do you have more time to spend setting up your system than you have money to spend hiring a consultant?

If your answer to all of these questions is yes, you should do it yourself; otherwise, hire a consultant. Where our two scenarios are concerned, you can probably install an ISDN system in a home office without requiring the services of a consultant. But the small business owner would be well served if he or she at least prepared a brief RFP (request for proposal), if only to see what consultants who respond to the request will propose. This kind of operation probably could do it without outside help, but it may be more cost effective to contract the work out if the business can make more money doing business during the installation period than the consultant is going to charge. If that's the case, it clearly makes more sense to "hire it done"!

Finding Good CT Consultants and Vendors

Why should you write an RFP to give to consultants and vendors? The primary reason to prepare an RFP is to avoid overlooking important details that could lead you to make wrong (and expensive) decisions. For most SOHO situations a full formal RFP is a waste of your valuable time. However, you should at least prepare a minimal telephony plan that documents your needs, wants, likes, dislikes, budget, current computer and telephone equipment, and so on. This will suffice for most consultants and for those vendors that specialize in servicing the SOHO market.

If your situation requires more complex hardware and software, especially if it involves a LAN/WAN connection with more than a couple of workstations, you may want to hear what a few consultants and vendors have to say about your project. They won't charge to prepare a proposal, and you will probably learn quite a bit from reading them. You may even decide to hire one of them to do the job.

Finding and evaluating consultants and vendors need not be a walk across hot coals. Use your network of business contacts —and don't overlook local Internet newsgroups. Most telephony consultants use the Internet to find clients. A simple question in a couple of newsgroups will probably get you a number of suggestions, both pro and con, regarding local consultants and vendors.

No matter what else you hear, be sure always to check out a prospective consultant's or vendor's references. There's nothing like a quick call to the last few clients to really find out who's doing a good job and who's talking the talk without walking the walk. Be sure to ask about the size of the project, its cost, and whether it was completed on time and to the buyer's satisfaction. Don't forget to ask about service after the sale, too.

Should you decide to produce an RFP to give to some consultants and vendors, make sure it addresses certain key issues, as described next.

The Basic RFP

An RFP is a widely used business document that sets forth a set of requirements for a system or services and that details what that system or services must deliver but which leaves implementation details up to the respondents. An RFP is usually open-ended and deliberately a little vague, leaving plenty of room for creativity and innovation. Normally the only thing that's immutable about an RFP is the budget!

Project description

Business addresses of main locations

Type of business

Description of current telephone and computer systems

Basic objectives of the project

Number of phones, messages per day, and types of usage expected

Type of system you think you want

When you would like to have it completely installed and running

How much you expect to spend

Date by which you want respondents' proposals in your hands

Contractor section

Performance bond (require one)

Liability insurance

Purchase terms and conditions (in the contract)

Warranty

Payment terms

Equipment acceptance

Conformation with local laws

The consultants or vendors you expect to respond to your RFP should be able to propose solutions to your RFP quickly and matter of factly, as long as you have given them the information they need. Don't be verbose; just present the facts and let the respondents do their jobs.

Evaluating Proposals

Larger companies go through intricate proposal evaluation processes to ensure that they award their contracts fairly and equitably. Since you are a comparative small fry, you can use a streamlined evaluation process of your own making. Of course, you'll look at the bottom line first and the completion date second. If a low bid has the best completion date, you're going to be tempted to lean toward that one, but don't be hasty. Take the time to check out the details in each proposal to get a feel for each consultant's or vendor's understanding and ability. It's vital that you have confidence in the consultant or vendors you select and that you believe you can work closely with them on this and future projects.

When you've selected the two or three best proposals, you would be well advised to ask at least one business associate who has used a consultant or vendor for a similar project to check over them with you. This might cost you a lunch or even a dinner at a nice restaurant, but it will be well worth the time and effort. Among other things, you can learn when prices are too high or, even worse, too low. "Bait and switch" isn't epidemic in the consulting industry, but it's practiced often enough that you'll want to avoid the hook that an overly low price sometimes conceals.

Hiring a CT Consultant

Even for small businesses, hiring a CT consultant may be the most cost-effective way to acquire an advanced computer telephony system, especially if you have more than a couple of people and computers in your business and want to take full advantage of CT's capabilities. After preparing a list of consultants and vendors and using advice from your friends and the Internet, you can mail the consultants your RFP and see what happens. Or you can telephone the names on your list to find out whether they're interested in responding to your RFP.

Keep in mind that since PC-based computer telephony is relatively new on the scene, you will probably encounter a variety of consultants. Some will have come from UNIX programming backgrounds, some from telecommunications, some straight out of college, and some seemingly from a desert wilderness. Some will try to sell you on a complete telephony or computerized system, whether you need it or not. Some will want you to hire them to produce custom programming for your location, whether you need it or not. Ignore these time- and money-wasting proposals.

Fortunately some will propose to study your needs, provide you with hardware and software alternatives that suit your needs and budget, install the chosen system, and help you and your employees learn to use the system. Hire one of these consultants, only after checking his or her references thoroughly and getting all specifications and costs in writing. Don't forget to stipulate some measure of service after the sale, so that the consultant's hourly rate doesn't apply to every call you make with a question later on!

Doing It Yourself

If you're going to give it the old college try, all we have to say is "Good for you!" The experience of purchasing and installing your own computer telephony system can be both frustrating and rewarding. You'll learn quite a bit about your computers, telephone systems, working habits, and why you aren't a computer telephony consultant. During the process, you may, as we read recently on the Internet, "feel like roadkill on the shoulder of the information superhighway." However, when you finally get your system running perfectly, you will be ecstatic.

Addressing Hardware and Software Compatibility Issues

As mentioned in earlier chapters, this book is aimed primarily at people using PCs and Windows 3.1, Windows for Workgroups, Windows 95, or Windows NT. ISDN is gaining a strong foothold in the United States as more people opt for its increased speed and reasonable costs. Manufacturers are developing and selling PC/Windows-based hardware and software as rapidly as they can. Internet Service Providers are trying to get ISDN up and running as a measured service to their clients. This is hampered by the lack of good software for billing customers for connect time, since ISDN connections may be made in less than a second and dropped equally quickly when there's no online activity. Billing by the minute is outdated and will be expensive for customers who pay on such a rate schedule.

Add to this the problem that Microsoft and all ISDN manufacturers/developers were still working with the alpha release of the 32-bit TAPI driver software (for Windows 95 and Windows NT) in December 1995. Knowing this, you'll soon see why the majority of available CT products depend on dial-up POTS line connections and require modem-based hardware with Windows 3.1 or WFW 3.11 interfaces using the older 16-bit TAPI driver.

Most of these problems will be solved in early 1996, when Microsoft delivers its commercial 32-bit TAPI drivers. Then the manufacturers of ISDN hardware can deliver 32-bit TAPI-compliant software for their ISDN bridges and routers, and CT software developers can release their new, more powerful 32-bit applications.

Until then, you have two basic choices:

1. You may continue to use modem-based dial-up applications under Windows 3.1 or WFW and wait for the 32-bit world to blossom.

2. You may switch to 16-bit ISDN hardware and software now, even under Windows 95 and NT. This approach works, but it makes Windows 95 run in real mode to handle the 16-bit DOS driver that must be loaded "the old-fashioned way."

Some CT applications may work with 16-bit ISDN drivers under Windows 95, but others won't. The best solution is option 1, unless all you want to do is connect to the Internet via ISDN while using Windows 95.

Selecting the Right Mix of Advanced Telephony Services

As we mentioned briefly in Chapter 6, one possibility for the home office scenario shown at the beginning of this chapter is to purchase a Compaq Multimedia computer with its built-in voice/fax/modem and its Compaq Phone Center software, or to purchase an Acer computer with the Phoenix Technologies Telephone Center package. Otherwise, you can purchase one of the following hardware and software packages or one with similar features.

Rochelle Communications Caller Profile

The Caller Profile software and hardware packages from Rochelle Communications, Inc. (Austin, TX, 800-627-7542) are produced for single-, two-line, and multiline phone systems. They integrate caller ID with personal computers and information-management software. Rochelle offers Caller Profile packages for Windows (3.1, WFW 3.11, and Win95) that can be used with your existing PIM.

Rochelle also offers packages that include Sidekick 2.0 (a popular personal organizer with flexible calendar, cardfile and notepad, and phone dialer) from Starfish Software. Caller Profile integrates directly into Sidekick. Their combined functions keep appointment schedules, manage addresses and phone numbers, create to-do lists, track your incoming and outgoing phone calls, and provide contact-management assistance.

The stand-alone Caller Profile package (model 5001 for Windows) lists for $69.99. The combined Caller Profile/Sidekick 2.0 for Windows package for a single phone line (model # 5101)lists for $149.99. The two-line model 5102 lists for $199. Both include Rochelle's serial port plug-in adapter so all you need is a free serial port and a caller ID equipped standard telephone line to get started. You'll also need your own modem to take advantage of Sidekick's dialing capabilities.

Diamond Multimedia TeleCommander

The Diamond Multimedia (San Jose, CA, 408-325-7000) TeleCommander 2500XL uses a 14.4 Kbps modem, and the 3500XL integrates a 28.8 Kbps modem and the company's TAPI-compliant software. The card includes 16-bit sound, fax send/receive/forward, fax-on-demand, voice mail, data transfer, pager notification, and call screening via caller ID and call forwarding. In addition, the product includes NetCruiser and VocalTec's Internet Phone capability (phone calls via the Internet). All of this for $209 (14.4 Kbps) or $299 (28.8 Kbps), depending on modem speed.

If you've decided to set up your own business office CT system similar to the one outlined at the beginning of this chapter, you may be interested in the following advice and suggestions from Bob Cameron, president of the Cameron Communications Group in Brentwood, Tennessee, a computer telephony consultancy that's been in business since 1987 (which counts as the Paleolithic for this kind of technology):

Alpha Telecom Super NT1

The Alpha Telecom Super NT1 forms the nucleus of my ISDN HOME office. It connects to the ISDN line at the U Interface and features two analog ports, two S/T ISDN digital ports, and an integral battery backup for the analog ports. One analog port is used for a conventional analog answering machine. The other is used for a fax-modem. A multibutton ISDN phone is connected to one of the S/T ports. A Combinet CB 2050 ISDN/Ethernet router is connected to the other. The number on the ISDN phone has Call Forward-Busy and Call Forward-No Answer to the analog answering machine. This setup works well as long as the calling rate is not excessive. As traffic increases, I would substitute a public voice mail service for the answering machine in order to decrease contention for the two B Channels.

Lodestar LTI 1001LS ISDN Multibutton Telephone

The 14-button Lodestar LTI 1001LS, with its speakerphone and ISDN caller ID capabilities, provides the ultimate in price/performance in a multibutton ISDN telephone. I ordered three call appearances of the Primary Directory Number on Buttons 1, 2, and 3. With this configuration, I can be having a conversation on one button and receive an incoming call on another button. I can then look at the caller ID display to decide whether I want to interrupt the current call to answer the new one. If I decide to answer it, pressing the ringing call appearance automatically puts the first call on hold and answers the incoming call. I then have a third call appearance free to get dial tone in order to transfer the caller to a second number or create a conference call. If I choose to ignore the incoming call, it will, after a predetermined number of rings, automatically forward to the analog port on the Super NT1, where a conventional analog answering machine invites the caller to leave a message.

Beware of Systems that Don't Support ISDN Telephones!

Many ISDN terminal adapters these days have integrated NT1s and one or two analog ports for voice capability. They may provide a call-waiting tone to notify you of an additional caller if you're on the phone. But you have no idea who is calling without interrupting your current conversation. Some TAs with analog ports even let you use switchhook flashes to activate transfer and conference features. In short, they're using modern ISDN technology to duplicate features that have been available on analog phone lines since the 1980s. In my opinion, an S/T port on the TA is essential.

The strength of an ISDN telephone is that it provides single-button access to multiple call appearances and switch features, just like a large business system. Once you've experienced the flexibility and ease of use of a multibutton ISDN phone, you'll never be satisfied with an analog phone again!

Combinet CB 2050 ISDN/Ethernet Bridge/Router

Any ISDN/Ethernet bridge or router with an S/T interface will work in this arrangement. I happened to have a pair of Combinet CB 2050s. The CB 2050 routes TCP/IP and IPX and bridges other Ethernet protocols. It is set up so that it originates a single B channel call to my remote-office LAN. With up to 4:1 compression, this is sufficient for most file transfers. However, if I need more bandwidth, I can add the second B channel for 128 Kbps before compression and up to 512 Kbps after compression. The actual compression ratio depends on the file type. Word processing files tend to compress the best, whereas bit-mapped graphics yield no more than 2:1 compression. Of course, if both B channels are being used for data, all incoming voice callers will get a busy signal. For this reason, I use only 128 Kbps data after business hours.

Source: http://www.ccg4isdn.com/isdn/info.html

We agree wholeheartedly with Bob regarding the need for the following items of equipment:

- an external NT1 with a couple of POTS ports and S/T jacks with extended telephony features

- an ISDN bridge/router with S/T interface and extra jack for future expansion.

Several models for both of these hardware items are discussed in other chapters. If you want to keep costs down, use POTS telephones instead of the much more expensive ISDN phones (but you'll lose the advanced features they provide).

Some of these features can be regained through the CT software you use on your PC, depending on the package you purchase. The key idea here is to let your PC handle any complex telephony services, before calls are passed to your POTS phone or to the speaker on your PC.

Ordering Services from Your Phone Company

ISDN is the most versatile, feature-rich service ever offered by your telephone company. A number of options will need to be specified when you first order your service. These options will vary depending on the equipment you plan to use and the RBOC that's providing your service. Most RBOCs have a "standard" BRI package that they install if you don't specify which services you want. This standard service usually includes voice and data on both B channels, which is what you want anyway.

The best approach is to wait to order your service until you know what kind of hardware you'll be using. That way, your equipment vendor can provide guidance for selecting those service options that are compatible with your ISDN terminal equipment. Even so, many of these options depend on what you want to do with the service and the mix of equipment you will be using.

You'll need to contact your ISDN dialtone provider (the local telephone company: usually RBOCs and independents) to determine whether ISDN service is available in your area and available options and prices. The following list of ISDN contacts in the United States should help you start your search for the perfect service provider.

Bellcore (Bell Communications Research)

National ISDN HotLine	1-800-992-ISDN
Fax:	201-829-2263
E-mail	isdn@cc.bellcore.com
URL:	http://info.bellcore.com
System prompt:	ftp info.bellcore.com

Company	Contact	Telephone no.
Ameritech	National ISDN hotline	1-800-TEAMDATA
		(1-800-832-6328)
Bell Atlantic	ISDN Sales & Tech Ctr.	1-800-570-ISDN
	(In NJ, call your local	(1-800-570-4736)
	telephone office.) For small businesses	1-800-843-2255
Bell South	ISDN hotline	1-800-428-ISDN
		(1-800-428-4736)
Cincinnati Bell	ISDN Service Center	513-566-DATA
		(513-566-3282)
GTE	Menu-driven information	1-800-4GTE-SW5
	FL, NC, VA, KY	1-800-483-5200
	IL, IN, OH, and PA	1-800-483-5600
	OR and WA	1-800-483-5100
	CA	1-800-483-5000
	HI	1-800-643-4411
	TX	1-800-483-5400
Nevada Bell	Small business	702-333-4811
	Large business	702-688-7100
NYNEX	ISDN sales hotline	1-800-GET-ISDN
		1-800-438-4736
	New England states	617-743-2466
Pacific Bell	ISDN Service Center	1-800-4PB-ISDN
		1-800-472-4736
	24 hr. automated ISDN	1-800-995-0346
	availability hotline	
	ISDN telemarketing	1-800-662-0735
Rochester Telephone	ISDN information	716-777-1234
SNET	Donovan Dillon	203-553-2369
STENTOR (Canada)	ISDN Facts by Fax	1-800-578-ISDN
	Steve Finlay	604-654-7504
	Glen Duxbury	403-945-8130
Southwestern Bell	Austin, TX	1-800-SWB-ISDN
	Dallas, TX	214-268-1403
	North Houston, TX	713-537-3930

	South Houston, TX	713-567-4300
	San Antonio, TX	210-351-8050
	For ISDN availability for remaining locations	
	pls. contact the Bellcore ISDN hotline at	1-800-992-ISDN
U S West	Ron Miller	303-965-7153
	Ron Woldeit	206-447-4029
	Denver, CO	1-800-246-5226
	Julia Evans	303-896-8370

National ISDN Long-Distance Carrier Contacts

Company	Contact	Telephone no.
AT&T	AT&T Front End Center	1-800-222-7956
GTE	N'wide avail./pricing	1-800-888-8799
	Ron Sterreneberg	214-718-5608
MCI	Tony Hylton	214-701-6745
	ISDN availability	1-800-MCI-ISDN
US Sprint	Rick Simonson	913-624-4162
WILTEL	Justin Remington	918-588-5069

ISDN Line Configurations

With ISDN comes the ability to select from virtually thousands of configurations for setting up your phone line. Your ISDN service provider will undoubtedly give you a list of the possibilities on request and would like to sell you as many as possible. If you don't plan to use an ISDN telephone (EKTS), you don't really need any of the "fancy" ISDN telephony features just to plug your current analog phone into the POTS jack on your NT1 or TA. However, you will need to be sure to get the basic features you need.

Depending on which regional phone company is serving you, you will probably find that your choice of line configurations is an issue of economics. We recommend that you get only the features you believe you will need. You can always add more features later if you need them. See Table 10.1.

Table 10.1: Typical ISDN Line Features

# of Channels	Channel Type	Typical Use
(1B)	CSD	64K Internet access (data only)
(1B)	CSVD	64K Internet or voice
(2B)	CSD+CSV	64K Internet and voice
(2B)	CSD+CSD	64K or 128K Internet (data only)
(2B)	CSD+CSVD	64K Internet and voice, or 128K Internet (good choice for 128K Internet and sporadic POTS)
(2B)	CSVD+CSVD	64K data and voice, or 128K data, or two voice lines (best choice if your ISDN provider allows two voice lines)

Notes:

- 1B: one B channel
- 2B: two B channels
- CSD: Circuit switched data on the B channel
- CSV: Circuit switched voice on the B channel
- CSVD: Alternate voice or data, on demand on the B channel
- EKTS: Electronic key telephone system. A phone with intelligent keys and dialing features normally found on a business phone. Most ISDN phones were designed for businesses and take advantage of EKTS features.
- POTS: Plain old telephone service. Special NT1s will support your analog equipment, such as fax, modem, and analog phone. POTS in this table refers to use of those NT1s.

For individual personal/business use at a residence with a connection to the Internet and a POTS phone plugged into the NT1 or TA, the (2B) CSVD+CSVD 64 Kbps data per B channel line configuration with only one voice call at a time allowed should provide very good service at a reasonable price.

Summary

If you have decided to install your own analog CT or digital ISDN system and have chosen—at least on paper or on your computer screen—the appropriate analog CT hardware and software or an ISDN phone service provider, along with an ISDN-capable ISP and an NT1, a TA, and the appropriate CT application software, you're ready to begin the process. Chapters 12 and 13 provide you with step-by-step help to assist you in preparing for and then installing a system.

Preparing for a
Home/Office CT System

If you've read the previous chapters, you should have a pretty good idea about the types of CT hardware, software, and services available. You should also have a good idea of what you want from the combination of your computer(s) and your telephone system. This chapter gives information on how to get ready for the installation of three CT systems:

1. an analog system using existing telephone lines

2. a one-person ISDN system

3. a small-office ISDN system

Researching Your CT Hardware, Software, and Services Needs

To get the latest information on CT equipment and other CT information prior to making any decisions, rely on your trusty vendors, friends, consultants, Computer Telephony magazine, and the plethora of Internet Web sites dealing with various forms of CT. Some of the best sites to start looking include:

- Dan Kegel's ISDN page:
  http://alumni.caltech.edu/~dank/isdn/

- Cameron Communications Group:
  http://www.ccg4isdn.com/isdn/info.html

- Computer Telephone Integrators, Inc.(CTI):
  http://www.inforamp.net/mainstay/cti/

- Ascend: http://www.ascend.com/

- Combinet / Cisco: http://www.combinet.com/

- Motorola: http://www.motorola.com/

- US Robotics: http://www.usrobotics.com/

- Diamond MultiMedia: http://www.diamondmm.com/

- Rochelle Communications: http://www.rochelle.com/

- Specific telephony applications (page from CTI):
  http://www.inforamp.net/mainstay/cti/spfcapps.html

- PacBell's ISDN Tutorial:
  http://www.pacbell.com/isdn/book/home.html

- SouthWestern Bell's WWW page: http://www.sbc.com/

- Texas ISDN Users Group:
  http://www.crimson.com/isdn/

- Telecommunications Industry Forum:
  http://www.t1.org/tcif/

Don't forget that you can also use a Web search engine (such as Yahoo, Excite, WebCrawler, etc.) with "telephony," "computer telephony," or "CT" as search terms to turn up lots of other resources besides these. Remember, too, that a well-informed consumer is a prepared buyer: Since you're going to be spending some money, you might as well spend some time, too, learning how to expend your cash wisely!

Choosing the Proper Hardware, Software, and Services

In this section we'll supply you with a questionnaire that you should complete before making any purchases. Here you'll identify your planned usage of a CT system and find important questions you'll want to get answered from your local phone company and other service providers that will play a role in your system's installation and use.

Ask Yourself These Questions First!

Which of the following are your planned uses for your CT service?

- Home

- Office (nonresidence)

- Personal

- Business

- Single user

- Multiple users

- Replace existing analog service

- Digital computer connections and additional voice line

- ISDN Internet connection for faster access

- Use current analog phone(s) with ISDN line

- Use ISDN (digital) phone(s)

Ask the Phone Company

- Is your location in an ISDN service area?

- What is the ISDN installation charge from your ISDN telephone service provider?

- What are the monthly charges (basic and usage) for ISDN service?

- Will your ISDN service be via a repeater?

- Will your ISDN service be via an SLC?

- Which central office ISDN switch does your service use (Siemens, AT&T, etc.)?

- Which protocol does the switch use? (i.e., NI-1 [National ISDN-1], AT&T 5ESS Custom, AT&T G3 PBX, or Northern

Telecom DMS-100 Custom, Northern Telecom BCS-34 [PVC-1], or other)?

- What calling features are available from your ISDN provider (e.g., EKTS, CACH)?

- Does your ISDN provider offer BRI (2B+D) with two SPIDs?

- Does your ISDN provider offer voice service on both B channels on the same BRI service with two SPIDs?

Ask the ISDN Software or Hardware Vendor

- Does your chosen NT1 device work well with your chosen TA and with the phone company's switch and protocol?

- Does your chosen NT1 device have zero, one, or two POTS jacks?

- Does your chosen NT1 device have an internal power supply?

- Does your chosen NT1 device have a battery backup?

- Does the ISDN TA you are looking to purchase communicate well with the phone company's switch and protocol?

- Does your chosen TA support B channel BONDing?

- Does your chosen TA's software support PPP or the protocol your Internet Service Provider offers?

- Does your chosen TA have zero, one, or two S/T jacks?

- Does your chosen TA have zero, one, or two POTS jacks?

Ask the Internet Service Provider

- What NT1 does your ISP suggest?

- What TA does your ISP suggest to work best with its system's ISDN router?

- What protocol does the ISP support (async. PPP, sync. PPP, ML, etc.)?

- Does the ISP have experience with connecting your chosen TA to its ISDN router?

- Does your ISP's software support two-B channel BONDing?

- What are the extra charges by your ISP for two-B channel BONDing?

- What are the ISDN setup charges from your ISP?

- What are your ISP's monthly ISDN account charges (basic and usage)?

Make Your Selections

After you've answered all of the relevant questions in the preceding lists, you'll be ready to choose appropriate CT hardware, software, and services for your needs.

1. Compare the previously checked items with the specifications of the hardware, software, and services you have researched.

2. Write down those that most closely match your needs.

3. Rank them in order of increasing cost (most expensive last).

4. Add the costs of the hardware, software, and services together and prepare a CT cost estimate.

At this point you may finally be ready to start acquiring system components, but there's still a bit more planning ahead (like where to put the equipment, what kind of hookups it will need, and more).

Home Office Use

Let's look quickly at the two scenarios from the previous chapter with regard to the four steps just listed. The first is aimed at home office use (Voice and Data + POTS phone with CT software).

Current

Location:	Home
Business:	Consultant
Number of people:	1
Online via:	Modem
Online services:	AOL, CompuServe, Internet
Fax:	Yes
Voice:	Yes
Answering machine:	Yes
Number of POTS lines:	3
Computers:	1 PC
Software system:	Windows 3.1

Desired

Number of phone numbers:	2
Voice/Data/Fax:	Yes
Computer voice mail:	Want it
Internet usage:	Faster
Phone call tracking:	In and out
Caller ID on screen:	Want it
Computer dialing:	Want it
Expected growth:	None

This person can achieve most of the CT functionality he or she wants by using analog telephone service with a CT package such as the Caller Profile system from Rochelle. It includes caller ID hardware and software, as well as computer dialing, call tracking, and contact management, and it will work with the existing modem. This system is inexpensive at $150 but doesn't provide voice mail or computer-based fax services, so three separate analog lines will be needed. This won't provide faster Internet usage, either, but it won't cost any more in monthly fees, and the total up-front outlay is low.

For only $150 more ($300 total) the Telecommander 3500 XL from Diamond Multimedia can provide all the desired CT functionality and a 28,800-baud modem for Internet access. If this user's existing modem is already a 28,800, the new setup won't be any faster, but it won't cost any more for monthly fees, either. This software and hardware (or a similar package) can increase functionality at a low initial cost while keeping monthly outlays the same.

Installing an ISDN BRI line with an ISDN external serial modem, such as the Motorola Bitsurfer Pro or TA-210 and a single-line Windows 3.1 compatible CT software package can also accomplish all of these goals, although it imposes an increased initial outlay and higher monthly costs as well. This is only one of many combinations of hardware, software, and telephone service that can satisfy the objectives stated previously.

The estimated costs incurred look like this (based on prices in late 1995; these will change with time):

Motorola Bitsurfer Pro Package $350

Single-line CT package $200

ISDN BRI installation $50–$450 (depends on location)

ISDN BRI monthly service fee $30–$200 (depends on location)

ISDN Internet account monthly $40–$200 (depends on location)

The up-front costs for this configuration range between $650 and $1050; monthly costs range between $70-$400. This wide range of costs is related to the different tariffs (allowable charges) that each RBOC charges for ISDN service and the associated charges for your ISDN Internet account from your ISP.

Small-Business Office

For the second scenario (small-business office with voice and data, and multiple ISDN phones), the following apply:

Current

Location:	Office building
Business:	Sales representatives
Number of people:	3
Online via:	Modems
Online services:	AOL, CompuServe, Internet
Fax:	Yes
Voice:	Yes
Answering machine:	Yes
Number of POTS lines:	3
Computers:	2 PCs

Software system:	Windows for Workgroups 3.11
Networked:	Yes with WFW

Desired

Number of phone numbers:	4
Voice/Data/Fax:	Yes
Computer voice mail:	Want it for each person
Internet usage:	Faster
Phone call tracking:	In and out
Caller ID on screen:	Want it
Computer dialing:	Want it
Receptionist in network:	Want it
PBX simulation:	Want it
Intra-office dialing:	Want it
Expected growth:	1–2 employees < 12 months

This scenario requires at least an ISDN BRI service for each person, with either an ISDN serial modem or an ISDN bridge/router card for each person's PC. The same type of CT software suggested for the first scenario will work in this one until a receptionist is added. Then more complex software will be required to route calls through the receptionist, along with reprogramming the system's telephony functions accordingly. The addition of another employee or two means that this system will soon cease to be simple. This scenario would therefore benefit from the services of a telephony consultant, especially if the operation wants to upgrade to Windows 95 or NT and plans more advanced CT functionality in the future.

A consultant would help determine hardware, software, and services needed for a variety of growth situations. System installation and employee training will be the key elements in this scenario, especially as the system grows in size and complexity. These activities must be executed quickly and expeditiously to minimize loss of work time and the inconvenience to this organization's clients. No client wants to hear that his order can't be shipped because you're changing your telephone system! Worse yet, calls that can't get through to your order department during a changeover may very well result in lost sales and even lost customers.

Establishing a CT Cost Estimate

To understand where future costs are headed, you must first understand your current telephone equipment and service costs. Here's how:

- Based on your current telephone equipment costs (payments, rental, amortized costs, etc.) and telephone service fees (lines, Internet connect time charges, other online charges, long-distance charges, etc.), determine your current telephony costs per month.

- Determine the expected cost of your new CT hardware, software, installation, consulting fees, etc.

- Amortize those costs over the appropriate number of months and add expected monthly costs for your new service fees (i.e., line charges, ISP charges, long distance, etc.).

- Determine whether you can sell some of your existing POTS phone equipment to defray the cost of going digital, if you decide to go this route. It's rare to recover more than 35-50 percent of your original outlays when selling used equipment.

- Now use your own method (or ask your accountant) to determine whether the expected initial costs and amortized monthly costs are reasonable given your organization's revenue/profit envelope.

If the costs are acceptable, proceed. If not, reprioritize what you need and want, and eliminate the most costly and least necessary items until you reach a figure that is within your budget. Since most digital CT equipment is upgradeable and expandable with components that are relatively easy to replace, you can start simply with a small system that can grow along with your needs and revenues.

Reviewing Your Wiring Needs

Unless you live in an old house in an older section of town or in a rural location where the telephone wiring hasn't been upgraded since the Kennedy administration, standard wiring will probably work for ISDN and other digital systems. Ask your telephone dial-tone provider (the phone company in your area) about its wiring at your location — especially about the condition of your local loop — when you ask whether ISDN or other digital services can be provided at your location. Also be sure to investigate these two important considerations:

1. Is the telephone wiring at your location a typical analog system with a parallel circuit of the same two wires throughout the building for a single phone number, as is typical for house wiring, or is it a star configuration, with each telephone having its own pair of wires from the demarc (outside wiring box) typical of office wiring?

2. Does your location already have an unused or reusable pair of telephone wires suitable for ISDN signals for each ISDN BRI you think you might need?

Digital telephone wiring requires a single pair of unsplit and unbranched wires for each telephony user. In the case of ISDN the twisted-pair wire must run directly from the demarc to the NT1 and end there. You can attach multiple ISDN hardware components to the NT1 or the S/T jacks of TAs attached to the NT1 but only a single NT1 to a BRI cable pair.

If your office is in an office building, you probably have a telephone punchdown block in a closet somewhere. Punchdown block? It's that large mass of little pins where the main phone cable comes in and office telephone wires go out. This is where each of your telephones connects with the outside world.

If you're familiar with how your office telephones are connected to the punchdown block, you can easily ensure that each of your ISDN lines is a single run that terminates at its associated computer or telephony device. If not, it's time to have your telephony consultant or service person give you a little help. The phone company person who installs your ISDN line will be glad to test your existing wiring, but it will cost you the going rate per hour. No matter how you do it, test to make sure that your wiring is working, because digital telephony doesn't work well, if at all, if it's poor quality or improperly configured.

Preparing for Hardware and Software Installation

Whether you install your own CT system or have a consultant install it for you, several considerations can make the experience less stressful for you and your customers. Most important, plan for the installation. If you're installing your own CT hardware and software as discussed earlier in this chapter, understand that Murphy runs the entire process from beginning to end. Nothing ever proceeds exactly as envisioned (or as advertised), and nothing installs without some problems cropping up along the way.

Despite our tone, this isn't rampant pessimism: It's cold, hard fact. You may not encounter any major problems, but find that everything takes at least three times longer to accomplish than you thought it would. Also, you'll have to call every hardware and software manufacturer involved in your system at least one time.

Of course, you'll be installing your system in the evening or on a weekend, to minimize downtime. Although this keeps your customers happy, it also means that you can't call the manufacturer's technical support line, which responds only during normal business hours, Monday through Friday.

So how can you "plan" for such an installation? To begin with, finish all your current projects. Tell your clients you'll be busy, out of town, or whatever, for two or three days. Read all the manuals on your new hardware and software. Start the installation on a Wednesday morning. That way you can use the weekend if necessary to finish up. Remember that you can't install any hardware or software until your ISDN line has been installed by the phone company (this may take from two to six weeks from the time you place your order). In the meantime, get ready for lots of waiting and a few phone calls to them, too!

You didn't think that preparation would be mostly mental, did you? The installation isn't all that difficult if you follow the steps in the users manuals and if you understand enough about your PC. This includes understanding how to determine IRQs, I/O base addresses and shared memory addresses and how to set them to avoid conflicts. You will also need to know how to make changes in your AUTOEXEC.BAT and CONFIG.SYS files, as well as how to use Windows to configure your I/O ports. Again, if this isn't something you're comfortable doing, it's time to bring in a consultant.

Summary

If it seems that we're pushing you toward using a telephony consultant every chance we get, maybe we are. After installing various types of CT hardware and software ourselves and dealing with our local phone company on ISDN BRI installations and our local Internet Service Provider for the ISDN account, we know how much time and energy it can take. We've also read the comp.dcom.isdn newsgroup for the past year and have experienced secondhand the trials and tribulations of many other do-it-your-selfers.

Even CT professionals have difficulties with some RBOCs and various types of seemingly simple installations. It's not that manufacturers try to exaggerate the ease of installation of their products they just don't take into consideration the complexity of the entire process. Sad to say, not all CT hardware and software is compatible, either. Finally, some of the hardest lessons about CT installation and configuration can be learned only in the school of hard knocks.

Most CT consultants have found compatible hardware and software for their RBOC's switch type and ISP's routers; therefore they're the best source of information on compatibility in your local area. You can either pay them to help you or pay yourself for the time it takes you to gain their knowledge the hard way. Don't forget that you can buy small chunks of their time to ask for advice and recommendations; just because you work with a consultant doesn't mean that you have to turn the whole CT situation, installation and all, over to the consultant. Your budget may dictate otherwise, but that needn't deter you from getting advice before you get started or help when you really need it!

The next chapter assumes that you're going to have a go at it yourself and explains the major steps involved in several CT installations, from start to finish. This should give you a pretty good idea of the magnitude of the task involved for each type of installation and what you'll have to master to succeed at it.

Home-Office Installation

In the preceding chapters you've learned what to expect from combining your computer(s) and your telephone system. By now you should be fully prepared to install the appropriate hardware and software. This chapter gives you information on how to install the following CT elements:

- a basic analog CT system that provides caller ID logging, using your own PIM or Sidekick for Windows and your existing telephone lines

- an analog CT system with extensive voice/fax/caller ID functionality, using your existing phone lines

- a one-person ISDN BRI system

The more complex small-office ISDN system discussed at the end of the previous chapter should probably be installed by a CT or ISDN consultant so you can get the best system for the least amount of time and money. Unless you're a telephony wizard or a determined do-it-yourselfer, such a complex system installation is probably well beyond your pain threshold!

Basic, Single-Line Analog CT System

Using your existing analog phone line and a Windows-based PC with your own modem, you can install and configure the Caller Profile combination hardware/software CT package in minutes (along with Starfish Software's Sidekick software, should you need a PIM as well). In many telephone service areas caller ID may be switched on the same day that you order it. Since Caller Profile uses your existing telephone line, you need no additional wiring, except for connecting the Caller Profile plug to the telephone and your computer with the cables included in the package.

Purchasing and Ordering the Hardware, Software, and Services

Caller Profile is available directly from Rochelle Communications, Inc. The package we used is Model 5101, which includes a single-line Caller Profile plug, Caller Profile software for Windows (3.1, WFW 3.11, or Win95), and Sidekick 2.0 for Windows. Its suggested retail price is $149.99 (if you already own Sidekick 2.0, get the model 5100 upgrade for $89.95). If you want only the Windows version of Caller Profile to use with another PIM or Contact Manager, order model 5001 for $69.99. Rochelle also offers two-line versions starting at $129.99 and six-line models starting at $399.99 for the multiline adapter, and $119.99 to $169.99 per workstation for the software.

You can order caller ID from your local telephone company, if it's available in your area. Simply call and ask. Caller ID generally costs about $5 for installation and from $6 to $8 per month per line (as you probably already know, prices vary with the RBOC because of local weather conditions, politics, season, etc. — or so it seems). Ordering before 3:00 p.m. may enable this service the same day in some RBOCs.

Wiring Your Home-Office for the Caller Profile System

Since the Caller Profile system uses your existing analog telephone line, the only wiring required is in connecting a telephone cable splitter (Y) cable from the Caller Profile package to the Caller Profile plug and connect your telephone and modem cables together to the Y plug. It's pictured and explained in the Caller Profile Hardware Installation Guide. If you don't already have your telephone wired into your modem, you may need either to plug it into the modem or use another splitter plug (available almost everywhere, even on your grocery store's telephone or hardware aisle) so that all three components (phone, modem, and Caller Profile plug) are connected to your telephone wall outlet.

Hardware Installation and Configuration

The Caller Profile hardware is a DB25 plug with lots of internal electronics (you can see its miniature circuit board through the smoked plastic case). All that's needed to install Caller Profile is plugging it into the DB25 serial plug on the back of your PC. If you're already using your DB25 plug, use the short DB25-to-DB9 cable that's included with the package to connect it to the DB9 serial plug on your PC (assuming that you have one unused serial port and plug in your PC).

If you're using a serial mouse on COM1 and your modem is either an external device attached to COM2 or an internal device designated as COM2, you have a problem. Your PC's built-in BIOS and pre-Win95 versions of Windows recognize only four COM ports, numbered 1, 2, 3, and 4. However, 1 and 3 share IRQ 4, and 2 and 3 share IRQ 3. Many older serial I/O cards support only IRQs up to 9 and since only IRQ 5 may be free in the range 1 to 9, you may not be able to configure your serial port with the Caller Profile plug or your modem to coexist with your serial mouse (or to make them peacefully coexist). If your serial card is new enough, try the following settings (which we were able to use after buying a new serial card):

- COM1: serial mouse on the DB9 plug, using IRQ 4

- COM2: internal modem, using IRQ 3

- COM3: serial port for the Caller Profile plug, using IRQ 10

For this to work, you'll need to set the jumpers on your serial card or motherboard and on your internal modem (follow the instructions in their users manuals); then restart your computer, so that your CPU recognizes the new hardware configuration.

Next, you'll need to run the Windows Control Panel application and select the Ports icon. Make sure that the IRQ settings are as shown here for the respective ports or that other unoccupied IRQs are used. Then restart Windows so these settings can take effect. Afterward, you should be able to follow the Caller Profile installation instructions for the software; you'll choose COM3 (or whatever port you've chosen) as the Caller Profile port.

If neither your serial ports nor your modem can use IRQ 10, you still have two reasonably priced options. The first option is to purchase a bus mouse to replace your serial mouse (it's possible to find such devices for as little as $10). A bus mouse includes its own adapter card that plugs into your computer. Although it uses an IRQ, it doesn't require a COM port and therefore can be set to either IRQ 5 (if you're not using a second parallel port) or an IRQ above 9, thus freeing both your COM ports. Most bus mice also include a switch or software driver so they emulate a standard Microsoft mouse.

The other option is to disable your older serial ports (change their jumper settings to turn them off) and install a new serial I/O card that can use IRQs in the range of 10 to 15. We took this route and used a SIIG, Inc., HighSpeed/Hi-IRQ I/O Expander 4S board (model IO1813) that we bought from our local hardware megastore for $54.95. The board includes two 16550 high-speed UART chips, with sockets for two more if you need to expand. The 16550 UARTs are necessary if you want to use an external 28.8 or faster modem or ISDN device.

After you get the COM ports happily configured with no Windows error screens popping up saying you have conflicts, you're ready to install the software. If you're lucky, this will take no more than two minutes; if not, you could spend a day or two locating and obtaining the right hardware to add a third serial device to your PC. Murphy's Law says that this activity almost always takes longer than you think it will, so consider yourself warned!

Software Installation and Configuration

Both Sidekick 2.0 and the Caller Profile software use Windows-based installation programs; they also include installation instructions in their manuals or on separate sheets that accompany their packages. If you'll follow the instructions, you should find that Sidekick installs quite easily. You will need, however, to configure Sidekick for your modem, using its Phone, Modem Setup menu. Just choose the appropriate COM port for your modem (COM2 in the preceding example) and enter the modem initialization string you have been using in your regular communications program. (If you don't know what that should be, you may want to check with the modem manufacturer's technical support staff.)

You need to make sure that Sidekick's Enable caller ID box is checked and that either "Office phone number" or "Home phone number" is included as one of the three sort fields in the "Sort Cardfile By" setup. Of course, Sidekick needs to know where to find phone numbers when caller ID activates it, and the program tries to display the caller's cardfile entry. While you're at it, you might as well enter call information into a new card (which is what happens when the caller's number isn't already present in Sidekick) so you can test your setup more easily.

Install Caller Profile next, which will automatically install itself into Sidekick if you want it to, and asks you to indicate which COM port contains the Caller Profile plug (this would be COM3, if you're following the previous example). Make sure that the Single Line box is checked unless you're using one of Rochelle's multiline packages.

At long last, you're now ready to test your CT system!

Testing

If you've received no error messages from any of the programs about COM port conflicts or other problems, you should be able to run Sidekick and Caller Profile. Try instructing Sidekick to dial the number that you previously entered into a new card: This tests your modem initialization string and port assignments. If it works, great; if it doesn't, double-check your port jumpers on your PC (turning it off first), then check your port and IRQ settings, using the Windows Control Panel, Ports menu.

Next, have someone call you and to see whether the Caller Profile screen pop appears, displaying the caller's phone number and name. If it does, you're up and running; if not, first double-check the port assignment for the Caller Profile plug using the Caller Profile Options, Preferences menu. Chapter 14 supplies other avenues for you to follow if you still can't get things to work. Bear in mind that you can always call the manufacturer's technical support lines for help.

Summary: Basic Single-Line System

This particular CT installation features Caller Profile and Sidekick, which together provide an inexpensive and relatively simple method for acquiring incoming caller identification. This ID information is then linked to a cardfile database of your clients and contacts. Sidekick also allows you to take notes directly into the same cardfile database, and supports a speed-dial function for any number in the Sidekick cardfile. If you want this kind of basic CT capability with a minimum of setup and cost, this system (or one like it) is probably just what you need. If you want additional functionality from your existing analog phone line(s), please read on: In the next section we'll cover a more complete single-line computer telephony system.

Complete Single-Line CT System

The Diamond Multimedia Telecommander 3500XL is a complete package for analog computer telephony. Using an existing analog phone line and a Windows-based PC, you can install and configure the Telecommander 3500XL hardware and software in a couple of hours. In many telephone service areas caller ID may be switched on the very day it's ordered!

Purchasing and Ordering CT Hardware, Software, and Services

Caller ID

You can purchase caller ID from your local telephone company, if it's available in your area: Simply call and ask. caller ID generally costs about $5 for installation and between $6 and $8 range per month per line. Ordering this service before 3:00 p.m. may result in service delivery the same day in some RBOCs.

Telecommander 3500XL

You can purchase the Telecommander 2500XL (14,400-baud modem for $199) or the 3500XL (28,000-baud modem for $299) directly from Diamond Multimedia (1-800-468-5846) in San Jose, CA, or from your local hardware store or a mail-order source. The Telecommander is a complete CT hardware and software solution for a single-line analog phone system. The Telecommander software provides the following capabilities:

- multiple voice/fax mailboxes

- auto-detection of incoming voice and fax calls

- record and playback voice messages on your PC

- speakerphone with microphone included

- speed dial from a list of the 20 most recently called numbers

- screen incoming calls before answering

- automatic caller ID display (if your phone line has caller ID service)

- call logging for incoming calls

- fax-on-demand mailbox setup

- automatic answer with your own recorded greeting

- remote data host mode operation

- fax polling

- notification of calls/faxes by phone, pager or fax

- attached binary files to faxes

- group phone list for scheduled group faxes

- fax forwarding

- password protection for each mailbox

- audio editing/mixing/play/record capabilities, including audio CD playing

The Telecommander adapter card provides:

- 16-bit sound board capabilities, including SoundBlaster and SB Pro

- CD-ROM interface connectors for Sony, Mitsumi, Panasonic, and IDE

- CD-ROM audio input connectors for Sony, Mitsumi, and Panasonic

- wavetable interface connector

- joystick connector

- microphone jack

- audio "in" jack

- audio "out" jack

- phone jack

- 28.8 modem (TC 3500) or 14.4 modem (TC 2500)

- 14.4 fax (V.17) for both models

- 16550A UART (with 16-byte FIFO),

- Hayes AT-compatible command set

- voice compression/decompression

- enhanced ADPCM

- concurrent DTMF detection

- dual DMA for full-duplex voice

- MIDI UART with MPU-401 interface

As if this weren't enough, the Telecommander has no jumpers on the card. Everything is configured with software, and the configuration windows work quite nicely.

Wiring Your Office for CT

Since the Telecommander uses your existing telephone line, there's no need for wiring work, except for connecting the Telecommander card to your phone line and telephone with the cables included in the package to the microphone (included in the package) and to your own speakers. It's all illustrated and explained step by step in Telecommander's excellent Comprehensive Installation Guide.

CT Installation, Configuration, and Testing

Hardware: Installing the Telecommander 3500 Card

To install the Telecommander 3500 card, simply plug the card into an available slot in your computer and turn your machine back on.

Software: Installing the Telecommander Programs

Installing the software is a little more complicated but not much. You must start at a DOS prompt without Windows running. Running the Install program from the diskette in A: copies the appropriate files to your hard drive and then launches Windows to finish the installation and configuration. Every step of the initial installation is carefully described and illustrated in the Telecommander Comprehensive Installation Guide. The Windows portions start in Chapter 2 of the Telecommander User's Guide (also referred to as the Diamond User's Guide to Telephony).

The automatic configuration method using all defaults will get you up and running within a few minutes. The User's Guide contains excellent step-by-step instructions in Chapters 2 and 3. After completing the installation and configuration, you should be able to make calls from your PC, using the microphone, and to hear calls on speakers or headphones. You can use most of the small speakers or earphones that work with portable CD players. We plugged in an old pair from Radio Shack and they worked just fine. You should also be able to call into the system and have it answer the phone, display the caller ID if you subscribe to CID, and record either a voice or fax message from the caller.

To configure the FaxTalk Messenger software for fax-on-demand and remote access, readi the User's Guide and follow its somewhat terse instructions. These chapters include some step-by-step instructions, but sometimes there doesn't seem to be quite enough explanation or enough step-by-step detail to make it easy to configure FaxTalk Messenger's more complex features. It will take a little more time and some testing for you to get everything just the way you want it. None of this is difficult; it's just complex. In fact, the Telecommander provides so much functionality in a single card and software package that it's difficult to really apprcciate all that this system can do!

We did not attach a CD-ROM device to the 3500, but its ability to play.wav file and caller voices on the speakerphone demonstrated that the audio portions of the card were undoubtedly of high quality. Its suite of audio software includes Media Launcher, Media Rack, Talking Clock, MIDI Player, Wave Player, CD Player, System Mixer, Presto Arranger, Wave Edit, and COMit. These should take care of your audio needs, especially since you probably purchased the Telecommander for its modem and telephony functions rather than its audio and CD-ROM functions.

One caveat is necessary at this point. Although the Telecommander information states that 4 MB of RAM is the "minimum configuration," it apparently doesn't function properly without at least 8 MB of RAM. We found that the voice portions of the FaxTalk Speakerphone software wouldn't properly install in a 4 MB system running only DOS 6.2 and Windows for Workgroups 3.11. Although it appeared to install correctly (no error messages appeared during install), when the Speakerphone software was run, an error message appeared, stating that it could not allocate enough memory to run and that we should remove some programs and try again. We continued in spite of the error message and found that some but not all of the voice functions worked and it wouldn't automatically answer the telephone.

We then put another 4 MB of RAM in the computer and tried again. We did not reinstall the software. We merely ran the FaxTalk setup program from Windows, after closing the FaxTalk program, and chose our settings from the easy-to-use menus. We ran FaxTalk Messenger and FaxTalk Speakerphone again and everything worked perfectly. To our way of thinking, this is proof positive that 4 MB of RAM on your PC is not enough for Windows and CT on the same system!

Summary: Complete Single-Line CT System

The Telecommander 3500 is an amazing combination of hardware and software for only $299. Its inclusion of a voice/fax modem, a CD-ROM controller, and sound card functionality on a single card is quite a combination. The software works well, and does not consume much Windows RAM. For a single-person office where a voice answering system with automatic fax, including fax-on-demand, and remote access are important, the Telecommander 3500 is a great deal. Since it is also a 28.8 Kb modem, you can use it to connect to online services, including the Internet. You can build a whole business around its fax-on-demand features.

The only thing the Telecommander is missing is an automatic link that opens your PIM or Contact Manager to the proper page based on caller ID information. But you can always use your own favorite PIM or CM in another window, with manual cut-and-paste on that information instead.

One-Person ISDN BRI System

In most cases five vendors will be involved in helping you get your ISDN based-CT system completely installed and running:

1. your local phone company

2. an Internet Service Provider

3. an ISDN software provider

4. an ISDN hardware provider and

5. a CT software provider

This assumes that you already have a 386 (or better) PC running Windows 3.1 or WFW 3.11. The rest of this chapter provides a brief overview of the steps you'll need to follow to get an ISDN-based CT system up and running.

For the purposes of this chapter a "home-office CT system" is defined by these specifications:

- Assumption that you want to install the ISDN-based CT system yourself

- single PC-type computer running DOS 6.x and Windows 3.1 or WFW 3.11

- 24-hour use of POTS line via ISDN

- attached multiple POTS phones to the same line (same phone number)

- attach FAX machine to ISDN line or POTS line

- full 128 Kbps throughput with analog phone to ring through one B channel

- Internet connection at full 128 Kbps

- capability of using ISDN phones and other ISDN devices (fax etc.) and

- use of existing analog Modem via ISDN (POTS) line

The ISDN Phone Service

The best approach is to wait to order your service until you know what type of hardware you will be using. That way your equipment vendor can guide your selection of service options that are compatible with your ISDN terminal equipment. However, many options depend on what you want to do with the service and the mix of equipment you will be using.

You will need to contact your local telephone company; usually RBOCs and independents) to determine whether ISDN service is available in your area, and the available options and prices for the service.

ISDN Line Configurations

With ISDN comes the ability to select from virtually thousands of configurations for setting up your phone line. Your ISDN service provider will undoubtedly give you a list of the many possibilities. If you're not planning to use an ISDN telephone and EKTS, you don't really need any of the "fancy" ISDN telephony features just to plug your current analog phone into the POTS jack on your NT1 or TA. However, you will need to be sure to get the basic features you need.

Depending on which regional phone company serves you, you'll probably find that your choice of line configurations is an issue of economics. We recommend that you get only those features you really need. You can always add more later if you need them.

For individual personal/business use at a residence with a connection to the Internet and a POTS phone plugged into the NT1 or TA, the (2B) CSVD+CSVD 64 Kbps data per B channel line configuration with only one voice call at a time allowed should provide good service at a reasonable price.

ISDN Internet Service Providers

ISPs across the United States are scrambling to provide ISDN dial-up service. Some are caught between their ISDN line provider (the phone company) and their hardware and software provider (router hardware and accounting software to automatically track connect time). Many ISPs can't get the lines they need from the phone company at a price they can afford. Most can't get the ISDN hardware and software at prices that they can remarket profitably. In other words, users won't pay high ISDN Internet access fees to their ISPs on top of high ISDN fees charged by the phone company, so ISPs are caught between a rock and a hard place. There's not much you can do about the phone company's fees, but ISP costs are coming down because of competition in the ISDN hardware and software market. So shop around before signing up for an ISDN account with an ISP.

"Shop around." Right. That's easier written than done, you say? It's really fairly easy via the Internet. The following URLs get you to the home pages for the majority of ISPs that offer ISDN connections. You can also ask for help finding the best ISDN ISP in your area on the comp.dcom.isdn news group.

- Dan Kegel's ISDN Internet providers WWW site: http://alumni.caltech.edu/~dank/isdn/isdn_ip.html

- Internet Service Providers organized by services by CyberBiz Productions: http://www.cybertoday.com/cybertoday/ISPs/Products.html#ISDN

Make sure you find out where an ISP is physically located. If the provider is in another town, you may have to pay long-distance charges in addition to its standard connect fees each time you use its service. When recurring service charges rear their ugly heads, they definitely change your outlook on prices.

ISDN Internet Access Software

You will usually need two software resources: a TCP/IP program that connects your computer's TA to the Internet and one or more application programs to navigate the Internet (FTP, WWW, Telnet, Archie, Gopher, News, Mail, etc.). If you're currently using a set of programs to connect to the Internet via SLIP, you may be able to use many of them in the same manner.

If, however, you're using a Winsock-compliant program such as Trumpet Winsock on a PC with Windows for Workgroups 3.11 (WFW), you'll probably be better off switching to Microsoft's TCP/IP-32 software and using PPP instead of SLIP for your WWW browser, FTP program, etc. (This has been discussed more fully in other chapters of this book).

Ask your ISP for help in this area: Many ISPs will provide you with TCP/IP software, since the majority is either freeware or shareware. If you're using a PC with WFW 3.11, you can choose from the following ISDN-compatible software packages, all of which are Winsock 1.1 compatible, and will therefore work with most ISDN PPP applications, as well as the MS TCP/IP-32 software:

- Mosaic
  http://www.compuserve.com:80/prod_services/consumer/consumer.html

- Cello
  http://www.law.cornell.edu/cello/cellotop.html

- Internet-in-a-box
  http://www.compuserve.com:80/prod_services/consumer/consumer.html

- NCSA Mosaic
  http://www.ncsa.uiuc.edu/SDG/SDGIntro.html

- Netscape
  http://www.netscape.com/

- Superhighway Access
  http://www.frontiertech.com/

- TradeWave winWeb
  http://galaxy.einet.net/EINet/clients.html

- WebSurfer
  http://www.netmanage.com/netmanage/apps/web-surfer.html

These packages will all let you navigate the Internet. Specifically they are WWW browsers, but several contain additional applications, such as e-mail, Gopher, and FTP clients. Most have a shareware or freeware test version for you to try. Try as many as you can, and choose the one you like the best.

ISDN Hardware

As you've already learned in previous chapters, you'll need an NT1 and a TA for your ISDN system. Ask your ISP and your trusty hardware vendor about the various models they have used successfully. Refer to earlier chapters for discussions of ISDN NT1s and TAs and for the method to determine which type is best for your situation.

Installing the System

For the purposes of this discussion, we'll assume that you want to install your ISDN system yourself for a single computer with a single analog (POTS) phone plugged into your system. We'll also assume that you need to make calls only when your computer is up and running. In this case you'll want the least expensive ISDN hardware for use primarily with your computer to connect to the Internet and other networks via ISDN. An external device, such as the US Robotics Sportster 128 card, makes the most economic sense in this case as it is among the most affordable of ISDN computer interfaces.

Ordering ISDN Service from Your Local ISDN Provider

Call your local telephone company's information line and get connected to the ISDN order line, if it has one. Most likely it will be in the "business" rather than the "residential" department, but don't let that bother you. Tell the nice person that you want to order an ISDN BRI 2B+D line installed at your house.

After you two determine that you do indeed live in an ISDN service area, get answers for these questions: (assume that you got the following answers)

_____	$150	What is the ISDN installation charge?
_____	$70 flat	What are the monthly charges (basic and usage) for ISDN service?
_____	no	Will your ISDN service be via a repeater?
_____	yes	Will your ISDN service be via an SLC?
_____	Siemens	Which central office ISDN switch does it have (Siemens, AT&T, etc.)?
_____	NI-1	Which protocol does the switch use (i.e., NI-1 [National ISDN-1], AT&T 5ESS Custom, AT&T G3 PBX, or Northern Telecom DMS-100 Custom, Northern Telecom BCS-34 [PVC-1], or other)?
_____	NA	What calling features are available (e.g., EKTS, CACH, etc.)?
_____	yes	Does your ISDN provider offer BRI (2B+D) with two SPIDs?
_____	yes	Does your ISDN provider offer voice service on both B channels on the same BRI service with two SPIDs?

_____   same price   What are the prices of 2B data versus 2B
                                  1data/1 voice vs. 2b both voice or data?

Write the answers down so you can refer to them later. If you like what you see, ask when the service could be installed. There will be a wait while the person checks the installation database. No matter what you are told, you can't do much to change it, so you either order the installation or you don't.

When you place your order, have the phone company representative confirm the installation price and monthly service for the features you have ordered. You will probably be given an order confirmation number and a phone number to dial to check on the progress of your order. Write these down also. You will probably need them. (We're not pessimistic, just realistic.)

While the phone company is getting ready to install your line or turn it on, get ready for the big day by purchasing your equipment, software, and signing up for an ISDN account at your ISP.

Purchasing Your ISDN TA/NT1 Interface Card

If your local hardware vendor doesn't stock the US Robotics Sportster 128 ISDN card, have one ordered for you or get one from a mail-order company, such as the ISDN Warehouse. If you have to wait for delivery, go on to the next step. If you're lucky enough to find the card locally, buy it, take it home, take it out of the box, look at it, put it back in the box, and then give your ISP a ring to make sure you can get that ISDN dial-up account using PPP it promised you last month.

Ordering Your ISDN Internet Service

You did your homework and The ISP is supposed to have the service available at a price that seemed OK at the time. Check the price again and be sure to ask about setup charges and monthly charges or connect-time charges. Also ask whether two B channel BONDing or MLPPP service is available and what it costs. Write everything down immediately. If everything still looks good, place your order and find out when the ISP can have their end ready.

Bear in mind that few ISPs have automated the ISDN setup on their end as they have for SLIP accounts. It may take as much as 30 minutes for an ISP network person to configure an account for you after getting the magical "round-tuit."

The ISP will probably want to know what TA and NT1 you are using in addition to what software you will use to dial up and connect your PPP link. You say that you're using a Sportster 128 card with built-in NT1 on your 486-66 with WFW 3.11 and the MS TCP/IP-32 stack, and the network person should be happy.

If for some reason he or she says that the Internet server (hardware or software) doesn't work well with your planned system, ask for a better suggestion. Then listen, write what you hear down, and ask for free help in installing and configuring it. The system specified here has not been bashed on comp.dcom.isdn and several people have said it works fine for them. Therefore if the ISP has trouble with it, you may want to call another ISP. If the ISP will help you install and configure another card or software with the same features for the same price, give it a try as long as you get a guarantee that it will meet your specifications and that you will get a refund if it doesn't.

The ISP will probably tell you that it can be ready for you in a couple of days, which is sooner than you need. Give them the installation date for your ISDN service and ask whether you can call back when it gets installed and you get your card installed in your computer. The ISP will say, "Sure."

ISDN Service: Wiring, Installation, Configuration, and Testing

Wiring Your Home for ISDN

In this installation scenario the house has only one POTS telephone currently installed. This leaves a second pair of wires in the normal four-wire cable to use for your ISDN service. Now everything you read will tell you that you should use only twisted-pair wire for ISDN. Although this is true, most standard house wires will support ISDN and POTS with no crossover at all. It doesn't hurt to give it a try. Of course, you can always buy a few meters of four-wire twisted-pair phone cable at your local Radio Shack or hardware store and run it from your demarc to the room where your computer is located.

You may be a little worried about getting shocked when dealing with your telephone wiring. It's possible, but only when the telephone rings. The current is approximately 110 volts but the amperage is low, so unless you're wearing a pacemaker, it should just tingle a lot and scare you. Don't do any wiring standing on a ladder unless you can avoid touching the bare metal of the wires or the screw posts with your bare skin or unshielded metal tools. Use common sense and you should be just fine.

Whether you use existing wiring or a new cable, there needs to be two wires at the demarc to connect to the ISDN line the phone company installs. You need to put either an RJ-11 or an RJ-45 jack on the other end of the cable next to your computer. If you are using your existing house phone wiring, you can purchase a double-RJ-11 wall jack plate to replace your existing single-jack plate. Simply wire the existing two POTS wires (usually red and green) to one of the jacks and the other two wires (usually black and yellow) to the other jack, making sure that you use the inside (middle) two terminals on the jack. Test the POTS phone to make sure that it "breaks" the dial tone and will call out on your existing POTS line.

If you're using a new cable, you can purchase an RJ-11 jack that attaches to the wall or one that looks like the female equivalent of an RJ-11 plug that fits on the end of the cable itself. Most good electronics stores carry these.

To test the integrity of the second pair of wires (the ones you are going to use for your ISDN line), plug your POTS phone into the jack with the second pair. Go out to the demarc and detach your current POTS wires (red and green?) from their connectors. Replace them with the other pair (black and yellow?). Go back inside and try dialing out on the phone. If it doesn't break the dial tone, go back outside and reverse the black and yellow wires and try again. If this still doesn't work you may have a short in the black-and-yellow wire pair.

You can test this directly with a volt/ohm meter by twisting the black and yellow wires together at the demarc, after removing them from the screw posts, and using the ohm meter on the other ends (at the RJ-11 jack inside) to see whether you get any resistance. It's really quite straightforward.

After your wiring passes the tests, you are ready for the telephone company to connect the ISDN line. For a comprehensive look at ISDN wiring, contact the North American ISDN Users' Forum (NIUF) at 301-975-2937 or e-mail dawn@isdn.ncsl.nist.gov and request the ISDN Wiring Guide for Residential and Small Businesses. It will tell you much more than you probably care to know, but it may make for interesting conversation at your next ISDN users group meeting.

ISDN Installation by the Phone Company

The simplest case for ISDN installation is when you live within 18,000 feet of one of the phone company's ISDN switches, you have only a single POTS number at your house, and your local cable bundle has an unused cable pair suitable for ISDN. Just about all the phone company has to do in this case is get on its computer and digitally flip a few switches to connect everything and test it up to your house connection. The phone company will then send an installation person to your house to connect the two wires of your existing cable to the proper screw posts in your demarc and test the ISDN line with a really cool ISDN line tester (all $3000+ worth).

However, if you have your wiring ready the installer will usually connect it at the demarc and may even go inside and test it for you for free. Don't assume anything, though, since many of the RBOCs charge $35 or more just to walk into through your front door and charge $15 every quarter of an hour ($1 per minute) after that.

If you have your wiring all ready, your computer running, and your Sportster 128 card all set up, you can try using your POTS phone plugged into the Sportster 128 card to see whether the ISDN line works. Before trying this, start your computer by turning it completely off and turning back on after all of the wiring is completed and plugged in. This ensures that the Sportster 128 looks at your ISDN line and properly runs the RXLOADER and other drivers. If all of them load without error messages, your POTS line should work, and you should be able to use your ISDN line for Internet calls after you configure your Internet software with your ISP's help.

Just a word or two about your friendly phone company ISDN installer. Since ISDN is quite new and used predominantly by businesses, most of the ISDN installers are from the business department rather than the residential department. They are generally very knowledgeable and esperiences in dealing with ISDN systems. You'll probably find them extremely polite and quite accommodating if you treat them with respect and in a businesslike manner. They are more used to installing larger systems for businesses than with dealing with hundreds of irate homeowners' noisy phone line problems every time it rains. They really want your ISDN line to work well and will do everything they can to see that it does.

ISDN TA/NT I Interface Card Installation and Testing

Your Sportster 128 card arrived today and you can't wait to plug it into your computer, flip the power switch, and start communicating at 128 Kbps over the Internet. Well, sorry, but you will have to wait just a little while longer. Installation and configuration is not a trivial matter.

Whether to wait for your ISDN line to be installed before you install your Sportster 128 card is a sort of Catch-22 situation. You can't completely test the ISDN line inside your house without the SL card up and running, and you can't completely test the card without a working ISDN line. You can, however, partially test the SL card without a working ISDN line, so you may as well get as far as you can before the phone company installer arrives.

Unless you are a hardware expert or incredibly lucky, installation, setup, and checkout of your Sportster 128 card will take you anywhere from several hours to a few days. This is not to say that anything is wrong with the card; installing network cards is complicated by IRQs, I/O base addresses, shared memory addresses, memory managers, DPMS, and network batch files. Working through each of these takes time, especially when you're doing it for the first time.

The Quick Start Up Guide for the Sportster 128 card takes you step by step through the installation and configuration process, and the online Reference

Guide contains examples of files for WFW as well as other networks. We'll quickly take you through the main steps to show you how complex it is.

Note: The step numbers that follow do not necessarily correspond to the step numbers in the Sportster 128 Quick Start Up Guide.

Step 1

This isn't in the Sportster 128 guide. Make a backup of your AUTOEXEC.BAT, CONFIG.SYS, WIN.INI, SYSTEM.INI, and PROTOCOL.INI files on another directory of your hard disk, as well as on a floppy disk. Several changes will be made in these files during installation and setup, and you want to make sure that you can get back to square one if things get too fouled up.

Step 2

Install the Sportster 128 card in your computer, following the directions.

Step 3

If your ISDN line hasn't been installed, skip the section on plugging the RJ-45 plug of the cable into the U interface on the card. By the way, a standard RJ-11 plug will plug into an RJ-45 jack just fine. Since the ISDN line uses only the middle two wires — in any order, it seems — just about any phone wire with RJ-11 plugs on both ends will work with ISDN. To be on the safe side though, you should keep the wire colors the same throughout your wiring: that is, red to red, green to green, etc.

Step 4

Plug your POTS phone into the RJ-11 jack on the card. Of course, it won't work unless you have the ISDN line installed.

Step 5

Turn your computer on. It's the red switch on the side, button on the front, toggle switch on the front: Keep looking; you'll find it.

Step 6

Install a memory manager. You're probably already using EMM386 with your WFW, or you may be using QEMM386 or another program. The idea is to free up at least 550 megabytes of conventional memory so that the installation program for the Sportster 128 software can run. It will help your system's overall performance to use a memory manager. This step may take you a while if you're not familiar with DOS and Windows. You can check your system's available memory from DOS by typing MEM /C at the DOS prompt and looking at the number after "Largest executable program size" to see whether it is 550,000 or larger. If it isn't, you can run MEMMAKER (if you have DOS 6.x) from the DOS prompt (without having Windows running) and let it try to get you some more conventional memory space.

Step 7

After you have freed enough memory, you can install the Sportster 128 network software. It is a two-step process, but maybe it will be integrated into a single-step some day. Just follow the directions in the Quick Start Up Guide. Phase 2 is going to ask you for the information about your ISDN service, which you obtained from your phone company order line person when he o she confirmed your installation date and your own imagination.

Step 8

Run the RXSETUP program again and choose its board diagnostics routines to let it find any conflicts. Since it made the settings, it probably won't find any problems at this time. If it does, try changing and testing them, one at a time.

Step 9

This step tests the ISDN line itself and can't be used until you have your ISDN line installed and the phone company says it is working properly. These diagnostics actually test the line all the way to the phone company's switch and back.

Step 10

This steps leads you through performing self-call testing and setup for remote calling. The instructions are clear in the Guide.

Step 11

Setting up the connection protocol is a tricky step. For this step to work, you must first install the Sportster 128 card and the TCP/IP-32 network driver in the WFW networks section.

Installing the Sportster 128 card and TCP/IP-32 into WFW

Before you can completely configure the Sportster 128 card, you must let WFW know it exists and install the TCP/IP-32 stack as its protocol. You then need to run Windows and use the Drivers section of the Windows Setup/Options/Change Network Settings window to add your Sportster 128 card and install the TCP/IP-32 driver. When you click the Drivers button, you will see a window with buttons to Add Protocol and Add Adapter. The Sportster 128 is the adapter and the TCP/IP-32 is the protocol that you need to add. Add the adapter first, then select it and add the protocol to it. Click the help button if you need it. It's very comprehensive.

Now you can complete the connection protocol portion of the Sportster 128 setup as shown in the Quick Start Up Guide. Follow the instructions very, very carefully and select the PPP option when possible for a standard 64 Kbps one B channel. If your ISP has ML/PPP at 128 Kbps, select it after discussing it with your ISP.

At this point, you are instructed to accept the settings and press ESC to exit the RXSETUP program, which saves the settings.

Step 12

You are now finished configuring your Sportster 128 card and WFW. However, there may be some confusion on the modification of your CONFIG.SYS and AUTOEXEC.BAT files and the creation of STARTNET.BAT. The Sportster 128 Quick Start Up Guide isn't very clear about what goes where.

What needs to be accomplished is simple, in theory. First, your computer must keep from using the part of its memory that the Sportster 128 card needs for its scratch RAM buffer space. It does this when you add the RAM and X=####-#### sections to the EMM386 line in your CONFIG.SYS file, as shown in line 3. The DOS Protected Mode Services Device driver must be loaded. Finally, the Sportster 128 RXBUFFER must be loaded. The following CONFIG.SYS file works for the authors:

1. DEVICE=C:\DOS\HIMEM.SYS

2. rem adds RAM and X=####-#### for Sportster 128 card

3. DEVICE=C:\DOS\EMM386.EXE NOEMS RAM X=CC00-CDFF

4. BUFFERS=40,0

5. FILES=80

6. DOS=HIGH,UMB

7. LASTDRIVE=Z

8. FCBS=16,0

9. STACKS=9,256

10. SHELL=C:\DOS\COMMAND.COM /p /e:512

11. rem loads DOS Protected Mode Services Device Driver (DPMS.EXE)

12. DEVICE=C:\RX\DRIVERS\DPMS.EXE

13. rem adds Sportster 128 drivers

14. DEVICEHIGH=C:\RX\DRIVERS\RXBUFFER.SYS /S3FFF

Your CONFIG.SYS file may contain other commands in addition to those shown here. The exact address of the X=####-#### line will be given to you by the RXSETUP program. You can add these commands to your CONFIG.SYS file with the SYSED program in WFW or NOTEPAD, etc.

Next, the RXLOADER program must run and load the RXPCKT.OVL overlay with the /P parameter and set up a DATA file path. It then must use RXCALL to load the PostDrvLoad. After this, you must run the network part of WFW (NET START) and then run Windows. All of this is accomplished in the following four command lines:

- \RX\DRIVERS\RXLOADER C:\RX\BIN\RXPCKT.OVL /PC:\RX\DATA %1

- \RX\RXCALL /PostDrvLoad

- \WINDOWS\net start

- WIN

It would be too simple to put these four lines in your AUTOEXEC.BAT file, and it may not run properly. When the RXLOADER program runs, it checks the status of your ISDN line. If it finds something wrong, it doesn't load the RXPCKT.OVL. When this happens, the RXCALL program aborts. With neither of these loaded, WFW's NET START can't find the Sportster 128 drivers, so it doesn't load properly. Finally, WFW may load but give you network error messages.

The way around all of this is to place the first two lines at the end of your AUTOEXEC.BAT file and the last two in another batch file, such as STARTWIN.BAT. Using this method, your computer automatically boots and starts everything up through the RX drivers. If RXLOADER doesn't load properly, you will see an error message on your screen. You should try running the two RX command lines again to see whether they will work the second try, which they usually do unless your ISDN line is "really dead." Putting just the first two RX lines in another batch file (as in STARTNET.BAT) just for this use is a good idea. You're wondering why this is necessary. Just remember that the ISDN system is relatively new and doesn't work perfectly every time, yet. Timing is important, especially during startup. So second tries are needed some of the time.

After you see that the RX drivers have loaded properly, you simply run the STARTWIN.BAT file to complete your startup. This completes your setup and configuration of your Sportster 128 card, WFW, and your DOS startup files. Now you are ready to get with your ISP to configure your Internet software and ISDN Internet account.

ISDN and Your ISP

Now that you have your ISDN line installed and configured and your Sportster 128 card running smoothly with your WFW system, you're ready to complete your Internet connection. Call and get your ISP to activate the ISDN account that you ordered a few days/weeks ago. You'll need several pieces of information from your ISP to enter into your system:

- the ISP's ISDN phone number   ###-####

- your ISDN account number   ###

- your IP address   123.12.1.###

- your default gateway 123.12.1.###
- your subnet mask 255.255.255.###
- the ISP's DNS (name server) address 198.3.118.11
- your user name yourusername
- your password ********

You will need to put these pieces of information into your TCP/IP-32 configuration via WFW so it can perform the "dial-up" function that you were having Trumpet Winsock perform with your SLIP account. Have your ISP help you with this step.

CT Software for ISDN

At the end of 1995 there were only a few functioning CT software packages for ISDN. Some of the manufacturers of ISDN hardware did provide phone dialer software: For example, US Robotics provides a simple phone dialer with speed dial for the Sportster 128 under Windows 3.1 or WFW. Most of the CT software available for ISDN is targeted at call-center operations rather than at the SOHO market. Most of the current ISDN CT software development is for Win95 and NT.

However, since Microsoft had not yet released its 32-bit TAPI server software, no Win95- or Windows NT-compatible ISDN dialers were available when this book was written. All manufacturers contacted said that they were working on the software and would release their packages shortly after Microsoft released the final 32 bit TAPI software. In the meantime, you can use analog software through your modem if it's plugged into the POTS plug on your ISDN TA or NT1 until the CT software you want is completed in 1996.

Summary: ISDN BRI System

With all the complexities of installing and configuring ISDN components, don't be surprised if everything doesn't work perfectly the first time. Try to be patient and check your setup parameters carefully when you enter them. Proceed deliberately, step by step. Test after each step. Write everything down as if you were the one writing this chapter for someone else to follow for a first-time installation.

To help keep your blood pressure down, don't expect your ISDN service to be up and running as continually and reliably as your tried-and-true POTS line. Accept it as a fact of life that ISDN service is new to everyone — including you and the phone company — and that everyone wants it to be as reliable as possible. But it's a newly developed, highly technical, completely computerized form of digital transmission that will be more susceptible to weather-related problems and other perturbations than POTS lines until all of the kinks are worked out of the system.

Keep the phone company's repair number handy and give them a call whenever you can't call out on the POTS phone plugged into the Sportster 128's POTS jack with your computer is running and the Sportster 128 software properly loaded and functioning. Then be prepared to wait and wonder while your problem is captured, diagnosed, and (we devoutly hope) cured. That's why patience is such a virtue, especially when it comes to ISDN.

Summary

In this chapter we've examined three CT installation scenarios. Starting with a simple one-line, inexpensive analog installation, you should have begun to see and understand that even a little computer telephony can go a long way. We personally think that the Telecommander product covered in the second one-line analog section represents much of the best that CT can bring to your desktop: integrated fax, phone, and voice mail handling, with ready access to call information and tight phone-computer integration. Digital CT is still a mystery at the desktop in many ways, but the pending introduction of Microsoft's 32-bit TAPI interface for telephony and ISDN should bring the same kind of power and capability to digital CT that products like the Telecommander already do for analog CT. We can hardly wait!

Troubleshooting, Tips, and Testing

The amount of time you spend troubleshooting your CT system will depend greatly on whether you installed an analog or an ISDN CT system. The analog telephone system has existed in one form or another for decades; ISDN has been around only for a few years. Only since the meteoric rise in Internet usage began in 1994 has there been a greatly increased interest in ISDN.

Your analog CT system may require some troubleshooting in the area of the modem and the PC's "COM" ports, with their ever-present but difficult-to-set IRQs and memory addresses. Installing your CT software in Windows should be a snap if the developer has done a good job with the Setup program. You won't know until you get into it, unless you've asked around and checked the Internet for anyone who has installed your particular software on your particular hardware configuration (or one very much like it). Such people are usually more than happy to tell you the good, the bad, and the ugly about their experiences, but they can't tell you anything unless you ask—so ask!

The most important thing you can do to keep troubleshooting to a minimum is always to read the manual and all information sheets in the package and to follow instructions very carefully. If you notice something happening that doesn't look right (an error window pops up or something equally subtle), write everything down that led up to the problem and write down the exact wording of the error message, including any error code number(s). This is crucial information you'll be asked to provide when you call the product's technical support line.

The second most important troubleshooting advice we can offer is to be patient and take your time installing your CT hardware and software. Remember that computer telephony is a rapidly evolving, state-of-the-art technology that wasn't even thought of a few short years ago. It does have its occasional rough spots, and problems will show up from time to time. If you're patient and painstaking, you'll be able to survive the occasional bump in the road; if not, you may get derailed by even trivial problems.

Troubleshooting Your Analog CT System Installation

Even though the POTS system is robust and easy to use, you'll still encounter the occasional glitch. More often than not, such problems will wind up traced back to your PC (especially configuration-related issues), your modem, or some of your cabling: Believe it or not, it's seldom the phone system itself that's the problem. Remember the adage about glass houses and stone throwing: It's always wise to check and double-check your own equipment and software before complaining about the phone company.

Analog Telephone Line Problems

Computer-related problems with your analog telephone line can be difficult to detect and identify. The usual CT problems relate to nonfunctioning caller ID and poor line quality (i.e., static, weak signal strength, "crossed" lines, etc.).

Caller ID

If your caller ID won't work, call your local telephone company repair number. If the phone company insists that it's on and functioning properly at the central office and up to your demarc (the box on the outside of your house/office), you must suspect your CT hardware or software. Call the manufacturer's support number and ask for troubleshooting help. It helps to have registered your CT package prior to calling, but we all know that most calls occur while you are installing the package within hours of purchasing it.

Speed Dial

If your speed dialer doesn't complete the call and you don't get an error message back from your modem telling you why, try the following steps:

1. First, check to see that the phone cable is plugged securely into your modem and the telephone wall plate.

2. If it is, unplug it from the modem and attach it to a telephone.

3. Call someone you know or call your local time/temperature service and listen to the quality of the voice on the line.

4. If you can't complete the call or the line is not clear, call your local phone repair service number and tell them that your line is too noisy, weak, or whatever. Don't mention using it with a computer or you may be told that you're paying for residential voice service, not a "conditioned data" line. Work with the repair service to get the problem fixed. Those really nice folks are trying their best to provide you with a clean phone line.

5. If the line sounds fine to you, plug the cable back into your modem and try the speed dialer again.

6. If it still doesn't complete the call, check the CT software's modem setup section to ensure that you have selected the correct communications port and modem type and are sending the modem the correct setup string. It should use the same modem setup string as your other communications program uses.

7. If the settings are correct, suspect your modem. Try using your standard communications software to connect to an online system as you normally do.

8. If this works, the modem is functioning properly, and the problem may lie in your PC's COM port setup. These are discussed briefly in the next section.

COM Port, IRQ, Address, and Other Hardware Conflicts

You should have no problems if you're using only two serial devices on your Windows-based PC, since the DOS BIOS and standard Windows 3.1 COM driver support COM 1, 2, 3, and 4. However, COM 1 and COM 3 share the same IRQ (interrupt) and address, as do COM 2 and 4. This means that you can't use COM 1 and 3 or COM 2 and 4 simultaneously. Therefore, if you have a serial mouse on COM 1 and a modem selected as COM 4 (even if it's an internal modem card), you won't be able to plug a caller ID device into the second serial plug on your I/O card (usually setup as COM 2) and have it work simultaneously with the modem on COM 4.

You may be able to get around this problem by installing an expanded COM port driver, such as KingCOM, TurboCommander, or Cyberdrive, all of which allow you to select up to 12 COM ports. However, before you go running off to install a COM driver, take a deep breath, call the technical support number for your CT package, and ask what to do. Those people have undoubtedly heard the problem before, and have figured out a solution, since most of their users will have the same or a similar configuration to that shown here.

Troubleshooting Your ISDN CT System

The telephone companies are knowledgeable about "standard" phone services, whether they're analog (POTS), switched 56, or T1 service. They're also fairly well versed in the intricacies of that new kid on the block, ISDN — or some of their employees are. At least you'll be able to call your local telephone service provider, ask for ISDN assistance, and eventually find a person who knows what ISDN means.

Shortly after your ISDN BRI service is installed, you will undoubtedly be calling your local ISDN service number. Although the phone company folks install and test your ISDN line, there is many a slip between the order and the final installation. Most of the early problems occur in the provisioning of the line. That is, the phone company failed to turn on the features you ordered. They can check these from their service center via computer, so give them a call if you don't think a feature you ordered is working.

You'll find that the ISDN customer service folks are highly trained and very nice. They are usually the senior people and have been working with digital lines (usually T1s and PBXs) in the business community for years. They will come out to your house or office and test your ISDN line, using your very own connection cable out of the back of your ISDN modem or NT1. That way they can test all of the wiring. When you call them, be sure to write down the service ticket number so you can tell them what it is if you have to call them back to check on the status of your service order. They will ask you for your SPID(s) or your circuit ID number when you call, so have them handy.

ISDN Line Problems

ISDN lines fail differently from analog lines. With an analog line you can get poor voice reception, noisy lines, and even crossover to other conversations. With an ISDN line you occasionally will get a "pop" or "snap" on the line but when an ISDN line fails, it usually doesn't work at all.

If you're not sure whether your ISDN line is down or your NT1 or TA isn't working properly, try plugging your POTS phone into the ISDN jack. If you hear "white noise," the ISDN line is still there, in some fashion. If it is dead calm, obviously the ISDN line is completely out, and it's time to call your local phone company repair number.

If your ISDN drivers try to load and give you a Layer 1 Failure error, something is probably wrong with the ISDN line itself. If you get a Layer 2 Failure error, the problem is probably with the provisioning of the phone company's central office switch for your service.

In testing your TA, you may be instructed to perform a "self-call" test. Some instructions have you call your secondary ISDN number via your primary number. For some reason this may not work, although if you try to call your primary ISDN number, it will work. Try both and see what happens. This is probably a function of the way the ISDN service is provisioned for data. Call your ISDN provider if neither works and you can't get any data call to function.

Most TA software packages include a "logging" function, which is useful in tracking down problems. The log files keep a running account of what happens during your ISDN sessions and generally contain the type of information shown in the following example, taken from US Robotics Sportster 128 ISDN log):

08/26/95 11:18:45 *** Logging STARTED ***

08/26/95 11:18:45 SecureLink(TM) ISDN Adapter, Version 3.00b Feb 09 1995

08/26/95 11:18:45 TAPI Version 3.00b Feb 09 1995

08/26/95 11:18:45 Switch type: National ISDN-1

08/26/95 11:18:45 Board 1:

08/26/95 11:18:45 S/T interface, iobase = $2a0, IRQ = 11, address = $cc00

08/26/95 11:18:45 SPID #1 = 512123123401

08/26/95 11:18:45 SPID #2 = 512123123501

08/26/95 11:18:46 Physical layer connection established for board 1

08/26/95 11:18:46 Layer 2 connection established for board 1, TEI 105

08/26/95 11:18:46 Layer 2 connection established for board 1, TEI 106

08/26/95 11:18:46 SPID #1 accepted for board 1

08/26/95 11:18:46 SPID #2 accepted for board 1

08/26/95 11:18:46 Initialization successful.

08/26/95 11:18:58 Attempting to establish PPP connection to REALTIME.

08/26/95 11:19:01 Call established (64 Kbps) to REALTIME at 3774141.

08/26/95 11:19:01 PPP - Authentication Complete to REALTIME.

08/26/95 11:19:01 PPP - IP Link UP to REALTIME (213.88.3.133)

08/26/95 11:19:01   Local IP Address (213.88.3.124) was configured.

08/26/95 11:20:03 Call down (64 Kbps) to REALTIME at 3774141.

08/26/95 11:20:03   Reason -> NORMAL.

08/26/95 11:20:03 PPP connection terminated to REALTIME.

08/26/95 12:18:03 Attempting to establish PPP connection to REALTIME.

08/26/95 12:18:04 Call established (64 Kbps) to REALTIME at 3774141.

08/26/95 12:18:04 PPP - Authentication Complete to REALTIME.

08/26/95 12:18:04 PPP - IP Link UP to REALTIME (213.88.3.133)

08/26/95 12:18:04   Local IP Address (213.88.3.124) was configured.

08/26/95 12:19:07 Call down (64 Kbps) to REALTIME at 3774141.

08/26/95 12:19:07   Reason -> NORMAL.

08/26/95 12:19:07 PPP connection terminated to REALTIME.

The log will include any error messages that happened to occur during operation. Ideally, these will be defined in your card's user manual along with suggestions on how to remedy the problem. You can always give the vendor, manufacturer, or your ISDN TA a call on your working POTS line to help you diagnose and repair your problem.

IRQ, Address, SRAM, and Other Hardware Conflicts

Newer PCs all feature various built-in system diagnostics and settings designed to provide faster, smoother operation. When you start adding complicated network cards and drivers, however, some conflicts will invariably occur. The standard IRQ, I/O address, and SRAM (scratch RAM) conflicts are usually noticed by the installation program for the ISDN card. Alternatively, you can use the Microsoft Diagnostics program (MSD.EXE) or a Windows-based diagnostic program (such as Quarterdeck's WinProbe) to examine and document your hardware and software settings and usage and to then set the card to avoid conflicts. Warning: This will sometimes mean rearranging other system components to make room for new cards that support only IRQs that may already be taken.

Conflicts with BIOS and CMOS settings are much more difficult to find. This generally requires using a process of elimination via testing one setting at a time. Since this demands a complete reboot of your computer each time, it can be quite time-consuming. Comments from users of various systems point to the following known conflicts, so you might start by disabling these if they are present on your computer: Auto Config Function—AMIBIOS ADVANCED CHIPSET SETUP— and Hidden Refresh—AMIBIOS ADVANCED CHIPSET SETUP. These two functions, when enabled, can keep WFW from loading properly with the ISC SecureLink card and NDIS drivers. When they are disabled, the systems works just fine, with no noticeable degradation in functionality—which makes you wonder what enabling these two "features" really did in the first place.

ROM shadowing in a Compaq ProSignia seemed to cause memory conflict problems when the drivers for a Digi PC IMAC/4 board under the Windows NT Advanced Server were installed.

If you don't know how to check your CMOS settings, give your hardware vendor a call for help. Vendors deal with these kinds of problems every time they change a modem or other I/O card in a PC. If you know enough about it to fix it yourself, remember to write everything down on screen prints of the initial settings, to change only one setting at a time, and to cold boot your computer after each change. A "three-fingered salute" (pressing Ctrl+Alt+Delete to force a reboot) may not reset the hardware, and pushing your Reset button may not completely clear the RAM in some computers. When in doubt, turn the machine off for at least 10 seconds before restarting.

Windows for Workgroups and Windows NT Problems and Solutions

If you installed a network ISDN TA/NT1 card, you may run into a problem in which your network causes your TA to establish periodic ISDN connections to your ISP (by periodic, we mean every one to five minutes). If your minimum timeout is one minute and your system automatically reconnects one minute after it has been disconnected, you will be "online" for about 30 out of every 60 minutes. This rapidly adds up on the charge side of bills from both your ISDN and Internet providers.

Several causes and a couple of solutions have been suggested for this problem. On systems using Windows NT, the "browser" is looking for other NT machines in your workgroup or domain. Since you apparently have an ISDN interface that looks like an NDIS interface, your ISDN interface tries, when it sends local subnet broadcasts, to call the other end of the line to send each broadcast along.

The solution is really easy, since NT has a neat configuration screen in the Network Control Panel. Start Control Panel and open the Network panel. Then click on Bindings. This screen divides its focus between a left- and right-hand side: Things on the left are services, protocols, etc.; things on the right represent interfaces and lower-level protocols. If the light bulb is on, the software pieces are talking to one another; if the bulb is dim, they aren't. You want to turn off all bulbs other than TCP/IP that lead to your ISDN interface. Just figure out which ones these are and double-click on them.

On WFW systems, the problem doesn't appear to be the "browser" as in NT and the solution isn't as simple. The only solution one user has found is to use the Network Settings section of the Windows Setup program to turn off the sharing for both files and printers on the ISDN-equipped PC. This stops spurious connections, but it also keeps other PCs from sharing files and printers, which is why you installed WFW in the first place. Fortunately, this problem doesn't occur on Windows 95 networks.

Tips for Better Use from Your ISDN System

Even though you may have shot all the trouble on your system, there are numerous ways to tweak and tune an ISDN hookup and also some innovative ways to get better use from this technology. In the sections that follow, we'll examine some tricks you can use to get the most from your expensive, but fast, new digital communications services.

Replacing POTS phones versus Using ISDN?

If one person is talking on an ISDN phone and someone in another room picks up another ISDN phone and attempts to access the B channel in use, would he or she be denied access to that B channel? Yes. How is the whole family supposed to talk to Grandma on their ISDN phones? Use a speakerphone, or does everybody crowd around the same handset? The answer is crowd around the same handset, unless a multiparty call is set up, and there are enough ISDN numbers to service each handset being used.

These are some of the reasons that ISDN isn't suggested for general home use. If you really want to use your ISDN BRI service for all your home needs, you can install a TA or an NT1 with a POTS jack. Then you can plug the existing house phone wiring into one of the POTS jacks (instead of into the demarc outside your house), thereby keeping your house phone system analog up to the TA or NT1. As long as your TA or NT1 remains powered up, your home analog phones will work the same way they did previously, except that they won't ring when somebody calls on one of your ISDN line numbers! That's because the ring voltage isn't usually passed on from the TA or NT1, another big reason not to replace your home POTS with ISDN just yet. Also, every time the power goes out, you'd lose your phones along with everything else plugged into the power grid.

If you are using only ISDN telephones with the proper wiring and the necessary number of S/T jacks on TAs in your house, ISDN allows for multiple directory numbers and multiple call appearances for each number. With a keyset feature option, the same number can appear on two phones, but for both to be on the same call at once, a conference bridge is required (this capability is automatically supplied with this feature). Also note that it requires two SPIDs and is usually implemented with two lines, though two SPIDs can share a line and do this.

When you "bridge on" to the call by pressing a lighted button, the CO switch automatically picks out a conference bridge. This is required because ISDN sets are digital. On an analog line you can put two phones in parallel and their microphone audio signals (analog) will add together, creating a composite. That wouldn't work on a digital line: adding 1s and 0s together would create random noise, at best. So the switch "magically" inserts a bridge when you press a common line appearance on two sets.

Using an Analog Modem with ISDN Service

You can plug your current analog modem into the POTS jack of either your NT1 or your TA if you have a combined TA/NT1 and use it in exactly the same manner that you currently use it for outgoing calls. If you have a fax or voice/fax modem, you can use it the same way. If you're using an ISDN "modem" with voice/fax features, you can put your analog modem on the shelf.

Only the calls receiving changes with some NT1s and TAs: Most fax and modem cards or stand-alone devices rely on analog ring voltage to initiate their answering responses. Some NT1s and many of the combined TA/NT1 cards don't pass analog ring voltage (about 110 volts) through to the analog circuit. This keeps the fax or modem from knowing that there is the phone is "ringing" for them.

If you receive faxes only after someone calls you on your voice line to tell you it's on the way, you can always manually run your fax software and click the manual Receive button when you hear your TA card "ring." If you really need unattended fax receipt on an ISDN line, you should either purchase an NT1 that passes the ring voltage through to your analog fax machine or purchase an ISDN fax device that plugs into the S/T jack on your TA.

Minimizing Connect Time

Since your ISDN service can connect in just a second or three, you don't need to stay continuously connected to the Internet during an online session. If you set the timeout on your ISDN card's software to a very short interval, you won't need to stay on line while you're reading information you've just downloaded; when you move your mouse or otherwise request new data, the interface will automatically reestablish your connection and continue your session. This means that you may need to stay connected only 20 or 30 percent of the time you're online, and you can save on ISP connect-time and ISDN talk-time charges.

Here's an important word of warning, though: Many service providers (both Internet and phone company varieties) use billing increments of one minute, with a one-minute charge minimum. Some phone companies charge only a penny a minute for ISDN talk time but charge 25 cents for call setup. In this case you'd want to set a 25-minute timeout because you could spend $6.25 for time (or more, since ISDN can actually set up and tear down as many as 30 calls a minute!) that would otherwise cost you only 25 cents.

Once you've considered the implications of the charges from your service providers, you can decide how to handle timeout and reconnect issues. That's when your access software's timeout settings really come into play. If you're being charged by the minute, without call setup charges, this generally won't pose a problem, because most programs can handle one-minute intervals without a problem. But if you're being charged by the second, you might need to find software with a shorter timeout than yours currently supports, or try to get your software provider to reduce the minimum setting in its next upgrade, in order to help control costs. All things considered, a timeout setting of 10 seconds should be reasonable for an ISDN line.

Using an off-line news reader can also greatly reduce connect-time charges if you subscribe to many newsgroups. The FreeAgent news reader from Forté (http://www.forteinc.com) quickly downloads article headers from whatever newsgroups you select. You can scroll through them while it is still downloading others. You can instruct it to download the bodies of selected articles while you are reading others. It even keeps a database of headers and articles on your hard disk so that you can read them at your leisure after you have disconnected from the ISDN provider.

Download large files during low traffic times on the Internet. Even though your ISDN line provides fast transfer capability, your overall transfer rate may be slowed by bottlenecks on the Internet itself or on the server where you're downloading the file. Try to determine an "off-peak time" for that server and proceed accordingly.

Turn the image display off on your Web browser. Of course, images will display much more quickly via your ISDN line, but they still take time. If you want to see them, you can always just click the images button (or some similar command) and they'll be quickly transferred and displayed. But text still moves more quickly than graphics, even at ISDN speeds!

ISDN Line Testing Equipment

Although you may want to own your own BRI analyzer, the truth is that you will probably never need one. If you suspect that your line isn't working properly, a quick call to your phone company's repair line will have it checked and fixed quickly in most cases and at a much lower cost than the lowest priced BRI analyzer. The only BRI analyzer we've found that costs under $3000 is the PA 100 protocol analyzer at $2495. Until it arrived, ISDN protocol analyzers had been priced from $8000 to more than $35,000. This makes it difficult to justify such a purchase, especially if you need one just occasionally.

However, without a protocol analyzer it's almost impossible to resolve the "finger pointing" that commonly occurs between the service provider and the equipment vendor or the customer. If you're employed in a company that is plagued by ISDN problems that drag on for months, a knowledgeable technician with a protocol analyzer may be able to resolve the problem quickly and at a lower cost than the time and productivity that might otherwise be lost.

The UPA 100 is a compact unit (9.5" x 7.5" x 1.5") that connects to the serial port of an IBM-PC compatible or Macintosh computer. It captures the messages passing between the subscriber's equipment and the network, decodes them into plain English, displays them on the screen, and places them in a buffer for later analysis. Circuit-switched and packet-switched decodes of national ISDN, Northern Telecom DMS 100 Custom, and AT&T #5ESS ISDN are supported.

Summary

The best advice for keeping CT problems to a minimum, solving the ones you do have quickly, and maximizing CT use can be simply stated: Ask for help from your CT product manufacturer, your local telephone company, the folks on comp.dcom.modems, and your ISP whenever necessary. If you're using ISDN, add your ISDN hardware vendor and the folks on the comp.dcom.isdn users group to that list.

Remember, nobody can help you diagnose a problem that you can't explain in adequate detail. Nobody will want to even try to help you if you say, "Yes, there was an error message on the screen, but I don't remember what it said and I didn't write it down." Write everything down, including the circumstances under which the problem occurred, your hardware and software configuration, and anything else that might possibly affect the situation. Let the experts ignore the parts that aren't germane to the problem. Good luck! If you persevere, you should be able to get over the hump.

Frequently Asked
Questions and Answers

The questions and answers in this chapter have been excerpted primarily from various Internet newsgroups and online sources. We have edited this material to make it more useful to novice users. The caller ID information was excerpted from Rochelle Communication, Inc.'s WWW FAQ (http://www.rochelle.com/). Much of the ISDN information was excerpted from the comp.dcom.isdn newsgroup and its FAQ.

Our thanks to all of the subscribers to comp.dcom.isdn for their great questions and cogent answers. Special thanks are required for a few of the professionals who always seem to be available to patiently answer the difficult ISDN questions, day after day, with great skill and forbearance: Chuck Sederholm, IBM Corp.; Laurence V. Marks, IBM Corp.; Fred R. Goldstein, Bolt Beranek & Newman Inc.; and Pat Coghlan, Newbridge.

Caller ID Questions and Answers

Where does caller ID originate?

Caller ID originates at your local telephone company.

What type of information is included in the caller ID signal?

The caller ID signal includes date, time, telephone number (including area code), and name (where available).

Has interstate (long-distance) caller ID been approved?

Yes. The FCC mandated that interstate caller ID begin December 1, 1995.

If I call-forward my phone, will I still capture the caller ID information?

No. The number to which you forward your calls will receive the caller ID, provided that number's line has caller ID service.

I have call-waiting. When I'm on one line and my second line rings, will I receive caller ID on the second call?

You won't if you use the telephone switchhook to "answer" the second call. You will receive the caller ID if you hang up the first call and allow the second call to ring twice.

Will caller ID work with my telephone system?

Caller ID will work if your phone system is a key system; that is, if you push a key for an immediate outside line.

Can I use caller ID on my ISDN or T1?

ISDN and T1 are digital, ground-start (not loop-start) technology and feature ANI and DNIS (Dial Number Inward Service) but not caller ID. You can get caller ID if you terminate a T1 into your business and convert it back to loop-start service via a channel bank.

Why can't I get caller ID on a PBX?

The reason is that most PBXs use ground-start (not loop-start) lines. However, some PBXs do have loop-start lines terminated in them. In this situation caller ID would be available in front of the PBX but not behind it. *Note*: Once the lines go through the PBX, caller ID information would be lost.

Can I get caller ID on my DID (Direct Inward Dial) lines?

Caller ID is available for Centrex (a.k.a. Plexar) DID lines only.

Can I get caller ID on my Centrex lines?

Yes.

What happens if my customer is calling from a large corporation with a PBX that has 50 or so outgoing lines? Which number will I get?

You may not get the main (i.e., switchboard) number from that company. It depends on that company's PBX. If you have name capability with your caller ID service, you should see the name of the company regardless of the line used by the PBX.

Is ANI the same as CID?

No. ANI (Automated Number Identification) is a technology used on digital lines (i.e., ISDN, PBX, T-1).

ISDN Questions and Answers

Can I put more than two ISDN devices on my BRI line?

I would like to put three ISDN phones (using the S/T bus) on one BRI ISDN line; however, I was told by Ameritech that no more than two devices which use the B channel. I know that you can't use more than two B channels at one time, but what I don't understand is since I will not use more than one or two phones at the same time, why can't I have up to eight ISDN phones installed? Don't they just monitor the D-channel for signaling information and use up only one B channel when you pick up the phone? By the way, I am on an AT&T 5ESS switch, if that makes any difference.

Your problem is not a technical one, it is a policy issue. Your technical assumptions are entirely correct, and you should be able to have eight phones on an AT&T 5E provide BRI.

AT&T has set a policy that it will not provide a service to a customer served by one switch type when that service is not available to all switch types. Therefore since a DMS 100 is not capable of more than two devices, AT&T will not offer more than two on any switch type.

The logic is that this will prevent someone served by a DMS100 from demanding a FX'd line off a 5E. Also, we understand that DMS100s are much cheaper, and AT&T doesn't want people to get used to the superior 5E. We hope that this policy will go away when (and if) NI2 becomes available on the DMS (but we wouldn't bet on it). We also imagine that AT&T hopes that people will buy more lines.

Is it possible to connect more than one NT1 to the U point/ISDN two-wire line?

No. The U loop terminates a single NT1 (network termination) device per ISDN U line. Therefore if the NT1 functionality is built into the ISDN equipment, a telephone set, or a data terminal adapter, no additional NT1s can be attached to that ISDN U line. The ISDN equipment with the integrated NT1 would need to have an S/T bus output connection to allow additional ISDN equipment to be attached via an S/T interface.

As a product example, IBM's TE 7845 provides integrated NT1 functionality together with an analog POTS connection that can use one of the ISDN B channels for voice. The second B channel is then made available via an S/T bus connector so an additional ISDN S/T bus device can be connected. In general, the only way to support multiple ISDN devices on a single ISDN U line is by using an NT1 and then connecting the multiple ISDN equipment at the S/T bus connector.

Can my existing analog telephone lines be used for ISDN?

According to Bellcore, usually yes. Most of the analog lines currently in service do not require any special conditioning. However, if a line has load coils or bridge taps on it, your telephone company installation person will be able to "decondition" the line for ISDN use, usually without your knowledge or intervention. In North America around 90 percent of existing telephone lines need no "deconditioning" in order to be used for ISDN BRI service.

How does ISDN compare to regular (analog) telephone lines?

A "single" ISDN BRI line may act like two independent analog phone lines with two numbers and be capable of handling data transmission at 64 Kbps per line (B channel). Depending on the central office equipment, many "special" features may be available. BRI ISDN phones can support key-set features (EKTS), such as you would expect to get on an office PBX, such as:

- multiple directory numbers per line

- multiple lines per directory number

- automated number identification

- conferencing features

- forwarding features

- voice mail features

- speed call

- call park

- call pickup

- ring again

- status displays

Is Caller ID available on ISDN?

Caller ID is an analog telephone service. On ISDN's digital service most telephone companies offer ANI, which is comparable to CID. The availability of ANI for residential ISDN BRI service depends on the capabilities of the local phone network and legislation allowing or disallowing ANI. The availability of ANI relies on the underlying switching protocol used by the switches that make up the telephone system. If ANI is available to your ISP, it should be used to help secure your

Internet account. Having the ISP's system check to see whether the ISDN call requesting your account is coming from either of your ISDN phone numbers greatly increases your security. It's practically impossible for someone who has stolen your account name and password to get around the ANI number check.

What is National ISDN?

Because of the breadth of the international ISDN standards, vendors of ISDN equipment can make a number of implementation choices. Given the number of choices vendors can make, different vendors' equipment may not interoperate. In the United States Bellcore has released a series of specifications to try to avoid these interoperability problems. These are the national ISDN specifications. Contact the Bellcore ISDN hot line for more information.

What is the NIUF?

North American ISDN Users Forum (NIUF) is an organization of ISDN-interested parties, coordinated by NIST (National Institute of Standards and Technology), which promotes the use of ISDN and provides a great deal of information about ISDN to anyone who asks for it. Contact:

NIUF Secretariat

National Institute of Standards and Technology

Building 223, Room B364

Gaithersberg, MD 20899

301-975-2937 voice

301-926-9675 fax

301-869-7281 BBS 8N1 2400 bps

What is ATM?

ATM (Asynchronous Transfer Mode) is a switching/transmission technique whereby data is transmitted in small, fixed-sized cells (5-byte header, 48-byte payload). The cells lend themselves both to the time-division multiplexing characteristics of the transmission media and the packet-switching characteristics desired of data networks. At each switching node, the ATM header identifies a "virtual path" or "virtual circuit" for which the cell contains data, enabling the switch to forward the cell to the correct next-hop trunk. The "virtual path" is set up through the involved switches when two endpoints wish to communicate. This type of switching can be implemented in hardware, almost essential when trunk speeds range from 45 Mb/s to 1 Gb/s.

One use of ATM is to serve as the core technology for a new set of ISDN offerings known as broadband ISDN (B-ISDN). For more information, read comp.dcom.cell-relay. This group has a Frequently Asked Questions list; it is posted to news.answers and is in various archives as cell-relay-faq.

What is B-ISDN?

Broadband ISDN refers to services that require channel rates greater than a single primary rate channel. Although this does not specifically imply any particular technology, ATM will be used as the switching infrastructure for B-ISDN services.

B-ISDN services are categorized as either interactive or distribution.

Interactive B-ISDN services are of three types:

- conversational, such as videotelephony or video conferencing

- messaging, such as electronic mail for images, video, and graphics

- retrieval, such as news retrieval, and remote education.

Distribution B-ISDN services are of two types:

- without user presentation control, such as electronic newspaper and TV distribution

- with user presentation control, such as remote education, teleadvertising, and news retrieval

What is BONDing?

BONDing a set of protocols developed by U.S. inverse multiplexer that supports communication over a set of separate channels as if their bandwidth were combined into a single coherent channel. For example, it supports a single 128 Kbps data stream over two Kbps channels.

The specification defines a way of calculating relative delay among multiple network channels and ordering data such that what goes in one end comes out the other. Most vendors also have their own proprietary methods that usually add features and functions not present in BONDing mode 1, the mode used for recent interoperability testing among vendors.

What is a SPID? Why won't my ISDN device work without one?

SPIDs (Service Profiles IDs) are used to identify what sorts of services and features the switch provides to the ISDN device. Currently SPIDs are used only for circuit-switched service (as opposed to packet-switched). Annex A to ITU recommendation Q.932 specifies the (optional) procedures for SPIDs. They are most commonly implemented by ISDN equipment used in North America.

Can I purchase European ISDN devices and use them successfully in the United States?

There are four major problem areas regarding interoperability of ISDN equipment among countries. The first has to do with voice encoding and is a problem only if the equipment is a telephone. Equipment designed for use in North America and Japan uses mu-law encoding when converting from analog to digital, whereas the rest of the world uses A-law. If the equipment has a switch for selecting one or the other of these encoding types, there will not be a problem with the voice encoding.

The second problem has to do with the way the equipment communicates with the telephone exchange. Interoperability problems arise because there are so many different services (and related parameters) that the user can request, and each country can decide whether or not to allow the telephone exchange to offer a given service; further, the specifications that describe the services are open to interpretation in many different ways. So as with other interoperability problems, you must work with the vendors to determine whether the equipment will interoperate. This is a basic problem; it impacts all ISDN equipment, not just voice equipment.

The third problem has to do with homologation, or regulatory approval. In most countries in the world the manufacturer of telephone equipment must obtain approvals before the equipment may be connected to the network. So even if the equipment works with the network in a particular country, it isn't OK to hook it up until the manufacturer has jumped through the various hoops to demonstrate safety and compliance. It is typically more expensive to obtain worldwide homologation approvals for a newly developed piece of ISDN equipment than it is to develop it and tool up to manufacture it.

A fourth issue is that in the United States, the TA and NT1 are both provided by the customer, whereas in Europe the NT1 is provided by the telephone company. Stated differently, if you walk into a store in the United States and buy something to plug into an ISDN line, it may be designed as a one-piece unit that connects to point U. In Europe you would get something that plugs into point T. Thus you might take a piece of U.S.-originated equipment to Europe and find that it won't work because the jack in Europe is a T interface and the plug on your U.S. equipment is a U interface.

There are attempts to remedy this situation, particularly for BRI ISDN. In North America the National ISDN User's Forum is coming up with standards that increase the uniformity of ISDN services. In Europe a new standard, called NET3, is being developed.

What are the basic differences between a BONDed 128KB ISDN connection and a switched 56 line?

Switched 56 and ISDN are both dial-up services; given a choice, go with ISDN. Switched 56 is an earlier service that is being phased out in favor of ISDN. The two interwork (call each other) freely, but ISDN gives you two B channels for a usually lower price than one switched 56 line. The delay is about the same, unless you're closer to one services switch than to the other.

How long should call setup (dialing) take when using a TA?

The "less than a second" call setup sometimes claimed seems to be rare. TAs have a negotiation phase, and it typically takes around four seconds to get through to the remote site.

Summary

In this chapter we've excerpted some of the most commonly asked CT-related questions and answered from a variety of online resources (primarily from the Internet). Although this Q&A information represents the hits in late 1995, the old favorites here may no longer be popular by the time you read this. If that's the case, please visit our recommended list of online resources and revisit the "hit parade" for yourself. This should convince you that you're not only in good company and not alone in this, it should also help run down solutions to your most common problems and recurrent questions. For a list of online resources, please consult Chapter 11, in the section entitled "Researching Your CT Hardware, Software, and Services Needs."

Appendix A: CT Bibliography & Online Resources

Our goal in providing this appendix is not to tell you how to use an online information service or the Internet in general, or CompuServe or the World Wide Web in particular. Nor do we want to provide the be-all and end-all of CT resources. Rather, we just want to tell you what information is available on CompuServe and the Internet, what it's made up of, and why you might find it interesting. We also want to point you at those books and materials about CT that we've found most useful in the course of researching and writing this book.

This appendix focuses first on what's up on CompuServe and the Internet, how best to interact with it, and what kinds of things you can and cannot find up there. It tells you how to be effective when you work with CompuServe or the Internet, from the standpoint of knowing what to look for, which kinds of questions you can ask, and the answers you're likely to get. It also helps you to understand just what kind of help you can expect to get from the online community and what to do if you can't get the help you need. Then, at the conclusion of this Appendix, we include a CT section at the head of the "Bibliographies and Resources" section.

By now, you've probably noticed that we've mentioned only CompuServe and the Internet as sources of online information. "What about the others?" you might ask. Yes, we know there's also America Online, Prodigy, Genie, the Microsoft Network (MSN), and a bunch of other lesser contenders in this field. But none of them have staked a presence in the area of technical information and support online like CompuServe, nor does any of them have the breadth and reach of the Internet (which can't yet compare with CompuServe's depth of offerings, but is quickly catching up).

That's why we focus the bulk of our discussion in this appendix to these two information sources, even though there are more to choose from. In the next-to-last section, entitled "Other Online Resources," we'll try to give you some ideas about other places worth looking, but this will be a set of cursory suggestions, rather than an in-depth investigation.

What Does "Online" Really Mean?

In the context of our discussion, "online" means that you have to log in to somebody else's network (frequently using a modem) to access their information collection rather than your own network. While this may sound inconvenient—and it sometimes is—the benefits invariably outweigh any inconvenience, costs, and effort the might be involved.

For the record, these benefits include:

- Free access to technical support operations for questions and answers via forums (CompuServe) or newsgroups and mailing lists (the Internet). Even if you never ask a question yourself, reading other people's questions (and the answers that go with them) can be enormously informative.

- Access to online sources for software patches and fixes for a broad range of products. Rather than waiting for the vendor to send you a disk, or paying long-distance charges to access their private bulletin board, you can get the latest versions of software (or the tools to turn your software into the latest version) with a local phone call and a (sometimes lengthy) download.

- Access to shareware and freeware that can extend your network's capabilities, or increase your personal productivity. Much of the software this book's authors use for things like screen shots, graphics, file compression, and more originated on the Internet or Compuserve. A little prospecting can work wonders in this area!

- The biggest benefit by far, is the opportunity to meet and interact with your peers and colleagues in the networking profession, and to learn from other people's experiences and mistakes. You'll also have the occasional chance to learn from the wisdom of real experts, including the developers of the software or hardware you're using, or world-renowned gurus from a variety of fields.

All in all, there's a lot to be gained from going online to look for information on just about any subject, but especially for technical and computer-related subjects. Since that's where networking fits pretty neatly, these resources are excellent (some would argue, indispensable) sources for information on the whole gamut of networking topics, products, technologies, and issues.

Now that we've gotten you all excited about the possibilities inherent in online information access, let's talk about the costs. Whether you join up with CompuServe, get onto the Internet, or—like this book's authors—do both; you can't join up without incurring some costs.

For CompuServe, this involves a series of account options, with associated monthly fees and additional charges for online time (usually above a certain number of "free" monthly hours). A light user shouldn't have to spend more than $10–15 a month for the service, but if you make regular downloads or spend significant amounts of time online, it's easy to spend $50–100 a month, or more.

For the Internet, you'll have to arrange for a connection with an Internet Service Provider (ISP), and select one of the many options available for an Internet connection. For individuals or small businesses, we recommend using ISDN—or at least a V.34 modem—with a PPP connection. While prices vary from location to location, you should expect to pay between $80–150 a month for ISDN service with this kind of a connection, or about half that with a dialup POTS connection. This usually entitles you to 10–20 hours per month of "free" online time, after which an hourly fee will be charged for additional hours.

There are lots of other Internet account options available from most ISPs, that can vary from dial on demand to dedicated accounts, or according to the bandwidth of the connection involved (modem, ISDN, T1, T3, etc.). If you're interested in attaching your network to the Internet, or need more bandwidth than an ISDN connection can provide, talk to your local ISPs, or to national ISPs that offer service in your area. If you shop carefully for the best combination of price and service, you should be able to find something you can live with!

As with any other service, whether it's CompuServe, the Internet, or both, you'll want to do your best to learn how to use these information conduits effectively, to get the best bang for your bucks. Please consult the bibliographies at the end of this Appendix for a list of resources that can help you learn what it takes to get the best use of either or both of these services.

CIS: The CompuServe Information Service

The CompuServe Information Service (CIS) is an electronic information service that offers a selection of thousands of topics for your perusal.

CompuServe, a for-a-fee service, requires an individual account (called a membership number) with an accompanying password to be accessed. There are many ways to obtain trial access at no charge, but if you want to play on CompuServe, sooner or later you have to pay for the privilege. CompuServe charges a monthly membership fee, in addition to a fee for connection time. Some of the services available on CompuServe have additional charges as well. Be warned! It's easy to spend time here.

Forums for conversation and investigation

When you access CompuServe, it's necessary to select an area of interest to focus your exploration of the information treasures available. On CompuServe, information is organized into forums. A forum is an area dedicated to a particular subject or a collection of related subjects, and each forum contains one or more of the following:

- **Message board:** Features electronic conversations organized by specific subjects into sections related to particular topics (CT, computer telephony, or the name of a CT vendor is probably what you'd look for as the focus for a section or forum on CT or related topics). A given sequence of messages, chained together by a common subject or by replies to an original message, is called a thread. It's important to notice that threads may read like conversations but that messages in a thread can be separated from one another by hours or days. Following threads is a favorite pastime for those who spend time on CompuServe.

- **Conference room:** An electronic analog to the real thing, it brings individuals together to exchange ideas and information in real time. It's much like a conference telephone call except that, rather than talk to each other, the participants communicate by typing on their keyboards. Conference rooms are not for the faint of heart, and they can be frustrating for those with limited touch-typing skills.

- **File library:** A collection of files organized by subject that can be copied ("downloaded" is the CompuServe term) for further perusal and use. Examples of file types found in CompuServe libraries include archived collections of interesting threads, documents of all kinds, and a variety of software ranging from patches and fixes for programs to entire programs.

In all, many, many worlds of information are available on CompuServe, any or all of which can by themselves be a completely absorbing source of information, gossip, software, and activity. With all its elements taken together, CompuServe is a perfect example of what might be called an "electronic information warehouse."

Getting a CompuServe membership

You can obtain an account over the telephone or by writing to CompuServe and requesting a membership. For telephone inquiries, ask for Representative 200. Here are the numbers to use:

- Within the U.S. (except Ohio), including Alaska, Hawaii, Puerto Rico, and the American Virgin Islands, call toll free at 800-848-8199.

- Outside the U.S., in Canada, and in Ohio, call 614-457-8650.

Telephone hours are from 8 a.m. to 10 p.m. Eastern time Monday through Friday, and from noon to 5 p.m. on Saturday. Written inquiries for a CompuServe account should be directed to:

CompuServe, Inc.
Attn: Customer Service
P.O. Box 20212
5000 Arlington Centre Boulevard
Columbus, OH 43220
U.S.A.

Accessing CompuServe

To get access to CompuServe, you must equip your computer with a modem and attach that modem to a telephone line. You also need some kind of communications program, to let your computer "talk" to CompuServe by using the modem and to help you find your way around its online universe. Finally, you have to obtain a telephone number for CompuServe—most of them are local numbers, especially in the U.S—that's appropriate for the type and speed of modem you're using.

At present, though, connection-time charges are based on how fast your modem is—faster modems cost more—but the higher charges are typically offset by even faster transfer speeds. If your CompuServe bill is $30 a month or higher, most high-speed modems will pay for themselves in six months or less based on the reductions in fees you realize by using one.

After you are connected to CompuServe, you enter your membership number and your password. First-time users should follow the instructions provided by your CompuServe representative or in the CompuServe Starter Kit that's available from CompuServe (for an additional fee).

After you're logged in, getting directly to a named CompuServe forum is easy-as long as you know the name of the forum you're after. When you simply type GO <NAME> from the CompuServe prompt, you are presented with a menu of additional choices for that forum. To get started with your information mining efforts, use the FIND command with CT, a vendor's name, or a product name, that you're after. This will normally produce a list of forums that you can visit, to further explore potential sources of information.

The Many Forums of CompuServe

There are plenty of vendors and networking communities represented on CompuServe. You'll find a rich selection of Novell forums (GO NetWire), and Microsoft-related forums and libraries, for everything from vanilla Windows, to Windows for Workgroups, Windows95, and Windows NT Advanced Server (use

GO MICROSOFT to get to the root of the Microsoft forums; don't skip the Microsoft Knowledge Base at GO MSKB, either). You'll also find plenty of IBM-related forums (GO IBM) or OS/2-related information (GO OS/2). Don't forget to use the FIND command to locate other vendors and products, either.

CompuServe Telephony-related Information Areas

- ISDN Forum: GO ISDN

- Telecommunications Forum: GO TELECOM

- UK Information Technology Forum: GO UKIT

- Intel Architecture Forum (TAPI info.): GO INTELA

- Microsoft's TAPI SDK (software developer's kit) is free in the WINEXT forum library.

The Internet

The Internet, as a wag might put it, is a "whole 'nother story." There are more riches to be found on the Internet than you could shake a stick at. This won't stop us from pointing you at a few good stops along the way, but it will effectively prevent us from covering all the possible bases. Rather than trying to tell you where all the goodies are, we're going to explain how to search for the information you seek.

Our primary approach to the Internet requires that you have access to the World Wide Web (WWW), usually known as "the Web." The Web is a world-wide collection of hypertext information servers that is made easy to navigate through the use of hypertext links, that let you jump effortlessly from document to document (or within a document) simply by activating a link on a document you're examining (and for most users, this requires no more effort than double-clicking a word or graphic on your display). Secondarily, access to electronic mail and/or USENET newsgroups will be quite helpful as well.

Searching for Satisfaction

In much the same way that the FIND command on CompuServe lets you ask for information by company or product name, the Web sports a number of database front-ends called "search engines," that will let you enter a keyword (or several, in fact) for search. These programs will return a collection of hypertext links to sites that match your keywords to various locations on the Web, ready for you to double-click on them and investigate further.

The name used to attach to a Web resources is called a "URL" (an acronym for Uniform Resource Locator, a way of designating sites and information accessible through the Web). Here are the URLs for a handful of popular—and useful—Web search engines. If you simply point your Web browser at one of these, you'll then be able to get pointers to the information you're looking for.

Sometimes, using the right tools can make using the World Wide Web for research much simpler. There is a class of software tools called *search engines* that can examine huge amounts of information to help you locate Web sites of potential interest. Here's how most of them work:

Somewhere in the background, laboring in patient anonymity, you'll find automated Web-traversing programs, often called robots or spiders, that do nothing but follow link after link around the Web ad infinitum. Each time they get to a new Web document, they peruse and catalog its contents, storing the information up for transmission to a database elsewhere on the Web.

At regular intervals, these automated information gatherers will transmit their recent acquisitions to their parent database, where the information is sifted, categorized, and stored.

When you run a search engine, you're actually searching the database that's been compiled and managed through the initial efforts of the robots and spiders, but which is handled by a fully functional database management system that communicates with a customized program for your search form.

Using the keywords or search terms you provide to the form, the database locates "hits" (exact matches) and also "near-hits" (matches with less than the full set of terms supplied, or based on educated guesses about what you're *really* trying to locate).

The hits are returned to the background search program by the database, where they are transformed into a Web document to return the results of the search for your perusal.

If you're lucky, all this activity will produce references to some materials that you can actually use!

The search engines of (our) choice

We'd like to share some pointers to our favorite search engines with you, which you'll find in Table A.1. This is not an exhaustive catalog of such tools, but all of them will produce interesting results if you use "computer telephony" or "voice recognition" as search input.

When you're using these search tools, the most important thing to remember is that the more specific you can make your search request, the more directly related the results will be to what your looking for. Thus, if you're looking for information about automatic call attendants, you might try using "call attendant" or "automatic call attendant" as your search terms instead of simply using "computer telephony." While you may get plenty of nothing when using search terms that are too specific, that's better than looking through a plenitude of irrelevant materials when nothing is all that's in there!

Table A.1: These Web search engines can make looking for CGI-related materials much less taxing.

Search engine name & info	URL:
Excite Excite corporation's "fuzzy logic" finds cool stuff!	http://www.excite.com
Lycos Carnegie-Mellon engine	http://lycos.cs.cmu.edu
W3 Org Virtual Library W3 Org outsourced project	http://www.stars.com
Wandex MIT spinoff's engine	http://www.netgen.com/cgi/wandex
WebCrawler University of Washington engine	http://webcrawler.cs.washington.edu/ WebCrawler/WebQuery.html
World Wide Web Worm (WWWW) University of Colorado engine	http://www.cs.colorado.edu:80/ home/mcbryan/WWWW.html
Yahoo	http://www.yahoo.com

The Web has to be experienced to be believed. Since the authors' initial exposure to it about two years ago, it's completely changed the way we approach research of any kind. We hope you'll find it to be useful, but we must warn you-it's also completely addicting!

Other Ways to Get Internet Satisfaction

When it comes to classifying the kinds of information you'll encounter on the Internet in any search for networking information, specifications, and examples, here's what you're most likely to find:

Focused newsgroups

Focused newsgroups are basically congregations of interested individuals, who congregate around a specific topic on USENET, BITNET, or one of the other regular message exchange areas on the Internet.

Where telephony is concerned, this involves a handful of primarily USENET newsgroups with varying levels of interest in (and coverage of) data communications in the `comp.dcom` newsgroup hierarchy. In addition to general-purpose groups like `comp.dcom.modems`, this hierarchy also includes groups of interest like:

`comp.dcom.isdn`

`comp.dcom.lans`

`comp.dcom.telecom`

`comp.dcom.telecom.tech`

`comp.dcom.videoconf`

Of all the newsgroups we follow regularly, these usually have the most relevant information about CT and related issues, especially the modem- and telecom-related newsgroups.

To begin with, you'll want to obtain a list of the newsgroups that your Internet Service Provider (ISP) carries. Normally, you will already have access to this list through whatever newsreader you're using, but you can usually get a plain-text version of this list just by asking for it.

Then, take this plain-text file and open it with your favorite editor or word processor that contains a search command. By entering the name of the company, technology, or product that you're interested in, you can see if there are any newsgroups devoted to its coverage (a recent check on our part discovered several hits for the term "isdn" including `comp.dcom.isdn`, `de.comm.isdn`, `fido.ger.isdn`, and `relog.isdn`). Of these, two are aimed at German audiences (`de.comm.isdn`, and `fido.ger.idsn`), we use `comp.dcom.isdn` as a terrific source of information, and know nothing about the `relog.isdn` list, since we found it empty.

In fact, the only way to tell if a newsgroup can do you any good is to drop in for a while and read its traffic. You should be able to tell, in a day or two, if the topics and coverage are interesting and informative. If they are, you should consider subscribing to the newsgroup, or at least dropping in from time to time to read the traffic. Remember, too, that these newsgroups are a great source of technical information, and that they often have vendor technical support employees assigned to read them, ready to answer technical questions on your behalf.

Focused mailing lists

Focused mailing lists originate from targeted mail servers that collect message traffic from active correspondents, and then broadcast the accumulated traffic to anyone who signs up for the mailing list.

Entering and leaving a mailing list takes a little more effort than subscribing to or leaving a USENET newsgroup, but otherwise, these two categories provide the same kind of information: daily message traffic—sometimes quite voluminous—focused on networking or related topics.

Locating mailing lists can sometimes be tricky. While you often learn about them only by reading message traffic on newsgroups, you can sometimes find them mentioned in search engine output, or by asking a users group or a technical support person focused on a particular topic or area. Even so, they can be incredibly useful.

Information collections from "interested parties"

Sometimes individuals with special interests in a particular area—like networking—will collect information about their area of concern, and publish it in a variety of forms that can range from Web pages to file archives available on private or public servers.

While such collections can often be eclectic and idiosyncratic, the best of them can offer outstanding "jumping-off points" for investigating any particular topic. This is as true for networking as it is for other topics.

Like mailing lists, finding these gems can be a matter of hit or miss. By watching the message traffic on newsgroups or mailing lists, you'll figure out who the gurus or forward-looking individuals are. By looking in their messages for pointers to Web pages or other resources (which you'll often find in the .sig, or signature files, at the end of their messages), you can sometimes get pointers to great sources of information.

In the same vein, if you see that a particular individual is a consistent and reliable source of good information on a particular topic, send him or her an e-mail message and request that they share their list of recommended on-line resources with you. While you may not always get a response (some of these people are very busy), it never hurts to ask, and the occasional answer can provide a real treasure trove of information pointers!

The best source of ISDN information on the Internet, bar none, may be found at the following WWW URL:

```
http://www.alumni.caltech.edu/~dank/isdn/
```

This is Dan Kegel's ISDN Web page, and it's got pointers to everything worth knowing about ISDN on the Internet (no kidding!). If you can get here, you can get all the online information about ISDN that you'll ever need.

Information from special interest groups

Special interest groups cover a multitude of approaches to their topics: they can be trade or industry organizations, research or standards groups, or even companies involved in particular activities.

Often, the groups with vested interests in a technology will provide information on that technology, along with pointers to other sources as well. This is as true for networking as it is for other topics, but because these groups are nonpareils of Web and Internet presence, they are often among the best places to start looking.

It's often been said that "It's not what you know, it's who you know, that counts." When it comes to locating Internet resources, this may sometimes seem more like "where you know," but the principle remains pretty much the same. Thus, for particular topics, you shouldn't only point your search engine at company, product, or technology names; try pointing them at the names of such groups as well. Here again, these can be incredible sources of useful information.

Dan Kegel's page includes a section entitled "ISDN User Groups;" look here for information about local and national groups, most of which have their own mailing lists, file archives, and Web servers that you can explore for good ISDN information (and contacts for consultants, equipment dealers, etc.).

Internet Telephony Resources

Communication Resources on the Web from Indiana University:
http://alnilam.ucs.indiana.edu:1027/sources/comm.html

Computer Telephone Integrators, Inc:
http://www.inforamp.net/mainstay/cti/spfcapps.html.
Computer Telephone Integrators Inc. provides information on specific telephony applications in order to further illustrate the advantages of the technology.

CTI@Dialogic:
http://www.dialogic.com/
Dialogic's WWW site provides links to many CT sites, a directory of vendors and market resources and other CT information.

Information Sources: The Internet and Computer-Mediated Communication:
http://www.rpi.edu/Internet/Guides/decemj/icmc/top.html.
PURPOSE: to collect, organize, and present information describing the Internet and computer-mediated communication technologies, applications, culture, discussion forums, and bibliographies. Areas of interest include the technical, social, rhetorical, cognitive, and psychological aspects of networked communication and information.

ISDN Suppliers list:
http://igwe.vub.ac.be/~svendk/suppliers_by_name.html

ISDN Informationbase:
http://igwe.vub.ac.be/~svendk/isdn_homepage.html.
Nice source of ISDN related: Internet information sources, Written sources, Upcoming events, Hardware, Software, Vendors, Suppliers, TO's (Telecommunication Operators a.k.a. Bell's ISDN Internet connection providers), Internet Access Provider Catalog, and an on-line Glossary

ITC: International Telecommunications Center:
http://www.telematrix.com/toc.html
The only Internet site devoted exclusively to telecommunications, data communications and networking. Provides

information on: Tools in the Computer/Telecom Revolution, Vendor Resources, High Tech Periodicals, Technical Standards, Jobs, Discount Hardware, Software and Books.

Telecom Digest Archives:
ftp://ftp.lcs.mit.edu/telecom-archives
All the back issues of *TELECOM Digest* are on file along with many other telephony related files.

Telephone Response Technologies, Inc.:
http://www.trt.com/info/
TRT provides Computer Telephony information and produces innovative high-performance Computer Telephony products, including ready-to-install applications (voice mail, fax-on-demand, voice/fax broadcast, etc.) and development tools.

The Telecommunications Glossary:
http://www.wiltel.com/glossary/glossary.html

Versit: http://www.versit.com/
An alliance founded by Apple Computer, AT&T, IBM, and Siemens to create Interoperability specifications in the convergence of communications and computing.

Other Online Resources

Many companies that are too small, too poor, or otherwise disinclined to participate on CompuServe or the Internet will maintain their own private Bulletin Board Systems (BBSs), which you can dial up and investigate. These are always free, but they're also almost always long-distance calls, so what you save in connect time costs to a service provider you'll probably end up paying to your long-distance company instead.

Nevertheless, when other avenues fail to turn up what you're looking for, it's a good idea to call the vendor and ask if they offer a BBS. This kind of setup often gives the opportunity to communicate with technical support via e-mail, instead of enduring "eternal hold" while waiting to speak to a real human being, and can often provide direct access to software patches, fixes, upgrades, FAQs, and other kinds of useful documentation.

In the same vein, many companies offer FAXback services that can ship paper-based documentation, order forms, and other goodies to your FAX machine. This has the advantage of costing you only as much long-distance time as it takes you to request the information you're after; after that, the transmission costs are usually born by the vendor.

Digging for information is an endeavor where persistence usually pays off. If you're bound and determined to get the facts, figures, or help you need, you'll eventually be able to get it. Just be sure to leave no resource uninvestigated, no possible avenue untraveled, and no stone unturned!

Non-computerized resources worth investigating

Even though they may not be as dynamic and interactive as on-line resources, don't overlook the information you can glean from more conventional paper-based publications. (We know you've got to be somewhat open-minded in this regard, because you're reading this book!) Nevertheless, we'll do our best to acquaint you with some books, magazines, and publishers to check out in your quest for the latest and greatest networking information. You should find this information in the bibliographies at the end of this Appendix.

Summary

In this appendix, we've tried to point you at the best and brightest of online (and other) information resources. Over the years, we've learned that both CompuServe and the Internet are essential to our research, but you will probably be able to get by with only one or the other. Whatever your choice of online information, however, we're sure you'll become dependent on it in no time (if you aren't already). It's definitely one of those things that, as soon as it becomes familiar, you wonder how you ever managed without it! In the bibliographies that follow, we try to provide some tools to bring you up to speed quickly enough to make the investment pay off right away.

Bibliographies and Resources

Computer Telephony Books

Bezar, David D. *LAN Times Guide to Telephony*. 1995, Osborne McGraw-Hill, Inc., Berkeley, CA. A fine overview of telecommunications and networking technologies for MIS managers, administrators and programmers at the corporate level.

Edgar, Bob. *PC Telephony* (3rd Ed.). 1995, Flatiron Publishing, Inc., New York, NY., The complete guide to designing, building and programming systems using Dialogic and related hardware. It's somewhat of a "Bible" of CT with emphasis on programming your own system using Dialogic hardware. It contains an extensive glossary, primarily taken from Newton's Telecom Dictionary by Harry Newton.

Gladstone, Steve. *Testing Computer Telephony Systems and Networks*. 1994, Telecom Library, Inc., New York, NY. Short guide to help you better understand your CT system and to help you plan and execute your testing.

Green, James Harry. *The IRWIN Handbook of Telecommunications Management*. 1989, IRWIN Professional Publishing, Burr Ridge, IL., This book provides a working guide for corporate, small business, and government telecommunications managers who need to install modern telephony equipment and systems. It is somewhat dated regarding the technology but the project planning and management aspects are still current and should be very useful.

Herrick, Clyde N. and C. Lee McKim. *Telecommunications Wiring*. 1991, Telecom Library, Inc., New York, NY. If you're going to do it yourself, you can use the information in this book to do it right the first time. If you're managing the project, you can use this book's information to insure that your contractor does it right the first time.

Laino, Jane. *Telephony for Computer Professionals*. 1994, Flatiron Publishing, Inc. New York, NY. A fine primer for people in the computer industry who want to learn a few buzzwords and see what telephony is all about.

Margulies, Edwin: *Client–Server Computer Telephony*. 1994, Telecom Library, Inc., New York, NY. One of the first books specifically discussing computer telephony and the client–server world.

Newton, Harry. *Newton's Telecom Dictionary* (9th ed.). 1995, Telecom Library, Inc., New York, NY. Updated every six months, this 1173-page tome is "The official glossary of computer telephony, telecommunications, networking, voice processing, and data communications." That's what Harry says about it, so it must be true.

Rasmussen, Gary. *How to Buy Telephone Equipment in the Secondary Market*. 1994, Telecom Library, Inc., New York, NY. This book is primarily for people who buy and sell used telephone equipment but anyone who wants a "better deal" can profit from its wisdom and insight.

Computer Telephony Magazines

Computer Telephony. Published by Harry Newton, Telecom Library, Inc., New York, NY.

Call Center. Published by Harry Newton, Telecom Library, Inc., New York, NY.

Teleconnect. Published by Flatiron Publishing, Inc., New York, NY.

Voice International. Published by Triton Telecom, London, England

Enterprise Communications Magazine. Published by Advanstar Communications, Cleveland, OH.

World Telemedia. Published by Triton Telecom, London, England

ISDN

Angell, David. *ISDN for Dummies*. 1995, IDG Books Worldwide, Inc., Foster City, CA. This is an excellent first book for anyone wishing to know more about the digital world of ISDN telephony.

Hopkins, Gerald L. *The ISDN Literacy Book*. 1994, Addison-Wesley Publishing Company, Inc., Reading, MA. A great comprehensive introduction to ISDN for managers and technicians alike.

Kessler, Gary C. *ISDN*, Second Edition. 1993, McGraw-Hill, Inc., New York, NY. Lots of practical information on ISDN. This book could serve as a complete guide.

Motorola University Press. *The Basics Book of ISDN*. 1992, Motorola, Inc. (published by Addison-Wesley Publishing Company, Inc.), Reading, MA. A short and useful introduction to ISDN terms and technology.

Stallings, William. *ISDN: An Introduction*. 1989, Macmillan Publishing Company, a division of Macmillan, Inc., New York, NY. Stallings has a prodigious understanding of ISDN. An exhaustive examination of ISDN from the high levels to the nitty gritty technical details.

Tittel, Ed and Steve James. *ISDN Networking Essentials*. 1996, AP Professional, Boston, MA. An excellent introductory book for the individual and small office user, even if we do say so ourselves.

General

Bernard Aboba. *The Online User's Encyclopedia*. 1993, Addison-Wesley Publishing Co, Reading, MA. A general book that covers online topics from A–Z, this tome defies description but is incredibly useful.

CompuServe

Rob Tidrow, Jim Ness, Bob Retelle, and Chen Robinson. *New Riders' Official CompuServe Yellow Pages*. 1994, New Riders Publishing, Indianapolis, IN. A directory to CompuServe resources organized like the Bell Yellow Pages, with great sections on vendors and networking (warning: be sure to get a current edition, as this information goes stale quickly).

Richard Wagner. *Inside CompuServe*, 2nd Edition. 1994, New Riders Publishing, Indianapolis, IN. A useful overview of how CompuServe behaves, what kinds of access software is worth considering, and what sorts of resources it contains.

Robert Wiggins and Ed Tittel. *The Trail Guide to CompuServe*. 1994, Addison Wesley Publishing Company, Reading, MA. A quick overview of the CompuServe Information Manager (CIM) software for Windows and Macintosh, and a quick, but useful, guide to resources online. Includes a chapter on network-related forums and topics.

Wallace Wang. *CompuServe for Dummies*. 1994, IDG Books Worldwide, Indianapolis, IN. One of the best all-round resources on CompuServe available, this book covers software, organization, and effective "surfing" techniques.

Internet

Angell, David and Brent Heslop. *Mosaic for Dummies,* Windows Edition. 1995, IDG Books Worldwide, Indianapolis, IN. Excellent coverage of the Mosaic Web browser, and Web-based online resources.

December, John and Neil Randall. *The World Wide Web Unleashed*. 1994, SAMS Publishing, Indianapolis, IN. The best of the general WWW reference books, this one covers all the topics, including one of the most comprehensive guides to online resources we've ever seen anywhere.

Dern, Daniel. *The Internet Guide for New Users*. 1994, McGraw-Hill, Inc., New York, NY. One of the three best all-around Internet books, this one covers a little bit of everything, including programs to use and places to look for information.

Hahn, Harley and Rick Stout. *The Internet Complete Reference*. Osborne/McGraw-Hill, Inc., Berkeley, CA. Another of the three best all-around Internet books, this one is aimed more at intermediate to advanced users, but covers a lot of ground anyway.

Krol, Ed. *The Whole Internet User's Guide*, 2nd Edition. O'Reilly & Associates, Inc., Sebastopol, CA. The third of the three best Internet books around, this was the earliest and is still a personal favorite.

Levine, John R. and Carol Baroudi. *The Internet For Dummies,* 2nd Edition. 1994, IDG Books Worldwide, Indianapolis, IN. An excellent overview of the Internet's many protocols, programs, and capabilities.

Levine, John R. and Margaret Levine Young. *More Internet for Dummies*. 1994, IDG Books Worldwide, Indianapolis, IN. A continuation of the coverage in the first book, this volume provides a good introduction to the World Wide Web, and how to use it.

Tittel, Ed and Margaret Robbins. *Internet Access Essentials*. 1994, AP Professional, Boston, MA. The fourth of the three best all-around Internet books, this one was co-written by one of this book's authors, which means he thinks it's pretty darned good indeed!

Appendix B: Vendor Information

A&A Connections
530 S. Henderson Rd. #A
King of Prussia, PA 19406
(610) 354-9070
Internet: attmail.com!aacorp/

Access ISDN
17130 N. Dallas Pkwy., Ste. 210
Dallas, TX 75248
(800) 333-4736

Active Voice
2901 Third Ave.
Seattle, WA 98121
(206) 441-4700

Adtran
901 Explorer Blvd.
Huntsville, AL 35809
(205) 971-8000
Internet: http://ww.adtran.com

Advanced Reconition Technologies
20380 Town Center Lane Suite 175
Cupertino, CA 95014
(408) 973-9786

AlgoRhythms
12221 Merit Drive, Suite 1380
Dallas, TX 75251
(214) 490-5487 Fax: (214) 490-3050

Alliance Systems
16801 Addison Rd. #120
Dallas, TX 75248
(214) 250-4141
Internet: alliance@asisys.com

Alpha Telecom
7501 S. Memorial Pkwy., Ste. 212
Huntsville, AL 35806
(205) 881-8743

Altec Lansing Multimedia
P.O. Box 277
Milford, PA 18337
(717) 296-1287

Ameritech
2000 W. Ameritech Center Dr., #2B30
Hoffman Estates, IL 60196
(708) 248-2000

Amtelco
4800 Curtin Dr.
MacFarland, WI 53558
(800) 356-9224

AnwserSoft
3460 Lotus Dr., Ste. 123
Plano, TX 75075
(214) 612-5100

Apex Voice Communications
15250 Ventura Blvd., 3rd Floor
Sherman Oaks, CA 91403
(818) 379-8400

Applied Voice Technology
1141 NE 122nd Way
Kirkland, WA 98083
(206) 820-6000

Ariel
433 River Rd.
Highland Park, NJ 08904
(908) 249-2900 Fax: (908) 249-2127
Internet: http://www.ariel.com
Internet: ariel@ariel.com

Ascend Communications, Inc.
1275 Harbor Bay Pkwy
Alameda, CA 94501
(510) 769-6001
Internet: info@ascend.com

AT&T
1-800-222-PART: Quick access to small
quantity orders of ISDN products.
Personal Desktop Video or TeleMedia
Connection System:
Visual Communications Products
8100 East Maplewood Ave. 1st Floor
Englewood, CO 80111
(800) 843-3646 or (800)VIDEO-GO
Prompt 3

AT&T
211 Mt. Airy Rd.
Basking Ridge, NJ 07920
(800) 247-7000

AT&T Global Information Services
1700 S. Patterson Blvd.
Dayton, OH 45479-0001
(800) 447-1124; (513) 445-5000
Internet: http://www.attgis.com

AT&T Network Systems
2600 Warrenville Rd.
Lisle, IL 60532
(708) 224-4000

Atlanta Signal Processors
1375 Peachtree St. NE, Ste. 690
Atlanta, GA 30309
(404) 892-7265

Aurora Systems
40 Nagog Park, Ste. 101
Acton, MA 01720
(508) 263-4141

B&W Electronics
2851 Nedecino Dr.
Prescott Valley, AZ 86314
(800) 228-1005
BBS: (214) 422-9835

BBN HARK Systems Corp. (subsidiary
of Bolt Beranek and Newman Inc.)
70 Fawcett St.
Cambridge, MA 02138
(617) 873-4636
FAX: (617) 873-2473

Bicom
755 Main St., No. 3
Monroe, CT 06468
(203) 268-4484
Faxback: (203) 268-3404

Brooktrout Technology
144 Gould St., Ste. 200
Needham, MA 02194
(617) 449-4100
Faxback: (617) 433-0789

BusLogic
4151 Burton Dr.
Santa Clara, CA 95054
(408) 492-9090
Internet: http://www.buslogic.com

Call Center Enterprises
1140 Kildare Farm Rd.
Cary, NC 27511
(800) 979-9699

CallWare Technologies
2323 Foothill Dr.
Salt Lake City, UT 84109
(800) 888-4226
Internet: http://www.callware.com

CCOM
120 Wood Ave. S.
Iselin, NJ 08830
(908) 603-7750

Cherry Communications
1260 Liberty Way, Ste. E
Vista, CA 92083
(800) 879-0504
Fax: (619) 551-8944

ClearWave
P.O. Box 272278
Fort Collins, CO 80527-2278
(970) 221-1998
Internet: http://www.clearwave.com

Combinet
333 West El Camino Real, Suite 240
Sunnyvale, California 94087
(408) 522 9020 or (800) 967-6651 for
product lit
Fax: (408) 732 5479

Comdial
1180 Seminole Trail
Charlottesville, VA 22906
(804) 978-2514

Commetrex Corporation
6400 Atlantic Blvd., Ste. 165
Norcross, GA 30071
(770) 564-5522; Fax: (770) 564-5649

Compaq Computer Corp.
20555 State Hwy. 249
Houston, TX 77070-2698
(800) 345-1518; (713) 374-0484
Internet: http://www.compaq.com

ConferTech
12110 N. Pecos St.
Westminister, CO 80234
(303) 633-3077

ConnectWare
1301 E. Arapaho Rd.
Richardson, TX 75081
(214) 997-4193
Internet:
http://www.connectware.com

Contact Network
165 Citation, Ste. 121
Birmingham, AL 35209
(800) 487-2050
Internet: oadi003@uabdpo.umb.edu

Cortelco
4119 Willow Lake Blvd.
Memphis, TN 38118
(901) 365-7774

Creative Labs
1901 McCartney Blvd.
Milpitas, CA 950035
(408) 428-6600
Internet: http://www.creaf.com

Dialogic
1515 Route 10
Parsippany, NJ 07054
(800) 755-4444
Faxback: (800) 755-5599
Internet: http://www.dialogic.com
Internet: sales@dialogic.com

Diamond Multimedia Systems, Inc.
2880 Junction Ave.
San Jose, CA 95134-1922
(800) 4-MULTIMEDIA; (408) 325-7000
Internet:
http://www.diamondmm.com

DigiBoard
6400 Flying Cloud Drive
Eden Prarie, MN 55344
(612) 943 9020 or (800)-344-4273
Fax: (612) 643 5398
Internet: info@digibd.com

Dinatel
96 Bonaventura Dr.
San Jose, CA 95134
(408) 428-1000

DSP Communications
1000 Coit Rd.
Plano, TX 75075
(214) 519-3000

DSP Group
3120 Scott Blvd.
Santa Clara, CA 95054
(408) 986-4300 Fax: (408) 986-4323

Eagle Teleconferencing
60 E. 56th St.
New York, NY 10022
(800) 778-6338

ELAN Software Corp.
383 Sunset Blvd., Ste. 101
Pacific Palisades, CA 90272
(800) 654-3526; (310) 454-6800
Internet:
http://www.goldminesw.com

Exacom
99 Airport Rd.
Concord, NH 03301
(603) 228-0706

First Pacific Networks
871 Fox Lane
San Jose, CA 95131
(408) 943-7600

Fujitsu
4403 Bland Rd., Somerset Park
Raleigh, NC 27609
(919) 790-2211
Internet: http://www.fujitsu.com

GammaLink
1314 Chesapeake Terrace
Sunnyvale, CA 94089
(408) 745-2250
Internet: http://www.gammalink.com

Gandalf Technologies
130 Colonnade Road South
Nepean, Ontario, Canada K2E 7M4
(800) GANDALF or (613) 723-6500
Fax: (613) 228-9510

Genesys
1111 Bayhill, Ste. 180
San Bruco, CA 94066
(415) 827-2711

Graychip
2314 Ramona St.
Palo Alto, CA 94301
(415) 323-2955
Internet: sales@graychip.com

Hark Systems
1801 Old Trolley Rd., Ste. F
Summerville, SC 29485
(800) 367-4275 Fax: (803) 873-5277

Hewlett-Packard
19111 Pruneridge Ave.
Cupertino, CA 95014
(800) 475-6697
Internet: http://www.hp.com

Imagelink
300 Mt. Lebanon Blvd., Ste. 2201
Pittsburg, PA 15234
(412) 344-7511

Incite
5057 Keller Springs Rd.
Dallas, TX 75248
(214) 447-8473
Internet: http://www.incite.com

Innovative Integration
31352 W. Via Colinas, Ste. 101
Westlake Village, CA 91362
(818) 856-6150

Intel
5200 NE Elam Young Pkwy. JF3-321
Hillsboro, OR 97124
(503) 264-1273
Internet: http://www.intel.com

Inter-Tel
7300 W. Boston St.
Chandler, AZ 85226
(602) 940-2152

International Business Machines (IBM)
Networking Systems Division
3039 Cornwallis Road
Research Triangle Park, NC 27709
(800) 426-2255 or (919) 543-7421
Fax: (919) 543-5417

ISDN Systems Corporation
8320 Old Courthouse Road, Suite 200
Vienna, VA 22182
(703)-883-0933

Key Voice Technologies
1805 Glengary St.
Sarasota, FL 34231
(800) 419-3800

LANart
145 Rosemary St.
Needham, MA 02194
(617) 444-1994 Fax: (627) 444-3692
Internet: http://www.lanart.com
Internet: sales@lanart.com

Linkon
226 E. 54th St.
New York, NY 10022
(212) 753-2544

LiveWorks
1950 Stemmons Frwy, Ste. 5001
Dallas, TX 75207
(214) 476-3733
Internet: http://www.xerox.com/live-works.html

Lodestar Technology
3101 Macguire Blvd., Ste. 251
Orlando, FL 32803
(800) 378-6316

MCI
1801 Pennsylvania Ave.
Washington, D.C. 20006
(202) 872-1600
Internet: http://www.mci.com

Megahertz
605 North 5600 West, PO Box 16020
Salt Lake City, UT 84116-0020
(800) LINKING; (801) 320-7000
Internet:
http://www.xmission.com/~mhz

Micom Communications
4100 Los Angeles Ave.
Simi Valley, CA 93063-3397
(805) 583-8600
Internet: http://www.micom.com

Microsoft
One Microsoft Way
Redmond, WA 98052
(206) 882-8080
Internet: http://www.microsoft.com

Mitel
350 Legget Dr.
Kanata, Ontario K2K 1X3
(800) MITEL-SX; (613) 592-2122
Internet:
http://www.semicon.mitel.com/

Modatech Systems, Inc.
1681 Chestnut St., Ste. 300
Vancouver, BC, CD V6J 4M6
(800) 804-MAXX; (604) 736-9666

Motorola UDS
5000 Bradford Drive
Huntsville, AL 35805
(205) 430 8000

MultiTech Systems
2205 Woodale Dr.
Mounds View, MN 55112
(612) 785-3500

National Instruments
6504 Bridge Point Pkwy.
Austin, TX 78730
(512) 794-5462
Internet: http://www.natinst.com
Internet: info@natinst.com/

Natural MicroSystems
8 Erie Dr.
Natick, MA 01760
(508) 650-1300
Internet: tech-support@nms.com

Newbridge Networks
593 Herndon Pkwy.
Herndon, VA 22070
(703) 834-3600
Internet: http://www.newbridge.com

NewVoice
1893 Preston White Dr. #120
Reston, VA 22091
(703) 648-0585
Internet: newvoice@planetcom.com

Northern Telecom
P.O. Box 833858
Richardson, TX 75082
(214) 684-8589
Internet: http://www.nortel.com

Novell Telephony Division
2180 Fortune Dr.
San Jose, CA 95131
(408) 434-2300
Internet: http://www.novell.com

Octel
1001 Murphy Ranch Rd.
Milpitas, CA 95035
(408) 324-3338

OCTus
8352 Claremont Mesa Blvd.
San Diego, CA 92111
(619) 268-5140

Olicom USA
900 E. Park Blvd., Ste. 180
Plano, TX 75074
(214) 423-7560

OnChip Systems
1190 Coleman Ave.
San Jose, CA 95110
(408) 988-5400

PCSI
9645 Scranton Rd.
San Diego, CA 92121
(619) 535-9500

Phoenix Technologies, Ltd.
Three First National Plaza
Chicago, IL 60602
(800) 452-0120; (312) 541-0260

Pika Technologies
155 Terrence Mathews Crescent
Kanata, Ontario K2M 2A8
(613) 591-1555
Internet: info@pika.ca

Polycom
2584 Junction Ave.
San Jose, CA 95134
(800) 765-9266

Promptus Communications
207 High Point Ave.
Portsmouth, RI 02871
(401) 683-6100
Faxback: (800) 647-1953
Internet: http://www.promptus.com/
promptus

PureSpeech
100 Cambridge Park Dr.
Cambridge, MA 02140
(617) 441-0000

Quarterdeck Corp.
13160 Mindanao Way, 3rd Fl.
Marina del Rey, CA 90292-9705
(800) 354-3222; (310) 309-3700
Internet: http://www.qdeck.com

Quiknet Technologies
153 Prospect Ave.
San Francisco, CA 94110

Radish Communication Systems
5744 Central Ave.
Boulder, CO 80301
(303) 443-2237

Readycom
1506 E. Franklin St., Ste. 201
Chapel Hill, NC 27514
(919) 968-8180

Rhetorex
200 E. Hacienda Av.
Campbell, CA 95008
(408) 370-0881 Fax: (408) 370-1171
Internet: http://www.rhetorex.com

Rochelle Communications
8906 Wall St., Ste. 205
Austin, TX 78754
(512) 339-8188
Internet: http://www.rochelle.com

SAT-SAGEM
20370 Town Center Lane, Ste. 255
Cupertino, CA 95014
(408) 446-8690
Internet:
http://www.catalog.com/satusa

Siemens PNCO
4900 Old Ironsides Dr.
Santa Clara, CA 95054
(408) 986-3151
Internet:
http://siemensrolm.com/info

Siemens Stromber-Carlson
900 Broken Sound Pkwy.
Boca Raton, FL 33467
(407) 955-5000

SIIG, Inc.
6078 Stewart Ave.
Fremont, CA 94538-3152
(510) 657-8688
FAX: (510) 657-5962

SoftTalk
85 Wells Ave., Ste. 200
Newton, MA 02159
(617) 482-5333
Internet: http://www.softtalk.com

Source
14060 Proton Rd.
Dallas, TX 75244
(214) 450-2600

Symantec Corp.
10201 Torre Ave.
Cupertino, CA 95014-2132
(800) 441-7234; (408) 253-9600
Internet: http://www.symantec.com

Tedas Inc.
19925 Stevens Creek Blvd.
Cupertino, CA 95014
(408) 973-7835; Fax (408) 973-7299

Technically Speaking
333 Turnpike Rd.
Southborough, MA 01772
(508) 229-7777

Teknekron Infoswitch
4425 Cambridge Rd.
Ft Worth, TX 76155
(817) 267-3025

Telaccount, Inc.
257 Robinson Ave.
Bronx, NY 10465
(718) 824-3493
FAX: (718) 823-0962

Telcontrol
P.O. Box 4031
Huntsville, AL 35815
(205) 881-4000

Teleconferencing Technology
1240 Cobblestone Way
Woodstock, IL 60098
(815) 338-2300

TeleMagic, Inc. (subsidiary of
Sage US Holdings)
17950 Preston Rd., Ste. 800
Dallas, TX 75252
(800) 835-6244; (214) 733-4292

Teltone Corp.
22121 20th Ave., SE
Bothell, WA 98021-4408
(800) 426-3926; (206) 487-1515

Telular
920 Deerfield Pkwy.
Buffalo Grove, IL 60089
(708) 465-4500

Tone Commander
4370 150th NE
Redmond, WA 98073
(800) 524-0024

U.S. Robotics Access Corp. (subsidiary
of U.S. Robotics Corp.)
8100 N. McCormick Blvd.
Skokie, IL 60076-2999
(800) DIAL-USR; (708) 982-5010
Internet: http://www.usr.com

Video Server
5 Forbes Rd.
Lexington, MA 02173
(617) 863-2300

VocalTec, Inc.
157 Veterans Dr.
Northvale, NJ 07647
(800) THE-CAT9; (201) 768-9400
Internet: http://www.vocaltec.com

Voice Control Systems, Inc.
14140 Midway Rd., Ste. 100
Dallas, TX 75244
(214) 386-0300
FAX: (214) 386-5555

Voice Technologies Group
2350 N. Forest Rd., Ste. 31B
Getzville, NY 14068
(716) 689-6700

Voiceboard
5574 Everglades, Unit A
Ventura, CA 93003
(805) 339-9797 Fax: (805) 339-9798
Internet: greg@voiceboard.com

VTEL
108 Wild Basin Rd.
Austin, TX 78746
(512) 314-2700

White Mountain DSP
131 DW Hwy., Ste. 433
Nashua, NH 03060
(603) 883-2430

Wildfire Communications, Inc.
20 Maguire Rd.
Lexington, MA 02173
(800) WILDFIRE; (617) 674-1500

Zeus Phonestuff
3841 Holcomb Bridge Road
Norcross, GA 30092
(770) 263-7111

Appendix C: Glossary

ACD

See Automatic Call Distribution.

amplitude

The width of a waveform or signal measured as the distance between the high and low points.

analog

A term used to describe the type of data/voice/signal transmission over a phone line when the original and transmitted signal are the same. See digital.

ANI

See Automatic Number Identification.

API

See Application Programming Interface.

Application Programming Interface (API)

The low-level operating system of a computer or telephone system.

Asynchronous Transfer Mode (ATM)

A high-speed one direction transfer method.

ATM

See Asynchronous Transfer Mode

Automated attendants

An automated phone system that answers incoming calls and presents the caller with a voice menu to access people, voice mail, or other services.

Automatic Call Distribution (ACD)

Can be used for both inbound and outbound calls. In an inbound call environment, the workers in a technical support center (for example, customer service representatives) are profiled based on their skill set. If a call comes in that requires a particular type of knowledge, the call is automatically routed to the next available operator with the required expertise. In an outbound call environment, such as a telemarketing firm, a list of contacts to be called is entered into the computer. The system then dials the numbers automatically and connects the telemarketer only when a call is completed; i.e., the call did not receive a busy signal or voice mail system.

Automatic Number Identification (ANI)

>The transmission of the telephone number of the person placing an incoming call.

B channels

>The "bearer" channel of an ISDN line. The B channel can carry 64 Kbps at full duplex.

B-ISDN (Broadband ISDN)

>Supports large data transfer rates up to 150 million bps.

Bandwidth

>The load capacity of a transmission device, usually measured in Kbps.

Basic Rate Interface (BRI)

>One of the two subscriber configurations of ISDN, the other being PRI. BRI provides two B channels and one D channel.

binary file transfer

>A method of data transfer that maintains the integrity of the original binary file.

BONDed B channels

>When the two B channels of an ISDN line are used simultaneously to double bandwidth.

BRI

>See Basic Rate Interface.

call forwarding

>A specialized telephone service that allows incoming calls to be routed to another number, such as voice mail, operator, or another phone anywhere in the world.

call logging

An automatic computer-based service that captures information about calls, such as duration, origin, destination, time, etc. Often tied with a note manager.

call management services

An interface design of a computer-based telephone control system that simulates a high-end multiline complex business phone system.

call waiting

A telephone service that informs you when another caller is trying to reach you, by signaling you with a short tone.

caller ID

A telephone service that provides the number and possible owner of the phone from which an incoming call is originated.

CDPD

See Cellular Digital Packet Data.

Cellular Digital Packet Data (CDPD)

An open specification that allows high-speed computer data transmittal over an enhanced cellular network.

Channel Service Unit/Data Service Unit (CSU/DSU)

An adapter to attach incoming digital lines to a digital phone system or device.

CLASS

See Custom Local-Area Signaling Services.

codec

Abbreviation for coder-decoder.

common control

A system configuration whereby all major applications and services are operated from a single area or use the same interface.

Computer Supported Telecommunications Applications (CSTA)

A European standard for linking telephone systems with computers.

computer telephony (CT)

The use of a computer to control internal and external telephone services and devices.

conference calling

A telephone call in which multiple connections are brought together so each person can speak to and hear all the others.

CSTA

See Computer Supported Telecommunications Applications.

CSU/DSU

See Channel Service Unit/Data Service Unit.

CT

See computer telephony.

Custom Local-Area Signaling Services (CLASS)

A set of telephone services that are standard within a local exchange.

D channel

The ISDN channel used to carry control signals.

DSVD (Digital Simultaneous Voice and Data)
> See Simultaneous Voice and Data.

deconverted
> To return a data packet or file back to its original format.

dedicated circuit
> A circuit used by a single entity.

dial pad
> The interface used to manually enter numbers on a telephone system.

diaphragm
> The thin, flexible sheet that vibrates as sound waves impact it in a microphone.

DID
> See Direct Inward Dialing.

digital
> A transmission method that converts voice and data into binary code signals for fast and efficient transmission.

Digital Signal Processor (DSP)
> A digital microprocessor that manipulates digital signals before sending them on.

digital switching
> A connection whereby binary signals are transferred from input to output connections.

Direct Inward Dialing (DID)
> A method of dialing directly into a company to reach an individual without going through an operator.

DSP
> See Digital Signal Processor.

DTMF
> See Dual-Tone Multifrequency.

Dual-Tone Multifrequency (DTMF)
> A telephone signal method that uses two tones that are easily distinguished by the receiving telephone switches.

ECMA
> See European Computer Manufacturer's Association.

electronic voice mail
> A computer-controlled message recording system that operates like an answering machine. See also voice mail.

Enhanced Call Processing (ECP)
> An interactive voice mail system.

ECP
> See Enhanced Call Processing.

error correction mode
> A method of data transmission that eliminates errors.

European Computer Manufacturer's Association (ECMA)
> A computer and telephony manufacturing group that upholds the European standards.

FDM

> See Frequency Division Multiplexing.

foreign exchange line

> A telephone line connection that links a phone system to a number in a different area code to eliminate long-distance charges.

Frequency Division Multiplexing (FDM)

> An obsolete method of dividing a circuit bandwidth into narrow bands to separate voice from data transmissions.

hertz

> A measurement of frequency in cycles per second.

inbound call screening

> A screening method that enables the receiver of a call to monitor a call's origin before answering it.

Integrated Services Digital Network (ISDN)

> A high-speed digital-transmission line commonly used for connecting to the Internet.

Interactive Voice Response (IVR)

> A computer interface that uses voice recognition to drive programs and menus.

ISDN

> See Integrated Services Digital Network.

IVR

> See Interactive Voice Response.

LAN

See local area network.

line conditioning

A filtering process that reduces line noise to improve the quality of data transmissions.

local area network (LAN)

A collection of computers connected together in order to share resources.

message filtering

The process of sorting and arranging voice messages by caller, time, date, or subject.

message monitoring

A surveillance method of listening to messages as they are being recorded.

microphone

The audio input device of a telephone or computer.

modem

Abbreviation for modulate/demodulate, the electronic device that allows digital computer signals to be transmitted over a POTS line.

modified read encoding

A two-dimensional coding scheme for transmitting fax information that handles the data compression of the vertical line and concentrates on space between the lines and within given characters.

MPPP

See Multilink PPP.

mu-law encoding

Sometimes written *μ-law encoding*, using Greek letter "mu." The PCM standard used in North America and Japan for voice and data coding, compression, and expansion.

Multilink PPP (MLPPP) or (MPPP)

A protocol that allows multiple PPP connections to be used together to increase bandwidth.

multiple-message format

A method of transmitting messages in groups, or a way of sending the same message to multiple recipients.

multiplexing

Transmitting two or more signals over a single connection.

multiport boards

A telephony or computer device that enables two or more input or output connections.

NetWare Loadable Module (NLM)

A software interface that allows NetWare-based networks to add CT.

NIUF

See North American ISDN User Forum.

NLM

See NetWare Loadable Module.

nodes

A point of connection on a network or phone system.

North American ISDN User Forum (NIUF)

A group that promotes the use of ISDN, often through information exchange. Contact NIUF, National Institute of Standards and Technology, Building 223, Room B364, Gathersberg, MD 20899 or call 301-975-2937.

notes databases

A phone memo collection often integrated within call management utilities.

passband

The range of frequencies that will pass through a filter unhindered.

PBX

See private branch exchange.

PC-telephone interface

The connection between a computer and a telephone system.

PCM

See Pulse Code Modulation.

PCM Expansion Bus (PEB)

A method of encoding an analog signal into a digital signal.

PEB

See PCM Expansion Bus.

phone switching

A process to connect a handset to an outgoing or incoming line. For example, a large PBX system may use a phone switching device to connect the internal phone network with a local exchange line to make an outgoing call.

Plain Old Telephone Service (POTS)

The basic phone service that supplies a single standard telephone line without any of the new, fancy services and features.

POTS

See Plain Old Telephone Service.

PRI

See Primary Rate Interface.

Primary Rate Interface (PRI)

The ISDN setup (with 23 B and 1 D channels) that has a bandwidth of 1.544 Mbps. See BRI.

private branch exchange (PBX)

A private telephone switching system, usually housed within a single building or company. For example, the internal phone system of a hotel.

protocols

The sets of rules that define the communications among electronic devices.

Pulse Code Modulation (PCM)

A method of sampling voice signals into digital signals.

RBOC

See Regional Bell Operating Company.

receiver

The device that converts a transmitted signal back into audio sounds on a telephone.

Regional Bell Operating Company (RBOC)
> Any one of the seven Bell telephone operation companies in the United States. The seven are Ameritech, Bell Atlantic, Bell South, NYNEX, Pacific Telesis, Southwestern Bell (or SBC Communications Inc.), and U.S. West.

rotary
> An obsolete telephone dialing method that uses circuit interrupts to dial.

SAP
> See Service Advertising Protocol.

SCbus
> An interface bus used for communicating with SCSA nodes.

SCSA
> See Signal Computing System Architecture.

SCSA Message Protocol (SMP)
> A standard for message transmission over an SCSA system.

Service Advertising Protocol (SAP)
> A repeating broadcast by a server to inform the other network nodes of the services available at its network address.

Service Profile Identifier (SPID)
> An identification number assigned to an ISDN line and used to identify when an ISDN connection is attempted.

Service Provider Interface (SPI)
> Microsoft TAPI term, a low-level specification used to interface hardware with software.

signal
> An electronic wave or pulse used to transmit information.

Signal Computing System Architecture (SCSA)
> A computing system architecture that defines how both hardware and software will communicate.

Simultaneous Voice and Data (SVD); (DSVD)
> The ability for a communications connection to transmit voice and data signals at the same time.

SMP
> See SCSA Message Protocol.

SOHO
> Abbreviation for small office/home office.

speech synthesis
> A process of simulating speech by a computer, often used to "read" material contained in documents.

SPI
> See Service Provider Interface.

SPID
> See Service Profile Identifier.

SVD
> See Simultaneous Voice and Data.

switch hook
> The button, switch, or lever used to disconnect a telephone transmission.

switched 56

A switched data service that allows 56 Kbps data transmission.

switching

The act of connecting the caller with the person being called.

T1

A 1.544 Mbps transmission connection.

TAO

See Telephony Application Objects.

TAPI

See Telephony Application Programming Interface.

TCP/IP

See Transmission Control Protocol/Internet Protocol.

TDM

See time division multiplexing.

TE

See terminal equipment.

teleconferencing

A telephone session in which two or more people are linked together.

telephone

An electronic device that allows audio communication over large distances.

telephony

The science of using a telephone to transmit information.

Telephony Application Objects (TAO)

A programming framework of the SCSA.

Telephony Application Programming Interface (TAPI)

Microsoft term used to refer to Windows-based telephony.

Telephony Services API (TSAPI)

A Novell standard for call control, monitoring, routing, and maintenance.

terminal equipment (TE)

A telephone or other receiving device at the end of a phone line.

Time Division Multiplexing (TDM)

A method of simultaneously transmitting multiple voice or data signals over a single communications medium.

time slicing

The process of dividing a computer resource so that it is possible for multiple applications or tasks requesting the resource to be allocated the amount of the resource's time that it requires. Multitasking requires that each task be allotted part (a time slice) of the CPU's processing power. Tasks with higher priority receive more time slices than do those tasks with lower priority.

Tmap

Developed by Northern Telecom, an interface that allows communications between TAPI and TSAPI applications, eliminating the need for application developers to write to more than one API.

tone

Audio signals of a certain frequency and duration.

tone dialing

Also referred to as Dual-Tone Multifrequency (DTMF), the tones you hear when you dial someone's telephone number. These tones have been internationally standardized for telephone communications.

Transmission Control Protocol/Internet Protocol (TCP/IP)

The communications protocol, developed for internetwork dissimilar systems, that is now supported on almost all platforms. The Internet uses TCP/IP to transfer information among systems. TCP/IP includes the File Transfer Protocol (FTP), that allows files to be downloaded and uploaded among TCP/IP sites.

transmitter

Opposite of the receiver, the device in the telephone handset that converts speech into electrical impulses for transmission of voice communications.

video teleconferencing

The technology that allows people who are widely separated to communicate face to face without the need for travel. Based on the H.320 standard, video conferencing is becoming more and more popular as the technology becomes more advanced and less expensive.

voice compression

The method of electronically modifying a 64 Kbps PCM voice channel to obtain a channel of 32 Kbps or less and provide a more efficient means of voice transmission.

voice-controlled outbound dialing
> The ability to speak a name or number aloud and have the computer recognize the term and dial the number for you.

voice digitization
> The process of converting analog voice signals into binary bits for voice storage and transmission.

voice mail
> A messaging system for voice messages. Answering machines are a less technical form of voice mail, but the underlying idea is the same: If you can't take a call, the person can leave you a message in his or her own voice; it is up to you what actions you take on that call once the message is left.

voice recognition
> The conversion of spoken words into computer text. This is done by first digitizing speech and then matching the speech against a dictionary of coded waveforms. Matches are converted into text on screen, as if the words were being typed on the keyboard.

wide area network (WAN)
> A communications network that is spread out over a large geographical area, such as a city, state, or country.

Windows Open Standards Architecture (WOSA)
> Microsoft's term for a variety of application programming interfaces designed to provide interoperability of applications across the Windows environment. WOSA provides access to network services from any software provider that supports the WOSA interface for Windows applications.

Index